imprint at
15 95

M 798
/HP
DW
2-7

$5 00
16
S
1/8

# FROM SAPPHO TO DE SADE

*Moments in the History of Sexuality*

MIGUEL SAN MIGUEL

D0060833

# FROM SAPPHO TO DE SADE

*Moments in the History of Sexuality*

JAN BREMMER

**LONDON AND NEW YORK**

First published 1989
First published in paperback 1991
by Routledge
11 New Fetter Lane, London EC4P 4EE
Simultaneously published in the USA and Canada by Routledge a
division of Routledge, Chapman and Hall, Inc. 29 West 35th Street,
New York, NY 10001

© 1989,1991 Jan Bremmer

Printed in Great Britain by
T J Press (Padstow) Ltd.,
Padstow, Cornwall

All rights reserved. No part of this book may be
reprinted or reproduced or utilized in any form or
by any electronic, mechanical, or other means, now
known or hereafter invented, including photocopying
and recording, or in any information storage or
retrieval system, without permission in writing from
the publishers.

*British Library Cataloguing in Publication Data*
From Sappho to De Sade: moments in the history of sexuality.
1. Europe. Man. Sexuality, history – Sociological perspectives
Sociological perspectives
I. Bremmer, Jan II. [From Sappho to De Sade *English*]
306.7'094

ISBN 0-415-02089-1

*Library of Congress Cataloging-in-Publication Data*
Van Sappho tot De Sade. English.
From Sappho to De Sade: moments in the history of sexuality/
[edited by] Jan Bremmer.
p. cm.
Bibliography: p.
Includes index.
1. Sex customs – Europe – History. 2. Sexual ethics – Europe –
History. I. Bremmer, Jan N. II. Title.
HQ18.E8V36   1989                    1989 89-3528
306'.094 – dc19                          CIP

ISBN 0415-06300-0 (p/b)

# Contents

CONTENTS

# List of illustrations

# Preface

Why was a homosexual relationship between two adults unacceptable in ancient Greece? Why did the prohibition of incest extend to the limits of kinship in the Middle Ages? Why was the nineteenth century terrified of masturbation? Why have the brothels with their madams virtually disappeared in western Europe? Psychiatrists like Freud and biologists like Kinsey would have been taken aback by these kinds of intriguing questions. Surely, people do 'it' now in the same way as they always have?

Their approach was understandable for a time in which historians had not yet made sexuality an object of research. In fact, it is virtually only in the last decade that historians have started to study sexual practices, a field that has been all too long the playground of psychologists, biologists, and doctors with their (often wrong) ideas. And it is only now becoming possible to see that sexuality is not a biological constant but an ever-changing phenomenon, that is being continuously shaped by people themselves. Historians, therefore, should not only pay attention to the social, economic, or religious sides of sexuality but they should also, as Gert Hekma argues in his contribution to this book, become interested in the preliminaries of sexual behaviour, in the design of sexual manners, and in the choreography and architecture of sexuality. Only then shall we have a reasonably firm basis for our opinions on this fascinating side of human existence.

This collection of studies is intended as a contribution to the historical debate on sexuality that is only now getting under way. The origin of the book lies in the largest historical congress that has ever taken place in Holland: 'Balance and perspective; on the nature and function of the knowledge of the past' (22–4 May

1986). At this congress, organized on the occasion of the 350th anniversary of the State University of Utrecht by a group of students from the Institute for History, numerous seminars were given on the most diverse aspects of history; the seminar on sexuality was assigned to the editor of this volume. He thought it a compelling task to illustrate the historical character of sexuality. For that reason, he made up the programme in such a way that successive papers discussed various aspects of sexuality in successive periods. When this plan attracted much attention during the congress and gave rise to many lively discussions, it seemed no more than reasonable to make the lectures accessible to a wider public. For this book all the papers have been revised and, in addition, some new contributions have been invited in order to give as varied as possible a picture of the history of sexuality. Successive contributors discuss homosexuality and lesbian love in antiquity, incest in the Middle Ages, sexual education and instruction in the Dutch Republic, voyeurism and French rococo art, de Sade, prostitution in *fin-de-siècle* Vienna, and mannish women of the Balkan mountains; an analysis of the rise of sexology closes the collection.

I would like to thank the organizers of the 'Balance and perspective' congress – Frans van Besouw, Aad Blok, Paul Boeding, Ivo Kuypers, and Marianne Neuteboom – without whose enthusiasm this book would never have materialized. Sarah Johnston and Ken Dowden once again helped me by revising the English of various contributions. Last but not least, Richard Stoneman, senior editor at Routledge, showed an early interest in this volume and waited patiently for its arrival.

J.B.
Ede, Holland

# 1

# Greek pederasty
# and
# modern homosexuality

*Jan Bremmer*

There was a time, not so long ago, that homosexuality was
regularly called 'Greek love' or 'Socratic love'. Such expressions
implied that modern homosexuality occurred already among the
ancient Greeks. But was this really the case? The words 'homosexuality' and 'lesbian love' do not predate the second half of the
nineteenth century. Moreover, it was only in this period that the
medical professions began to consider homosexuality a perversion
the study of which belonged in the field of sexual psychopathology.
Such developments strongly suggest that homosexuality as we
know it is a recent phenomenon. Did homosexuals not exist in
ancient Greece?[1]

The best study of Greek homosexual practices fails to perceive
these problems – witness its title *Greek Homosexuality*.[2] In classical
Greece, however, homosexual couples of two adult men were not
to be found. Greek texts and vases show that homosexual relationships normally took place only between adults and adolescents or
between young men and boys. Previous generations of scholars
have overlooked this Greek peculiarity and have preferred to
explain the homosexual practices as a consequence of the
militaristic way of Greek life, drawing parallels with cases of
homosexuality among soldiers during the Second World War.[3]
But although it is true that decent Greek women were tightly
guarded, there were plenty of courtesans about to serve the Greek
males' sexual needs.[4] Moreover, the 'militaristic' solution also
fails to explain why the participants in the sexual relationship
never were two adult men.

We, therefore, will seek a different approach. Short homosexual
affairs between adults and boys also occurred among 'primitive'

tribes in Australia, New Guinea, and Melanesia. Examining evidence from these areas may enhance understanding of the Greek practices – even if the approach is somewhat unusual.


## 1 PEDERASTIC PAPUANS

Between 1926 and 1932, the English social anthropologist F. E. Williams visited the Papuans of the Trans-Fly a number of times. This is his account of homosexual practices during the Papuan rites of initiation:

> It was frequently maintained that *setivira*, or bachelors, remained truly celibate until they entered upon sexual relations with their own wives. Without giving too much credence to this statement, we may note that the hospitable exchange above noted was nominally restricted to married adults. Some informants maintained that *setivira* could secure the favours of married women at feast times, but it seems evident that this was not definitely sanctioned.
>
> The bachelors had recourse to sodomy, a practice which was not reprobated but was actually a custom of the country – and a custom in the true sense, i.e., fully sanctioned by male society and universally practised. For a long time the existence of sodomy was successfully concealed from me, but latterly, once I had won the confidence of a few informants in the matter, it was admitted on every hand. It is actually regarded as essential to the growing boy to be sodomized. More than one informant being asked if he had ever been subjected to unnatural practice, answered, 'Why, yes! Otherwise how should I have grown?'
>
> The ceremonial initiation to sodomy and the mythological antecedents to it will be spoken of elsewhere (pp. 194, 308). In the meantime it is enough to note that every male adult in the Morehead district has in his time constantly played both parts in this perversion. The boy is initiated to it at the bull-roarer ceremony and not earlier, for he could not then be trusted to keep the secret from his mother. When he becomes adolescent his part is reversed and he may then sodomize his juniors, the new initiates to the bull-roarer. I am told that some boys are more attractive and consequently receive more attention of this kind than do others; but all must pass through it, since it is

regarded as essential to their bodily growth. There is indeed no question as to the universality of the practice.

It is commonly asserted that the early practice of sodomy does nothing to inhibit man's natural desires when later on he marries; and it is a fact that while older men are not debarred from indulging, and actually do so at the bull-roarer ceremony, sodomy is virtually restricted as a habit to the *setivira*.[5]

This description is confirmed by more recent anthropological studies.[6] Thus, the following points should be noted as important features of the practice. (1) We have here a case of pederasty, which should not be confused with modern homosexuality, as both initiators and novices normally marry afterwards. (2) The active pederasts are the novices of the previous initiation, and it may be of importance to note that it is these novices who usually play a prominent role in upholding discipline during the initiation. Finally, (3) copulation, in which the novice is always the passive partner, takes place anally.[7]

Among the Greeks, similar homosexual practices occurred during rites of initiation. We will therefore employ the description of the Papuan ceremony as a means of 'opening our eyes' during our analysis of the Greek rites.

## 2 INITIATION AND PEDERASTY AMONG GREEKS, GERMANS, AND ALBANIANS

In Greece, the most detailed description of a pederastic affair occurs in a report of a Cretan initiation ritual by the fourth-century historian Ephoros:[8]

They [i.e., the Cretans] have a peculiar custom regarding love affairs, for they win the objects of their love, not by persuasion, but by capture [*harpagei*]; the lover tells the friends of the boy three or four days beforehand that he is going to make the capture; but for the friends to conceal the boy, or not to let him go forth by the appointed road, is indeed a most disgraceful thing, a confession, as it were, that the boy is unworthy of having such a lover. When they meet, if the abductor is the boy's equal or superior in rank and other respects, the friends pursue him and lay hold of him, though only in a very gentle way, thus satisfying the custom [*to nomimon*]; afterwards they cheerfully turn the boy over to him and allow him to lead him away. If, however, the abductor is unworthy, they take the boy away from him. And the pursuit does not end until the boy is taken to the men's house [*andreion*] of his abductor. They regard as a worthy object of love not the boy who is exceptionally handsome, but the boy who is exceptionally manly and decorous. After giving presents to the boy, the abductor takes him away to any place in the country he wishes; and those who are present at the capture follow behind them and after feasting and hunting with them for two months (for it is not permitted to detain the boy for a longer time), they return to the city. The boy is released after receiving as presents a military habit, an ox, and a drinking cup (these are the gifts required by law, *nomon*), and other things so numerous and costly that the friends, on account of the number of expenses, make contributions thereto. Now the boy sacrifices the ox to Zeus and gives a feast for those who returned with him. Then he makes known the facts about his intimacy with his lover, whether, perchance, it has pleased him or not, the law [*nomou*] allowing him this privilege in order that, if any force was applied to him at the time of his capture, he might be able at this feast to avenge himself and be rid of the lover. It is disgraceful for those who are handsome in appearance and also are descendants of illustrious ancestors to fail to obtain lovers. . . . So much for their customs [*nomima*] regarding love affairs.

Before we look at pederasty in particular, we should note a few details characteristically found in initiatory rituals. A short stay in the 'bush' and hunting are typical of initiation among most 'primitive' peoples; indeed, these practices can be recognized even in modern fairy-tales that include an initiatory scenario, such as Grimm's 'The twelve brothers'. The gift of a suit of armour signified adulthood, as in Greece only adults fought in full armour. In the city of Thebes, a boy also received armour from his male lover when he was registered as an adult, and several Athenian vases show adult males offering their beloved a helmet or some other piece of armour.[9] But what about the drinking cup?

The drinking of wine played an important part in the existence of Greek men – witness the central place of the symposium in Greek society. This importance is reflected even in the way in which Greeks looked at neighbouring peoples; whereas the Greeks

4

themselves drank mixed wine, they ascribed the drinking of unmixed wine, milk, or water to others. In fact, wine was so important to the adult male Greeks that some cities forbade wine to women and boys altogether. In order to demonstrate this difference, boys were often employed at the symposium as wine-pourers. By letting them pour the wine but not drink it, the adult males stressed the adolescents' inferior position. The mythical counterpart of these boys is Ganymede, son of a Trojan king, who was kidnapped by Zeus to become his wine-pourer and, according to later versions of the myth, his beloved.[10] The possession of a drinking cup, then, was a sign of adulthood.

It is also important to note that the pederastic ritual was sanctioned by the Cretan community. The pursuit of the boy ended in the *andreion*, the men's house, which, as in many 'primitive' tribes, was the centre of political activity. The various references in the report to customs and laws also show that the Cretan community supervised the ritual. Evidently, pederastic kidnapping was a 'must' for every aristocratic boy.

What about the nature of pederastic copulation? Unfortunately, we have no direct information, but it is clear that the lover had to take account of the boy's feelings. It may be noteworthy that a poem glorifying the *derrière* of a boy is written by the Cretan Rhianos, but, naturally, admiration of a nice *derrière* does not necessarily imply anal copulation.

Pederasty in puberty rites also occurred in Sparta, a city well known for its archaizing customs, as appears from the words of Xenophon in his *Laconian Institutions* (2. 12, tr. Marchant, Loeb): 'I think I ought to say something also about intimacy with boys, since this matter also has a bearing on education [*paideian*].' The institutionalized role of pederasty also clearly appears from the fact that the highest Spartan authorities, the ephors, penalized those who, although qualifying, had not chosen a boy to be their beloved. Xenophon, who had lived for a time in fourth-century Sparta, stated that the homosexual relationships in Sparta remained platonic but honestly added that he did not expect people to believe him (2.13). His suggestion, is indeed hardly convincing, as pederastic graffiti already occur in the early Spartan colony Thera, the present Santorini. It is therefore difficult to believe that practising pederasts were absent in the mother city, Sparta.[11]

5

The Athenians were so fully convinced of pederastic practices in Sparta that a comedian even coined the word *kusolakōn*, 'anus-Spartan', a term that leaves little to the imagination. From a methodological point it is of course dubious to accept without reflection the Athenian allegations, for the comedians were more concerned with good jokes than with faithfully reporting other peoples' customs. Nevertheless, the expression is valuable in a different way, as it seems to be characteristic of peoples who themselves practise pederasty to impute the act to others. Thus the Athenians called pederasty 'doing it the Spartan way', or 'doing it the Chalcidian way' as the inhabitants of Chalcis also had the (deserved) reputation of being pederasts. In the Middle Ages the practice was ascribed to Arabian influence, the early modern French considered the Italians to be the *bougres par excellence*, and modern Albanians vilified the gypsies as pederasts (below). These imputations seem to point to a culture's subconscious discontent with its own pederastic practices; otherwise the origin of the custom need not have been ascribed to other peoples.[12]

The Greeks were not the only peoples who practised pederasty during initiation. The historian Ammianus Marcellinus (31. 9. 5) relates that among the Taifali, a tribe connected with the Goths, the boys lived in a state of pederasty until they had killed a boar or a bear. The killing of a boar was a typical heroic ordeal, and also had initiatory value in Macedonia, where a man could recline at dinner, i.e. have the status of an adult, only when he had speared a boar without a hunting-net. As the pederastic relationship continued only till the boy reached adulthood, this case is similar to the Greek customs, even though the method of copulation remains obscure.

Pederastic relations were reported even in nineteenth-century Albania, still one of Europe's most isolated countries. Unfortunately, we are not told whether the practice had supposed educational goals, but the relationship was sanctioned by society: the young lovers (16 and 12 years old, respectively) together took the eucharist. The nature of copulation in this case can be pinpointed, perhaps, with the help of a list of dirty Albanian words, published in 1911 in *Anthropophyteia*, a scholarly journal specializing in scatology. From this list I take the following: '*büthar* = pederast [literally: "Arschman"]'; the word speaks for itself. Yet not all Albanians were charmed with their pederastic practices, as one might judge from the fact that the same list contains the words *madzüp* (gypsy), *madzüpi* (pederasty), and *madzüpoj* (to practise pederasty). Whereas the Albanians were themselves convinced pederasts, they denounced the gypsies, a regularly stigmatized group. This ambivalent attitude is also apparent in the 1854 report of the Austrian civil servant von Hahn, the oldest source for Albanian pederasty. His informant, a young Albanian, assured him that the relationships were purely platonic – a fact denied by better-informed sources.[13]

Among Greeks, some Germans, and Albanians, then, pederastic acts were a fixed feature of a boy's road to adulthood. Until now, however, our informants have reported about the 'outside' of the rituals. It usually remained completely obscure what the participants themselves thought about the practices. Did they like it or loathe it? Or did it leave them indifferent? The coercion that Spartan authorities sometimes had to apply to force aristocratic youths to participate in the pederastic rituals suggests that not everyone liked what he had to do. That is all we can say about Sparta, but we are somewhat better informed about Athens, the cultural centre of the classical Greek world.

## 3 BETWEEN PEDERASTY AND HOMOSEXUALITY: THE CASE OF ATHENS[14]

In Athens, in the second half of the sixth century, pederastic scenes became very popular on vases, a fashion that enables us to trace the history of Athenian pederasty in some detail. On these vases, which circulated in the aristocratic symposia, we see adult men offering a boy a present with one hand and freely reaching for the boy's penis with the other – clearly, quid pro quo. The presents indicate the qualities that were expected from the boys: a cockerel, warlike behaviour; a hare, speedy running; or a lyre, musical qualities. As we already saw (p. 4), the adults also offered pieces of armour – surely a sign of the completion of the boy's education.

The close connection between pederasty and the entrance into adulthood is also attested by the fact that Athenian males quitted playing the passive role in a homosexual relationship when their beards appeared. We know of only one exception to this rule. Greek comedy often mocks the tragedian Agathon, who having

7

become an adult still continued to play the role of boy in his relationship with Pausanias (who is mentioned in Plato's *Symposium*) by shaving off his beard. This is the only known relationship in ancient Greece that closely resembles modern homosexuality, although even these lovers apparently could not appear in public as 'two consenting adults'. Although the traditional Athenian rites of initiation had disintegrated in the course of the sixth (?) century, the original connection between pederasty and initiation remained visible.[15]

The Athenian vases clearly show that only the adults were considered to derive satisfaction from pederastic intercourse; the boy usually looks as if he is solving some academic problem.[16] Evidently he was not allowed to take pleasure in the sexual aspect of the relationship. The apparent one-sidedness of the affair accords with its probable origin in initiation rites, which also aimed at teaching the youngsters to respect their elders: shared pleasure would only confuse the hierarchy of adults and novices. However, the difference in status between adults and adolescents was not stressed too much in public, for, rather strikingly, the vases never show anal intercourse, although such a mode of copulation is regularly presupposed by the literary texts. The man and the boy always stand up straight, wrapped in a cloak. The Greeks considered the passive role in anal intercourse to be a submissive one, and, therefore, probably considered the act itself to be too compromising a picture in public; after all, the boys soon would be respected aristocrats. But the mockery and disapproval that the passive partner in pederasty encountered in the non-aristocratic layers of Athenian society indicate that even ritualized pederasty always remained a delicate matter.[17]

On the oldest Athenian vases we often see various men wooing one boy (Plate 1). Later traditions, which are not always trustworthy, ascribed the origin of important personal feuds, such as those between the great Athenian politicians Themistocles and Aristeides, to quarrels over boys. Vases and texts, then, demonstrate that in Athens pederasty had become a field of competition. How do we explain this development?

In the course of the seventh century, changes in military tactics robbed the Greek aristocrats of the possibility to excel on the battlefield. They therefore looked for new opportunities to assert their pre-eminence. One new field was sport. At the beginning of the sixth century, all over Greece, important athletic games, including the Olympic, were founded or reorganized in order to make them inaccessible to non-aristocrats. In addition, in Athens education apparently became another field of aristocratic competition. In Sparta, the state had gradually taken over from the individual citizens supervision of the education of the youths, but in archaic Athens initiation had remained strictly in the hands of private individuals. Here the boys apparently had a say in the choice of the tutor who would oversee their final education. This possibility for private initiative opened the way for competition, as the adult males now tried to become accepted as tutor by those boys who were the most attractive. The boys, on the other hand, may well have played the various males off against one another. The intensity with which the adults competed for the favours of the boys must have stimulated a sexual preference for boys even among those who in other circumstances might have been disinterested in their own sex. Pederasty now started to play a much larger role in Greek society, and many myths, such as the one of Ganymede (above, p. 5), acquired pederastic overtones. In this way the situation in Athens (and elsewhere in Greece) more closely approached that of modern homosexuality than it seems to have done in Sparta and Crete.

However, this Athenian development did not permit men to show an unlimited interest in boys. On the contrary. Men who were too keen on chasing boys ran the risk of being considered *agrios*, 'wild', a word normally used only for animals. The designation is significant. According to the Greeks, civilized people knew how to control themselves and only 'wild men' indulged their passions without inhibition. Too intensive an interest in the same sex, then, was not permitted in Athens.[18]

Greek communities were, in general, so small that they considered it necessary for all members of their society to take on the duty of procreation. Marriage was a 'must' and bachelors were held in low esteem. In Sparta, indeed, bachelors had to parade annually through the market, where they were mocked and abused by the rest of the population. And although Athens was a big city in classical times, this common Greek attitude none the less may have played a role in the depreciation of over enthusiastic lovers.[19]

On the other hand, a radical rejection of all heterosexual

contacts, as is typical for many modern homosexuals, was perhaps not necessary for those Greek males who felt more attracted to their own sex. It is hardly by chance that modern homosexuality developed at the same time that the heterosexual relationship within marriage acquired a much more intimate character. It seems as if the rise of modern homosexuality is at least a reaction to this development, which led to the disappearance of a separate male world. In Greece, males could virtually live their own lives; they did not need to see their wives very frequently. Consequently, the sustaining of a heterosexual relationship must have been relatively tolerable for everyone.

## 4 PEDERASTY, INITIATION, AND DISCIPLINE

What conclusions can we draw from our survey so far? It seems clear that among various peoples – Papuans, but also Greeks and Germans – boys had to pass through a pederastic stage in order to become fully accepted adults. The reason for this sexual inversion remains insufficiently analysed, and the ancient participants themselves have not handed down any explanation for the practice. The Spartans called the male lover *eispnēlas*, 'breather-in', but the precise meaning of this term is not illuminated by our scarce sources. In an epoch-making article at the beginning of the century, the German classical scholar Erich Bethe wanted to demonstrate that the word indicated the practice of anal copulation, because the transfer of the male force through sperm is stressed by the Aborigines and neighbouring peoples. Unfortunately, Bethe could not produce any parallels to prove his point; we must look therefore in a different direction.[20] Among the Greeks, and among many other peoples, taking the passive position in a homosexual relationship strongly suggested submission. Can this depreciation perhaps be the key to a better understanding of pederasty in initiation rituals?

Recently, a German ethologist has noted that many mammals practise a peculiar mode of *Rangdemonstration*: the males mount their fellows in order to show them their superiority. Modern society usually connects rape with the man–woman relationship, but among many peoples homosexual subjection serves to demonstrate a superior position; in Western society, this phenomenon normally is restricted to subcultures such as prisons, students' associations, and sports clubs. In the Greek world, too, the passive, anal role in a homosexual relationship was considered to be absolutely unacceptable for an adult.[21]

Now, demonstration of status and rank is exactly what we would expect to find in rites of initiation. These rites must socialize the adolescent and show him his (low!) position in the world of the adults. As Gert Hekma rightly observes, 'the confirmation of the older generation's domination of the whole existence of the novices provides the basis for a total (re)socialization within the relevant male community. This serves the cohesion of the male group.'[22] It is not improbable that precisely this aspect of *Rangdemonstration* constitutes the background for the occurrence of pederasty in rites of initiation.

## 5 GREEK PEDERASTY AND MODERN HOMOSEXUALITY

As we have seen, Greek pederasty fundamentally differed in form and function from modern sexuality. Admittedly, the Greek situation offered great opportunities to those males whose sexual interest mainly concerned other males, but this preference had to be limited to boys and, moreover, the passive and active roles in these relationships were sharply defined. In addition, this preference had to be propagated with moderation, without completely excluding the opposite sex. At the same time, the aspect of initiation into the adult world illuminates an even more important difference between Greek pederasty and modern ways of homosexuality. Whereas modern homosexuals often occupy a marginal position in society and are regularly considered to be effeminate, in Greece it was pederasty that provided access to the world of the socially elite; it was only the pederastic relationship that made the boy into a real man.[23] The Greeks, then, certainly knew of 'Greek love' and their interest in boys was never purely platonic, but they did not, in any sense, invent homosexuality!

## NOTES

The annotation has generally been kept down to the most recent literature. I thank Sir Kenneth Dover, Albert Henrichs, and Sytze Wiersma for their critical comments on the text. Sarah Johnston skilfully revised the English style of this contribution.

11

Abbreviation: Kassel-Austin = R. Kassel and C. Austin, *Poetae Comici Graeci*, Berlin/New York, 1983ff.

1 The word 'homosexuality' was coined by K. M. Benkert, *Paragraph 143 des preussischen Strafgesetzbuches vom 14 April 1851* . . ., Leipzig, 1869; for the terms 'lesbian love' and 'sapphism' see Lardinois, this volume, ch. 2, n. 1. For the construction of modern homosexuality see Hekma, this volume, ch. 10; see now also David M. Halperin, *One Hundred Years of Homosexuality*, New York and London, 1990, 15–40.

2 Cf. K. J. Dover, *Greek Homosexuality*, London/New York, 1978; note also Th. Africa, 'Homosexuals in Greek history', *Journal of Psychohistory*, 1982, 9: 401–20. Although I disagree with Dover's discussion of the origin and spread of Greek pederasty, it must be stressed that his book is a brilliant analysis of the practice in the classical period. For Dover's most recent views on the origin of Greek pederasty see his *The Greeks and Their Legacy*, Oxford, 1988, 115–34. F. Buffière, *Eros adolescent. La pédérastie dans la Grèce antique*, Paris, 1980 has a very useful collection of evidence.

3 Cf. W. den Boer, *Laconian Studies*, Amsterdam, 1954, 245; H.-I. Marrou, *Histoire de l'éducation dans l'antiquité*, 6th edn, Paris, 1965, 63. The argument was already rejected in the too little known study by W. Kroll, *Freundschaft und Knabenliebe*, Munich, 1924.

4 Cf. H. Herter, 'Die Soziologie der antiken Prostitution im Lichte des heidnischen und christlichen Schrifttums', *Jahrbuch für Antike und Christentum*, 1960, 3: 70–111.

5 Cf. F. E. Williams, *Papuans of the Trans-Fly*, 2nd edn, Oxford, 1969, 158 f. On Williams (1893–1943) see A. P. Elkin, 'F. E. Williams – government anthropologist', *Oceania*, 1943, 14: 91–103; E. Schwimmer, 'F. E. Williams as Ancestor and Rainmaker' in F. E. Williams, *'The Vailala Madness' and Other Essays*, London, 1976, 11–47.

6 See also the many studies by G. Herdt: *Guardians of the Flutes: Idioms of Masculinity. A Study of Ritualized Homosexuality*, New York, 1981; (ed.), *Rituals of Manhood. Male Initiation in Papua New Guinea*, Berkeley, Calif./Los Angeles/London, 1982; (ed.), *Ritualized Homosexuality in Melanesia*, Berkeley, Calif./Los Angeles/London, 1984.

7 Cf. Williams, *Papuans of the Trans-Fly*, 309, on the mythological first occasion: 'Gambadi informants describe the initial occasion more vividly. The father bids his son stoop to drink and as he does so catches him at a disadvantage.'

8 Ephoros (*FGrHist* 70 F 149, summarized by Athenaeus 11.782C) *apud* Strabo, 10.4.21 (tr. Jones, Loeb, slightly modified). For a detailed, fully annotated discussion of this Cretan ritual see my 'An enigmatic Indo-European rite: pederasty', *Arethusa*, 1980, 13 (279–98): 283–87; for ritual capture scenes see now J. N. Bremmer and N. M. Horsfall, *Roman Myth and Mythography*, London, 1987, 105–11. For Cretan pederasty see now also H. Patzer, *Die griechische Knabenliebe*, Wiesbaden, 1982; B. Sergent, *L'Homosexualité initiatique dans l'Europe*

*ancienne*, Paris, 1986, 52–95; A. Henrichs, 'Three approaches to Greek mythography', in J. Bremmer (ed.), *Interpretations of Greek Mythology*, London, 1987 (242–77), 247. The objections of Halperin (n. 1), 58 against an initiatory reading of this ritual are unconvincing.

9 Thebes: Plutarch, *Moralia*, 761B. Athens: G. Kock-Harnack, *Knabenliebe und Tiergeschenke*, Berlin, 1983, 156.

10 On boy wine-pourers see my 'Adolescents, symposium and pederasty', in O. Murray (ed.), *Sympotica*, Oxford, 1990, 135–48. On Ganymede see most recently B. Sergent, *L'Homosexualité dans la mythologie grecque*, Paris, 1984, 237–47. Sergent's very useful collection of evidence does not sufficiently take note, though, of the often late intrusion of pederastic motives into existing myths.

11 See now P. Cartledge, 'The politics of Spartan pederasty', *Proc. Cambridge Philol. Soc.*, 1981, 17–36; Sergent, *L'Homosexualité initiatique*, 29–41 (Santorini).

12 Sparta: Dover, *Greek Homosexuality*, 187; see also Kassel-Austin on Aristophanes, fr. 358; Eupolis, fr. 385. Chalcis: Karystius *apud* Athenaeus, 13.603B; Plutarch, *Moralia* 761; Suidas and Hesychius s.v. *chalkidizein*; in fact, the Chalcidians even claimed that the rape of Ganymede had taken place in their territory at a place called Harpagion ('kidnapping'), and, indeed, there has recently been found a statue of Ganymede in their area: Athenaeus, 13.601F, cf. P. G. Themelis, *Athenian Annals of Archaeology*, 1969, 2: 163–5. Middle Ages: J. Boswell, *Christianity, Social Tolerance, and Homosexuality*, Chicago/London, 1980, 52. Boswell's book is very erudite but often too much inclined to explain away passages which are unfavourable to homosexuality; cf. R. MacMullen, 'Roman attitudes to Greek love', *Historia*, 1982, 31: 484–502; D. F. Wright, 'Homosexuals or prostitutes?', *Vigilae Christianae*, 1984, 38: 125–53. French: N. Z. Davis, *Fiction in the Archives*, Stanford, 1987, 201, n. 57.

13 Cf. J. G. von Hahn, *Albanesische Studien*, Jena, 1854, 166–8; P. Näcke, 'Über Homosexualität in Albanien', *Jahrbuch für sexuelle Zwischenstufen*, 1908, 9: 327–37, 'On homosexuality in Albania', *Intern. J. of Greek Love*, 1965, 1: 39–47; 'Erotisch-skatologisches Glossar der Albanesen', *Anthropophyteia*, 1911, 8: 35–9; E. Bethe, 'Die dorische Knabenliebe', *Rheinisches Museum* NF, 1907, 42 (438–75): 475; Bremmer, *Interpretations*, 289 f.

14 For the explanation of the development of Athenian homosexuality in this section see the fuller discussion in my study of 1990. 'Adolescents, symposium and pederasty' (n. 10).

15 This is denied, although without any arguments being offered, by D. Cohen, 'Law, society and homosexuality in classical Athens', *Past & Present*, 1987, no. 117, 3–21, who, moreover, completely fails to take into account the historical development of Athenian homosexuality. On the legal aspects of Athenian homosexuality see now also J. M. Rainer, 'Zum Problem der Atimie als Verlust der bürgerlichen Rechte insbesondere bei männlichen homosexuellen Prostituierten', *Revue Intern. des Droits de l'Antiquité*, 1986, III, 33: 89–114.

16 Cf. M. Golden, 'Slavery and homosexuality at Athens', *Phoenix*, 1984, 38: 308–24, who notes some exceptions (314, n. 26).

17 Literature and anal copulation: Dover, *Greek Homosexuality*, 140–7; note also that the names of well-known citizens were regularly used by comedians to denote the behind, cf. Kassel-Austin on Aristophanes, fr. 242; Photius *a* 3224 Theod. Intercrural mode of copulation: the prominence of the thigh as a sexual stimulus suggests that such copulations occurred perhaps more often than normally is accepted, cf. Dover, *Greek Homosexuality*, 70; add Kassel-Austin on Eupolis, fr. 127.

18 These restrictions have been insufficiently taken into account in the review of Patzer (n. 8) by D. Fehling, *Gnomon*, 1985, 57: 116–20. *Agrios*: Dover, *Greek Homosexuality*, 37 f; J. Taillardat, *Bulletin de Correspondance Hellénique*, 1983, 107: 189 f; add now Photius *a* 259 Theod.

19 On the obligation to marry see F. Graf, *Eleusis und die orphische Dichtung Athens in vorhellenistischer Zeit*, Berlin, New York, 1974, 114.

20 Bethe, 'Die dorische Knabenliebe' (60–4); see now also K. J. Dover, 'Homosexualität in Griechenland und die "Inspiration"', in H. P. Duerr (ed.), *Die Wilde Seele. Zur Ethnopsychoanalyse von Georges Devereux*, Frankfurt am Main, 1987, 47–63.

21 See the full collection of material in D. Fehling, *Ethologische Bemerkungen auf dem Gebiet der Altertumskunde*, Munich, 1974, 18–27; Dover, *Greek Homosexuality*, 100–9.

22 G. Hekma, 'Man of geen man. Een historiografie van de homoseksualiteit', *Sociologisch Tijdschrift*, 1988, 14, 620–44: 624 f.

23 This is rightly stressed by Hekma (n. 22), 625.

# 2

# Lesbian Sappho and Sappho of Lesbos

*André Lardinois*

The present use of the word 'lesbian' is first attested in the English language in 1890.[1] The noun 'lesbianism', in relation to the homosexuality of women, is slightly older. It dates from 1870.[2] It is written with a capital letter, thus revealing the connection which was felt with the island of Lesbos, where the poet Sappho wrote her songs around 600 BC. Is the connection between the isle of Lesbos and the homosexuality of women justified? Are there reasons to believe that Sappho of Lesbos was a 'lesbian'?

This is the Great Sappho Question, defined in less kindly terms by a German scholar as 'der Versuch der Beurteilung des der Lyrikerin unterstellten, nach ihrer Heimatinsel benannten Excesses'.[3] This question was already debated in antiquity but scholars have still not been able to reach agreement. They probably never will, not only because the evidence is too scanty, but because there is something intrinsically wrong with the question as put. In this chapter I would like to collect the most important evidence which we possess for Sappho's sexual inclination, and see what can be deduced from it and also, more importantly, what cannot be deduced.

Our sources of information concerning Sappho's life can be divided into three categories. First, there are the remnants of her poems. Actually the word 'songs' is more appropriate, as all of Sappho's poems were performed to music. Secondly, there are the so-called *testimonia*, a collection of fiction, truths, and half-truths, about Sappho and her poetry, gathered from the works of various ancient writers. Finally, there is the historical context, our knowledge of Sappho's time, which may be used for purposes of comparison or as background information to her life and work. So

15

far as is possible, I will deal with these three sources of information separately, confining myself to those facts which could be of importance in finding out whether Sappho of Lesbos was lesbian as well.

## 1 THE FRAGMENTS[4]

A scholarly edition of Sappho's poems, or a not too fanciful translation, contains only one complete poem, approximately ten substantial fragments, a hundred short citations from the works of ancient writers, and around fifty pieces of papyrus texts that emerged from the sands of the Egyptian desert. This is why it is more accurate to speak of Sappho's fragments.

The contents of these fragments differ greatly. Besides songs about the beauty of young girls, we possess pieces of cultic hymns, wedding songs, satires, songs about members of Sappho's family, and even one epic fragment.[5] Our interest is drawn primarily to the songs about young girls, since they most of all have given rise to the supposition that Sappho was a lesbian. I shall discuss their contents later. First I would like to examine the other songs.

The cultic hymns suggest that Sappho was a respected member of her community. Otherwise it is inconceivable that she was granted the honour of writing songs for the gods. These were choral hymns sung in public. If Sappho was a lesbian, and was able to proclaim her predilection, it must have been acceptable to the island community. This may also be inferred from the small size and the open character of this community.

The wedding songs too were sung by choirs. Female friends of the bride performed them during the wedding feast. They show us that at least part of Sappho's poetical activity centred around heterosexual love. There are also other fragments that treat of the love between man and wife.[6]

The satirical poems are of special interest as they speak about young girls who ran away from Sappho or about women to whom they had turned. Whatever the relationship was between Sappho and her girls, she clearly experienced rivalry. The actual names of the women mean little to us, but in one fragment a girl is mentioned who preferred the friendship of a woman belonging to the house of Penthilus (fr. 71). We are acquainted with this family through the work of a contemporary of Sappho, the Lesbian poet

Alcaeus. His political arch-enemy had entered into an alliance with this family through marriage. According to some sources, Alcaeus in turn had befriended Sappho. It is possible that complex political alliances played an important role in the termination or establishment of relationships between Sappho and her girls, whatever they may have been.

Sappho criticized in her poems not only perfidious girls or troublesome rivals, but her own brother Charaxus and his girlfriend Doricha as well (cf. fr. 202). In yet another song she praises her younger brother Larichus who served wine in the town hall. As this was a privilege reserved for young aristocratic adolescents (fr. 203), it can safely be inferred that Sappho belonged to an important Lesbian family. The epic fragment, recounting the wedding of Hector and Andromache, I will not discuss here: perhaps it was performed at an actual wedding feast, or perhaps it was simply a mythical story which Sappho could recite on various occasions.[7]

Most controversy has been raised by Sappho's songs about young girls. They can roughly be divided into two groups. First there are the songs which concern those girls who had left Sappho, either against her wishes (see above) or with her consent (possibly in order to marry). In these songs she mentions the girls by name: Anactoria (fr. 16), Gongyla (fr. 22), Megara (fr. 68a), Mica (fr. 71), Arignota(?) (fr. 96), Atthis (fr. 131), Archeanassa (fr. 213). Therefore they must have been occasional verses, in the sense that they concern one particular girl and one particular occasion. The same cannot be said of the songs in which Sappho refers to a girl who is still near to her (fr. 1, fr. 23(?), fr. 31). No specific person is addressed and they could have been recited on various occasions, even by different poets.[8] This bipartition is rather hypothetical, though, as in most cases too little of the poems is preserved to say with certainty whether a name appeared in them or not. Thus we expect the name of a girl to have figured in the lost part of fragment 94, whereas we do not expect its occurrence in poem 23.

It is, however, certain that these poems concern young girls. Sometimes Sappho herself refers to them as such and the *testimonia* confirm this repeatedly. Therefore the supposition that Sappho was lesbian requires at the very least some qualifications. If Sappho's feelings towards these girls were erotic, she appears to have been a kind of female pederast. But what exactly were these feelings? A French scholar recently declared that whatever has been adduced in defence of Sappho and her morals, the sensual character of most of her poetry is self-evident.[9] Against this can be set the words of a German classicist: 'In any case it has to be kept in mind that in the considerable amount of verses which we can study today, not the slightest indication can be found of any sexual "anomalies".'[10] Perhaps the only thing that is clear is that Sappho's poems are unclear in this respect.

Against the supposition that Sappho was lesbian it has repeatedly been argued that there is no sign of physical love in her poetry.[11] This statement has tempted others to scrutinize the fragments for the slightest possible allusion to homo-erotic practice. Fragment 94 is famous in this respect. In this fragment Sappho mentions her own name; so there can be no doubt about the identity of the narrator. She addresses a girl who had to leave her and she recalls all the pleasant things they did together: stringing flower-wreaths, putting on beautiful clothes and wearing lovely perfumes, and spending time in sanctuaries which the fragmentary words 'dance' and 'sound' probably relate to. In the middle of all this we read: 'and on soft beds . . . you would satisfy your longing . . .' (ll. 21–2). Here the text breaks off yet again and we are left to wonder what the girl was longing for. Even in antiquity one could experience longing (*pothos*) for other things besides sex. Perhaps the girl had been tired. An erotic interpretation of the line cannot be excluded, but as a whole the passage is a weak argument in favour of Sappho's involvement in lesbian love-affairs.

In another fragment a dildo is suddenly mentioned (*olisb* . . ., fr. 99, l. 5). I need not stress the fact that such an instrument could be of use to a heterosexual woman as well. Judith P. Hallett rightly remarked about this dildo: 'The poetic context fails to clarify Sappho's relationship to it and its to Sappho.'[12] Moreover, it is quite likely that this is a fragment in which Sappho tries to blacken one of her rivals. In that case the passage would rather be proof of Sappho's prudery; in contrast to this woman she would never make use of such an instrument.

The question is, however, whether it is safe to argue that Sappho did not participate in lesbian practices because she does not say so in her poetry. Reading the male poets who write about their love-affairs with adolescent boys we do not encounter a detailed description of the act either, yet their physical involvement is hardly ever doubted. Sappho did not have to write pornography in order to be a lesbian poet.

The poetry of Sappho was already compared to that of the male pederasts in antiquity. In their love-poems we find parallels for most of the wording and imagery which Sappho uses.[13] This is one of the strongest arguments in favour of Sappho's sexual involvement with the girls she addresses. But against this it can be said that in her wedding songs Sappho permits choirs to sing about a bride in no less erotic terms than she uses in her alleged homo-erotic lyrics. A good example is fragment 112. Here a maiden choir sings to the bride: 'Your form is gracious and your eyes . . . honey-sweet; love streams over your desire-arousing face. Aphrodite has indeed greatly honoured you.' Most fragments of Sappho are far more innocent in tone.

The looks of a girl were considered to be extremely important in antiquity. Would it not be possible then that Sappho in her poems, like the choirs in the wedding songs, wishes only to emphasize the attractiveness of these young girls, which was meant to be appreciated in the first place by the men in her audience? In her poems she regularly compares the girls with famous heterosexual women, like Helen of Troy (fr. 16 and fr. 23), and according to an ancient report those who were most attracted by her poetry were young men in love (*test.* 58). The parallel in her wedding songs is of even more significance when one realizes that some of these songs may have been sung by maiden choirs as well (n. 8).

One could object that Sappho occasionally states that she is herself attracted by the beauty of her girls. In fragment 1 she says that she suffers from a 'maddened heart' (l. 18, cf. fr. 36 and fr. 8) and in fragment 16 she declares that Anactoria 'is loved' (l. 4, cf. fr. 49). The one does not have to exclude the other, however. An archaic Greek did not think in terms of exclusive homosexual and exclusive heterosexual love. By declaring that she herself was enchanted by the beauty of her girls, she did not diminish their prospects of marriage. Quite the contrary. What is expressed in all these poems is the general attractiveness of the girls. It is not chance that both in the wedding song quoted above, and in fragment 1, in which Sappho herself speaks, Aphrodite is invoked. But this does not answer the question whether Sappho engaged in sexual affairs with the girls. And we may ask ourselves yet another question: how far are the sentiments which Sappho expresses in her poetry to be considered personal?

The late French scholar George Devereux interpreted fragment 31 as a poetical reflection of an anxiety attack that Sappho had suffered as a result of her repressed homosexuality.[14] In this fragment Sappho enumerates various so-called *pathemata*, afflictions of body and soul. The narrator suffers from these every time she sees an unspecified girl laughing and speaking to a man. Her heart misses a beat, her ears ring. She cannot speak and sweat pours down her face. She mentions ten of these *pathemata* in all. The situation looks grave, but a psychological interpretation of these conditions is not permissible as that is something alien to the Greek culture Sappho lived and wrote in. In fragment 47 she tells us that Eros moved her mind, like the wind which falls upon the oak trees in the mountains. What we experience as a personal feeling is here ascribed to the power of a god which is regarded as something akin to a force in nature.[15]

The poetry of Sappho is, like all archaic poetry, conventional in character. Eight of the *pathemata* enumerated in the fragment are already mentioned by Homer, and after Sappho we regularly encounter them in Greek literature as well. The Latin poet Catullus could translate the whole fragment to express his feelings for a woman.[16] Even if we are willing to assume that the narrator in the poem is Sappho herself and that she thought of one particular girl when she wrote the song, it is impossible to gather from her poem her personal feelings. This is emphatically true of all her poetry. Even if some of her songs appear homo-erotic in content, one cannot infer that Sappho was a lesbian at heart. Neither, however, may one conclude the contrary.

Sappho's own verse, which can be rightly termed the most reliable biographical source, yields depressingly little. It is a fact that she did not write exclusively about lesbian love, and also that she must have been a respected member of her community. Possibly she engaged in sexual relations with the girls she wrote about, like the male poets who wrote about their boys. If so, we would like to find some confirmation in other sources. Perhaps the *testimonia* can be of assistance.

## 2 THE TESTIMONIA

Much must have been written about Sappho in antiquity, ranging from brief allusions to voluminous works, but only a fraction came down to us. The most elaborate source we possess is a poem by the Latin poet Ovid.[17] It takes the form of a letter supposedly written by Sappho herself. In this letter various details are mentioned which we know of from other sources as well. Confining myself to facts related to Sappho's sexual disposition, I will try to examine their historical value.

The 'letter of Sappho' is addressed to Phaon, a man (!) she is said to be hopelessly in love with.[18] This love induces her to commit suicide by jumping from the Leucadian rock into the sea.[19] She also speaks about a daughter (!),[20] but there is mention of her preference for little girls as well:

Neither the girls of Pyrrha or Methymna [villages on Lesbos] delight me, nor the rest of the throng of Lesbian women. Naught to me is Anactoria, naught the fair Cydro; Atthis is not pleasing, as before, to my eyes, nor *a hundred others whom I have loved, not without reproach.* Shameless man, what once belonged to many girls is yours alone now. (Italics added)[21]

Here we have the most likely source of Sappho's reputation as a lesbian in the nineteenth century. At the beginning of that century this poem of Ovid was better known than any other writing about Sappho, including her own poetry. Faith in the document was increased by the fact that for a long time it was believed to be based on an original letter of Sappho, which Ovid merely translated. Sceptics could find confirmation in the Suda, a Byzantine compilation of a variety of facts worth knowing from antiquity. In it there is mention of three 'companions or girlfriends' of Sappho, 'Atthis, Telesippa, and Megara', through whom she earned a bad reputation for 'disgraceful friendship' (*test.* 2). At the beginning of the twentieth century a papyrus text was found which refers to rumours suggesting that Sappho had been a 'woman-lover' (*test.* 1).

The German classicist Welcker was the first to conduct a critical examination of the *testimonia*. In 1816 he published a book under the instructive title: 'Sappho freed from a modern prejudice'. In this study he exposed as fables practically all the ancient accounts of Sappho's life, in particular those concerning her alleged lesbianism. He blamed Athenian comedy for most of the fabrications. It would have presented its customary caricature, which in Sappho's case subsequent authors, including Ovid, took to be true.[22]

The weakness in Welcker's argument is that, so far as we know, Sappho was never portrayed as a lesbian on the Athenian stage, but, quite to the contrary, as an extreme heterosexual. She supposedly enjoyed various male lovers at one and the same time, and in all probability her love of Phaon was made fun of. It appears that the name which the Suda gives to a husband of Sappho is derived from a Greek comedy as well: a free translation of it would be 'Prick from the city of Man'.[23] But Welcker has to be given credit for raising doubts about the historical value of the ancient reports. One should not believe everything one reads, even when written two thousand years ago.

It can be assumed that the Greeks and Romans in subsequent ages knew little more than we do about events that had taken place on Lesbos in the sixth century BC. But they had one advantage over us: they must still have been able to read the works of Sappho in fairly complete form. Therefore, whenever they mention a fact which may stem from Sappho's own writing, it should be treated seriously.

A good example is the historicity of Sappho's daughter. Ovid does not mention her name but other sources do: Cleïs (*test*. 1 and *test*. 2). We possess two fragments by Sappho in which this name occurs (fr. 98b and fr. 132). These fragments by themselves do not reveal that we are dealing with a daughter of Sappho, but nothing contradicts this possibility and a single word in fragment 132 may even corroborate it.[24] We know that Sappho wrote songs about her brothers, so a poem about a daughter would not be inconceivable. In such a case the *testimonia* may tip the scales. In all probability Sappho did have a daughter named Cleïs. Given the social context, one may assume that she was also married therefore, and Greek comedy jumped to this conclusion, as we have seen. Yet it is strange that we do not possess any reliable name for Sappho's husband. Normally the names of mothers and wives are lacking in the ancient sources, not those of husbands.[25] Probably Sappho was married, but we cannot know for sure.

Very different is the case of Sappho's alleged leap from the Leucadian rock. It goes without saying that she could not have recorded it in her poetry. It is also unlikely that there was a contemporary report. In all probability the account is not historical. But we cannot leave it at this. We must ask ourself how such a story could arise. A leap from the Leucadian rock is also mentioned by another Greek poet (Anacreon fr. 13, Page). Here it is presented as a proverbial remedy against the pain of love. Love-pains figure prominently in the poems of Sappho, and it could be that she had used the same image in a lost poem. That would offer a plausible explanation for the origin of the story. Many such figurative statements by early poets were taken literally by scholars in late antiquity.[26]

The story of Sappho's love for Phaon is probably also based on an erroneous reading of Sappho's poetry. Phaon was a mythological figure, who belonged among the loved ones of Aphrodite, just like Adonis with whom he should perhaps be identified. We know that Sappho wrote songs about the love of Aphrodite for Phaon and Adonis (fr. 211). A fragment is preserved of one of those songs for Adonis in which the goddess is made to speak (fr. 140a). It may be that Sappho had put into the mouth of the goddess a profession of love for Phaon, which was later interpreted as being her own.[27]

When the same critical approach is applied to the reports about Sappho's homosexuality as to the stories of her suicide and her love for Phaon, there remains little to support their claim to be historical. After all, it is unlikely that Sappho proclaimed in any of her poems that she was a 'woman-lover'. But there is one difference. These reports about her homosexuality cannot be traced to a misreading of a proverbial statement or a confusion of identities. They are interpretations of genuine statements by Sappho about girls like Atthis and Anactoria. And as we ourselves are puzzled about their intention, should we not allow these ancient interpretations to guide our own?

Even when ancient reports about Sappho's life prove to be unhistorical, they can be of value, because they reflect how Sappho was viewed in antiquity. This view must somehow be based on responses to Sappho's poetry, as this was the only available source of information about her life in later antiquity. Now, with regard to Sappho's sexual predilections the opinions seem to have changed remarkably over the ages. In Athenian comedy (around the fourth century BC), as we have seen, she was portrayed as a staunch heterosexual. Rumours about her 'disgraceful friendships' with women emerge only in Roman times, and even then stories were still circulating about her involvement with men. Thus the Roman philosopher Seneca mentions a contemporary treatise addressing the question whether or not Sappho had been a prostitute (*test.* 22).

The meaning of the word 'lesbian' (*lesbis, lesbia*) underwent a similar change. The word was used in the first place for a female inhabitant of the isle of Lesbos, but from classical times onwards erotic connotations became attached to it. What influence Sappho's poetry played in this is hard to assess, but that it did have influence is not unlikely. In antiquity Sappho was already by far the most famous female inhabitant of the island. Her poetry was very popular and Lesbos minted coins bearing an image of the poet for several centuries (*test.* 11 + n).

The classical comedy writer Aristophanes (446–385 BC) used a verb *lesbiazein*, 'to do like the Lesbian women', for women who practised fellatio, and this meaning of the verb is attested until late antiquity.[28] The first overt association of Lesbos with female homosexuality is found in Roman times. The Greek writer Lucian (*c.* AD 120–80) states: '*They say* there are women in Lesbos with faces like men, and unwilling to consort with men, but only with women, as though they themselves were men' (italics added).[29] In the Byzantine period we also encounter the word 'lesbia' itself with reference to a female homosexual.[30] It can hardly be accidental that Sappho's sexual reputation runs parallel with that of the women of Lesbos in general. In my opinion the development of the meaning of the word 'lesbian' in antiquity can serve as evidence for responses to Sappho's poetry.

How can this development be explained and what does it finally tell us about our poet? The matter is complex and we can only speculate. As I said before, in archaic and classical times there was no strict boundary between hetero- and homosexual love.[31] Both belonged to the sphere of influence of Eros and Aphrodite, who together were opposed to Hera, the goddess of the orderly, less passionate married life. A womanizer like Alcibiades could just as well be accused of lacking restraint in his pursuit of homo-erotic affairs. Is Sappho's case similar? Could it be that her frivolous songs praising the beauty of young girls gave rise to the assumption that she would also have been more than willing to sleep with numerous men, preferably in a shameless manner?

After the classical period a change in the conception of sexuality occurs. The heterosexual love-novel presented itself with its 'happy ending' in marriage, while the practice of pederasty no longer was permissible. Aphrodite and Eros were assigned their own spheres of influence: Aphrodite was said to cover the area of heterosexual love (from now on to be sought in marriage), Eros the area of homosexual love (primarily an aberration of the archaic poets).[32] A dichotomy thus arises between homo- and heterosexuality, similar to that in modern society. As long as the distinction was not regarded as absolute, one could see in Sappho a generally erotic woman: Aphrodite and Eros were central to her poetry, and so they must have been to her life. From the moment that a choice had to be made between the two, Sappho belonged, according to some of her readers at least, to the category of homosexual women: her poetry, after all, was all about girls.

It is possible to derive both views of Sappho from the erotic interpretation of her poetry. This fact is in itself not without significance: it supports those who believe that there is more at stake in her songs about young girls than mere praise of their beauty. But each view has its own particular limitations. Sappho lived in the archaic Greek age, not in the Roman, Byzantine, or modern era. This means that any proclamation that Sappho was a homosexual, or the opposite, is necessarily anachronistic. And what are we to make of the classical Greek opinion that she was a 'generally erotic' woman? Are we also to infer from her poetry that she devoted not only her poetic talents to the works of Aphrodite, but her personal life as well? There is in any case not the slightest scrap of evidence in her poetry that Sappho slept with numerous men, and Welcker was certainly right in asserting that Athenian comedy could exaggerate grossly.

## 3 THE HISTORICAL CONTEXT

Our investigation of the *testimonia* has made one thing particularly clear: it is of the utmost importance to discover more about the social and cultural context in which the work of Sappho has to be seen. Unfortunately our information about the archaic Greek era is as defective as the transmission of Sappho's poetry and *testimonia*. And there is the additional problem that it is impossible to decide with certainty what is relevant to Sappho's poetry and what is not. I shall concentrate on two subjects, which have received most attention in modern research on Sappho: first the educational system which brought young girls together in groups, and secondly the existence of women in other parts of Greece who had sexual relationships with girls.

From the poems of Sappho it becomes clear that she had gathered several girls around her and some of the *testimonia* speak about education.[33] These facts tempted a prominent German classicist to declare that Sappho had been at the head of a 'boarding-school' for young women. He has been vehemently attacked because of the anachronism of this view. Nevertheless, most scholars today have accepted the idea that Sappho's relationship to her girls encompassed that of teacher to pupil.[34]

Thanks to a fairly recent study we know more about the kind of groups in which young girls were organized in archaic Greece.[35] They joined maiden choirs, which formed part of their education. Music was considered pedagogically important in early Greece. By singing together the girls learned discipline as well as a certain sense of beauty. Singing was usually accompanied by dancing. Through these dances the girls could show that they knew how to move gracefully. Spinning and weaving, two even more important skills for women, were taught at home. They did not belong to the activities practised by Sappho and her maidens.[36]

The poems of Sappho do not reveal the exact kind of organization her so-called 'circle' comprised. Music and dance figure prominently in the fragments, however, and at one time she speaks about the house 'of those who serve the Muses' (fr. 150). The same expression is encountered in an inscription from the second century BC about a theatre group.[37] There is nothing surprising about a poet leading a choir of girls. It could have performed the religious hymns, the wedding songs, and possibly other songs which Sappho wrote. It could also accompany performances by Sappho herself with dances.[38] Sappho's teaching need not have been restricted to music and dance, however. An impression of all the activities Sappho performed with her girls is to be found in fragment 94, summarized above (p. 18). Thus there are good reasons for the presence of young girls in Sappho's poetry, other than sexual. But the one does not have to exclude the other, and besides singing and dancing and putting on beautiful clothes, fragment 94 referred to a young girl's unspecified longings.

There are very few sources about lesbian love in antiquity and they are mostly of dubious quality.[39] It is clear, however, that lesbian love was known, but that it was, at least in late antiquity, not accepted. Lucian, whom we quoted above, calls the love between two women 'unnatural', and the Roman poet Martialis even speaks of a crime (*facinus*, I.90.6). This judgement is shared by Ovid and the other commentators on the 'disgraceful friendships' of Sappho.

It certainly comes as a surprise that a contemporary of Martialis, the Greek author Plutarch, asserts that in ancient Sparta 'distinguished ladies' had sexual relationships with young girls (*Lyc.* 18.4). The Spartans introduced the custom, he says, to match the pederastic relationships between adult men and young boys. An obscure statement by an obscure philosopher from the fourth century BC seems to confirm this. He declares that it was customary for young Spartan girls before their marriage to have sexual relationships like the boys.[40] In subsequent ages there were various fables told about archaic Sparta, and we should seriously doubt the reliability of these statements, were they not corroborated by evidence from the archaic age itself.

Thus we know that the poet Alcman, who wrote songs for Spartan maiden choirs in the seventh century BC, used the word *aïtis* for a young girl engaged in a sexual relationship (fr. 183 Calame). The male equivalent of this word, *aïtas*, was the official term for the young boy in a pederastic relationship. We also possess a vase from the Greek island of Thera, dated around 600 BC, which portrays two women, the one making an inviting gesture to the other, who is carrying a wreath in her hand.[41] We possess similar representations of men and young boys. It seems therefore that during the archaic Greek period there existed in some parts of Greece relationships between older women and girls, similar to male pederastic relationships.

Of the maiden songs of Alcman two fairly long fragments have been preserved. Their contents have led some scholars to believe that homo-erotic relationships also existed between the young girls themselves.[42] Thus in fragment 26 (Calame) a maiden choir displays the admiration which its members feel towards one of them, presumably their leader, the *choragos*, in the following way:

'with longing that loosens the limbs and she casts glances that are more melting than sleep and death; and not in vain is she sweet' (ll. 61–3). The English scholar Bowra wrote about the girl: 'We are left with the impression that the whole company is in love with her and no doubt this is what Aicman intended his audience to feel.' But he added: 'The aim of the song is the celebration of a girl's beauty and charm which everyone is intended to feel.'[43] There is a marked difference, however, between 'love' and 'the celebration of a girl's beauty', and between 'the whole company' and 'everyone'. (The celebrated girl is running among a large crowd – ll. 73–4.) There is a strong resemblance between the description of this girl and that of the bride in fragment 112 of Sappho, which I quoted above. Therefore I see no reason why the choir should be saying anything more than that their leader should be regarded as a very beautiful girl.

In my opinion the same holds true for the girls Hagesichora and Agido in fragment 3 (Calame). In this poem there is, however, another interesting passage. At a certain moment the maiden choir makes the following general statement: 'You [a woman] won't go to the house of Ainesimbrota and say "let Astaphis be mine", nor "let Philulla pay attention to me and Damareta and lovely Wianthemis", but [you will say] "Hagesichora distresses me"' (ll. 73–7). We do not know who Ainesimbrota was, but it is clear that she had some influence over the girls. It has been suggested that she was a sorcerer who could brew love-potions.[44] Otherwise she might have been a woman who allocated the girls among the women of Sparta. It is a fact that in Sparta the practice of pederasty was more tightly organized than anywhere else in Greece. Thus the passage could point to possible relationships between the girls and women in the audience. There is, however, no reason to suppose that relationships also existed among the girls themselves. The other sources also refer only to relationships between adult women and girls.

It has been suggested that these kind of relationships existed on Lesbos as well, and that Sappho, and possibly her 'rivals', were such adult women.[45] It is a fact that in the days of Sappho pederasty was practised on the island. This can be inferred from the poems of Alcaeus.[46] But this is all we can say with certainty. Some resemblances between Sappho and the Spartan women can be pointed to. In both cases we are dealing with highborn women.

From our sources concerning male pederastic relationships it appears that these were restricted to the aristocracy. Also the age of the Spartan girls and of those in Sappho's circle appear to be similar. The advantage of the comparison is that it can do full justice to the erotic interpretation of Sappho's poetry in antiquity and to the parallels which were drawn between her poetry and that of the male pederasts. It also provides sexual relationships between Sappho and her girls with the necessary social legitimacy.

There remain some problems, however. Sappho had a group of young girls around her, and it is unlikely that she had a sexual relationship with all of them. Both the women in Sparta and the male pederasts had relationships with only one youth. But there need not have been a connection between Sappho's relationships and her 'circle'. In Sparta there was a distinction between the poet who instructed the girls (e.g. Alcman), and their female lovers. Whatever the reliability of the Suda as a source may be, it does differentiate between 'girlfriends' of Sappho and her 'pupils' (*test.* 2). If her girlfriends did belong to the circle, probably each of them was in succession the most important girl of the group, or, according to the terminology of a Greek maiden choir, the *choragos*. One may also think of groups like those at Crete which centred around one aristocratic boy and his lover.[47]

Another problem is that some *testimonia* maintain that it was not only girls from Lesbos, but also girls from other parts of Greece, who joined Sappho's group.[48] It is extraordinary that this assertion has never been doubted. It does not comply with the types of organization we know of in archaic Greece, and it compels one to believe that Sappho was indeed heading a kind of boarding-school. The fame of Sappho throughout antiquity would itself be sufficient reason for the fabrication of the story. Ultimately all archaic female poets were said to have been pupils of Sappho, and it is only natural that other cities desired to establish some connection with the tenth Muse, as Sappho sometimes was called. But it is also possible that the assertion stems from an erroneous reading of her poetry. The regions to which some of the girls, according to the poems, went *after* their stay in Sappho's circle, may have been held to be their places of origin. In most cases the girls were married there, and the mobility of brides, still fairly great among the aristocracy of archaic Greece, may not have been taken into account by the Hellenistic scholars. But whether one believes the assertion or not, it does not affect the possibility that Sappho had sexual relationships with some of her girls, similar to those between adult men and boys, or between women and girls in other parts of Greece.

As regards these relationships one has to be cautious, however, about the application of modern notions, like 'lesbian' or 'homosexual', associated as these are with such concepts as 'natural inclination' or 'exclusiveness'. We are dealing with an institutionalized type of sexuality, in which the preferences of those involved may have been of little consequence. We have remarked that in the establishment of relationships between Sappho and her girls alliances between prominent families probably played a larger part than her own heart. Our sources about the pederastic relationships of the men indicate that they were primarily a mark of honour, and the whole practice may ultimately go back to an initiation ritual.[49]

There can be no question of exclusiveness either. Sappho was probably married, and it is unlikely that this was not the case with the 'distinguished ladies' in Sparta. The girls were also expected to marry. Hagnon states explicitly that the relationships lasted till their marriage, and it is commonly agreed that Sappho wrote her marriage songs for girls who shortly before had left her circle.

## CONCLUSION

We may conclude that in the case of Sappho we are dealing at the most with short relationships between an adult woman and a young, marriageable girl. To call these relationships 'lesbian' is anachronistic. Whether the word applies to Sappho herself, her inner life, is impossible to assess. Actually it constitutes a nonsensical question. Even if by modern standards Sappho were to be considered lesbian, her experience must have been very different, living as she did in a different age with different notions and different types of sexuality.

## NOTES

I have greatly profited from comments made by Dr J. N. Bremmer, Dr Th. C. W. Oudemans, Dr R. C. T. Parker, and I. Sluiter. Dr Parker, and my brother-in-law, Desmond McAleer, also helped to revise my

English. The Dutch version of this article was dedicated to my girlfriend, Cécile Cuppens, now my wife.

1 J. P. Hallett, 'Sappho and her social context', *Signs*, 1979, 3: 451-2. She also discusses another term derived from Sappho's reputation as a homosexual, the words 'sapphism', 'sapphist', and 'sapphic'.

2 *A Supplement to the Oxford English Dictionary*, Vol. II, Oxford, 1976, 645. The English were fairly late in adopting the term, compared to the continent of Europe. In French it is already attested in 1842: W. von Wartenburg, *Französisches Etymologisches Wörterbuch*, Vol. V, 1950, 261, s.v. Lesbos; in Dutch the word 'sapfisch' (Sapphisch) dates at least from 1847: *Algemeen noodwendig woordenboek*, Amsterdam, 1847, cited by M. Everhard, 'De liefde van Lesbos in Nederland', *Tijdschrift voor vrouwenstudies*, 1984, 5: 344.

3 'The attempt to evaluate the excess which, named after her place of origin, the poet is said to have committed' (my translation): H. Saake, *Sapphostudien: Forschungsgeschichtliche, biografische und literarästhetische Untersuchungen*, Munich, 1972, 14.

4 The numbers of fragments and *testimonia* refer to the latest edition of Sappho's poems, that of D. A. Campbell, *Greek Lyric*, Vol. 1, in the Loeb Classical Library, 1983. Campbell has provided all fragments and *testimonia* with a useful translation. In numbering the fragments he has followed fairly closely the editions of E. Lobel and D. L. Page, *Poetarum Lesbiorum Fragmenta*, Oxford, 1955, and E.-M. Voigt, *Sappho et Alcaeus: Fragmenta*, Amsterdam, 1971.

5 With a reasonable degree of certainty we can identify as *cultic hymns* fragments 2 (?), 140, cf. fr. 211; as *wedding songs*, fragments 27, 30, 103-17b, 161, cf. fr. 194, *testimonium* 58; as *satires*, 133 (?), 144, 178 (?), 213, cf. *test*. 20; as songs about *her brother Charaxus*, fragments 3 (?), 5, 7 (?), 15, 209 (?), 213A (b-e), cf. fr. 202, *test*. 1, 9, 14-16; and about *her brother Larichus*, fragment 203, cf. *test*. 1, 2, 14. Fragment 44 is commonly regarded as *epic* in character.

6 Fragments 102 (?), 121, 129b, 137, 138. A detailed discussion of the wedding songs can be found in D. L. Page, *Sappho and Alcaeus: an introduction to the study of ancient Lesbian poetry*, Oxford, 1955, 119-26.

7 The view, widely held at the beginning of this century, that fr. 44 was performed during an actual wedding feast, has recently been defended again by W. Rösler, 'Ein Gedicht und sein Publikum: Ueberlegungen zu Sappho fr. 44', *Hermes*, 1975, 103: 275-85. Most modern interpreters, though, prefer to regard the poem as an unspecified mythological story: A. Lesky, *Geschichte der Griechische Literatur*, Berne, 1971[3], 171; Saake, *Sapphostudien*, 78; G. M. Kirkwood, *Early Greek Monody: the history of a poetic type*, Ithaca, NY/London, 1974, 146. See also: A. M. van Erp Taalman Kip, 'Enige interpretatieproblemen in Sappho', *Lampas*, 1980, 13: 349-51; A. Pippin-Burnett, *Three Archaic Poets: Archilochus, Alcaeus, Sappho*, London, 1983, 219-20.

8 M. L. West, 'Burning Sappho', *Maia*, 1970, 22: 307–30. It is too readily assumed that Sappho intended her songs to be performed solely by herself. She mentions her name in only four fragments (frs 1, 65, 94, 133), which makes it possible that other songs were meant to be sung by other poets as well. Moreover, it appears from the fragments that her girls also dedicated songs to each other (fr. 22 and fr. 96). Were these songs composed by themselves, or did Sappho write them, as she wrote the wedding songs? It could be that an occasional poem like fragment 96 was actually meant to be sung by one, or a group, of her girls (note the plural in line 21, although this is not conclusive). This does not make the interpretation of Sappho's poetry any easier.

9 F. Buffière, *Eros adolescent: La pédérastie dans la Grèce antique*, Paris, 1980, 246.

10 My translation: A. Lesky, *Vom Eros der Hellenen*, Göttingen, 1976, 53.

11 Still recently: Hallett, 453.

12 Ibid. About the fragment see also: Page, *Sappho and Alcaeus*, 144–5; West, 'Burning Sappho', 324; G. Giangrande, 'Sappho and the "olisbos"', *Emerita*, 1980, 48, 449–50; A. Guarino, '"Professorenerotismus"', *Labeo*, 1981, 27: 439–40; G. Giangrande, 'A che serviva l' "olisbos" de Saffo?', *Labeo*, 1983, 29: 154–5.

13 G. Lanata, 'Sul linguaggio amoroso di Saffo', *Quaderni Urbinati di Cultura Classica*, 1966, 2: 63–79; Page, *Sappho and Alcaeus*, 10. Sappho is often mentioned in the same breath with Anacreon, a known representative of pederastic poetry: Plato, *Phaedrus*, 235c, *test*. 39, 42, 47, 51, 52, 54; fr. 156. E. S. Stigers, however, maintains that there is a marked difference between Sappho's love-poetry and that of the male poets, in H. P. Foley (ed.), *Reflections of Women in Antiquity*, New York, 1981, 45–61. On Sappho's love-poetry see also: Ch. P. Segal, 'Eros and incantation: Sappho and oral poetry', *Arethusa*, 1974, 7: 139–60.

14 G. Devereux, 'The nature of Sappho's seizure in fr. 31 LP as evidence of her inversion', *Classical Quarterly*, 1970, 20: 17–31.

15 For the radical difference between our modern and the archaic Greek culture, see now Th. C. W. Oudemans and A. P. M. H. Lardinois, *Tragic Ambiguity: Anthropology, Philosophy and Sophocles' Antigone*, Leiden, 1987, esp. chs 2–4.

16 Catullus LI. For Homeric and other parallels: A. Turyn, *Studia Sapphica I*, Eos Suppl. 6, Lwow, 1929, 29, 41–57; Page, *Sappho and Alcaeus*, 29. O. Tsagarakis has drawn some interesting parallels with modern Greek folk songs: 'Some neglected aspects of love in Sappho's fr. 31', *Rheinisches Museum*, 1979, 122: 97–118; more recently: 'Broken hearts and the social circumstances in Sappho's poetry', *Rheinisches Museum*, 1986, 129: 1–17. They confirm the conventional character of Sappho's verses. However, his interpretation of the song as heterosexual in content has to be rejected, cf. J. M. Bremer, 'A reaction to Tsagarakis' discussion of Sappho fr. 31', *Rheinisches Museum*, 1982, 125: 113–16.

17 *Heroides* 15. Campbell includes several passages from the poem in his collection of *testimonia*: ll. 61–2 (*test.* 13), ll. 63–70 and 117–20 (*test.* 16), ll. 15–20 and 201 f. (*test.* 19), ll. 29–30 (*test.* 44).

18 *Her.* 15, esp. ll. 9–12, cf. *test.* 3, 23; fr. 211a, 211c.

19 *Her.* 15, ll. 175 ff., 220; cf. *test.* 3, 23 + n.

20 *Her.* 15, ll. 70, 120; cf. *test.* 1, 2, fr. 150, 213A(g)?.

21 *Her.* 15, ll. 15–20 (*test.* 19); cf. ll. 201–2; Ovid, *Tristia* 2.365 (*test.* 49). In view of the verses 201–2 the stated reading, 'not without reproach' (*non sine crimine*) is to be preferred to the reading 'here without reproach' (*hic sine crimine*): H. Jacobson, *Ovid's Heroides*, Princeton, NJ, 1974, 292–3; recently W. M. Calder III, 'Welcker's Sapphobild and its reception in Wilamowitz', in W. M. Calder III *et al.* (eds), *Friedrich Gottlieb Welcker: Werk und Wirkung*, Hermes Einzelschriften, Wiesbaden, 1986, 49, (131–56): 143.

22 Ibid., 131–56.

23 W. Aly, 'Sappho', in Pauly Wissowa, *Realencylopädie des klassischen Altertumswissenschaft*, Vol. 2 A 1, 1920, 2361; Campbell, *Greek Lyric*, 5. On Sappho in Athenian comedy: *test.* 8, 25, 26 + n.

24 *agapata* (beloved): J. P. Hallett, 'Beloved Cleïs', *Quaderni Urbinati di Cultura Classica*, 1982, NS 10, 21–31; compare, however, 'beloved soul' (*psucha agapatasu* . . ., fr. 62).

25 J. N. Bremmer, 'Plutarch and the naming of Greek women', *American Journal of Philology*, 1981, 102: 425 f.

26 C. M. Bowra, *Greek Lyric Poetry*, Oxford, 1976, 177, 213. For a different explanation of the image: G. Nagy, 'Phaethon, Sappho's Phaon, and the white rock of Leukas', *Harvard Studies in Classical Philology*, 1973, 77: 137–77.

27 Bowra, *Greek Lyric Poetry*, 212–14.

28 H. D. Jocelyn, 'A Greek indecency and its students: "laikazein"', *Proceedings of the Cambridge Philological Society*, 1980, NS 26, 18 + n. 66, 31–4; A. M. Komornicka, 'A la suite de la lecture "La ragazza di Lesbo"', *Quaderni Urbinati di Cultura Classica*, 1976, 21: 37–41.

29 Lucian, *Dialogues of the Courtesans*, 5.2.

30 A. C. Cassio, 'Post-classical "Lesbia"', *Classical Quarterly*, 1983, 33: 296–7.

31 Cf. K. J. Dover, *Greek Homosexuality*, London/New York, 1978, 1.

32 Buffière, *Eros adolescent*, 245. On sexuality in ancient Greece: H. Licht, *Sittengeschichte der Griechen I: Das Liebesleben der Griechen*, Dresden/Zürich, 1926 (English translation: *Sexual Life in Ancient Greece*, London 1962[2]); R. Flacelière, *L'amour en Grèce*, Paris, 1960 (English translation: *Love in Ancient Greece*, London, 1962); Lesky, *Vom Eros der Hellenen*; C. Calame (ed.), *L'amore in Grecia*, Rome, 1983; M. Foucault, *Histoire de la sexualité*, II: *L'usage des plaisirs*, Paris, 1984, and III: *Le souci de soi*, Paris, 1984 (English translation: *The History of Sexuality*, Vol. 2: *The Use of Pleasure*, New York, 1985, Vol 3: *The Care of the Self*, New York, 1985).

33 *Test.* 2, 20, 21, 49, fr. 214B1.

34 U. von Wilamowitz-Moellendorff, *Die griechische Literatur des Altertums*,

*etc.*, Leipzig/Berlin, 1912, cited by Calder, *Welcker*, 140 + n. For the educative role of Sappho, see among others: C. Calame, *Les choeurs de jeunes filles en Grèce archaïque*, I, Rome, 1977, 367–72, 390–1, 400–4; Pippin-Burnett, *Three Archaic Poets*, 209–28.

35 C. Calame, *Les choeurs de jeunes filles en Grèce archaïque*, Rome, 1977.

36 Contra R. Merkelbach, 'Sappho und ihre Kreis', *Philologus*, 1959, 101: 4; in fr. 102 a daughter speaks to her mother(!); inc. fr. 17 probably refers to the goddess Athena: Campbell, *Greek Lyric*, ad loc.

37 Calame, *Les choeurs de jeunes filles*, 367.

38 Ibid., 127.

39 Some philosophers (Plato *Symposium* 191e, *Laws* I.636c; Pseudo-Lucian *Affairs of the Heart* 28; Synesius *De Providentia* 13, 17); some church-fathers (St Paul *Letter to the Romans* 1.26; Clemens of Alexandria *Paedagogus* III.3.21.3; Tertullian *De Pallio* 4.9, *De Resurrectione* 16); two myth-makers (Ovid *Metamorphoses* 9.724–35; Phaedrus 4.15); other poets (Horace *Epodes* 5.41; Asclepiades, *Anthologia Graeca* 5. 207(?); Martial 1.90, 7.58, 67, 70); some astrologers (Manetho 1.31, 3.330, 4.358, 5.216; Ptolemy *Tetrabiblos* 3.14; Vettius Valens 111.7); an interpreter of dreams (Artemidorus 1.80); a doctor (Soranus *apud* Caelius Aurelianus *De morbis chronicis* 4.9); a pseudo-orator (*apud* Seneca Rhetor *Controversiae* 1.2.23), and two comic writers (Petronius *Satyricon* 67; Lucian *Dialogues of the Courtesans* 5). See also W. Kroll, 'Lesbische Liebe', in Pauly-Wissowa, *Realencyclopädie des klassischen Altertumswissenschaft*, Vol. 13, 1924, 2100–2; Dover, *Greek Homosexuality*, 171–84; Licht, *Sittengeschichte de Griechen I*, ch. 11; 'Female Homoeroticism and the Denial of Roman Reality in Latin Literature', *Yale Journal of Criticism*, 1989, 3: 209–27.

40 Athenaeus XIII, 602 d/e: Calame, *Les choeurs de jeunes filles*, 434; J. N. Bremmer, 'An enigmatic Indo-European rite: paederasty', *Arethusa*, 1980, 13: 279–98; contra: G. Devereux, 'Greek pseudo-homosexuality and the "Greek Miracle"', *Symbolae Osloenses*, 1968, 42: 83; Dover, *Greek Homosexuality*, 188.

41 The vase is depicted in Dover, *Greek Homosexuality*, no. CE 34.

42 Fr. 3 and fr. 26 Calame = fr. 1 and fr. 3 Page. H. Diels already believed that he could detect hints of homo-erotic relationships among the girls in Alcman's maiden songs: 'Alkmans Partheneion', *Hermes*, 1896, 31: 339–74. Esp. C. Calame, *Les choeurs de jeunes filles en Grèce archaïque*, II, Rome, 1977, 86–95; B. Gentili, *Poetry and its Public in Ancient Greece*, Baltimore and London, 1988, 74–104 ('The Ways of Love in the Poetry of *Thiasos* and Symposium').

43 Bowra, *Greek Lyric Poetry*, 32.

44 M. L. West, 'Alcmanica', *Classical Quarterly*, 1965, ns 5, 199; M. Puelma, 'Die Selbstbeschreibung des Chores in Alkmans grossem Partheneion-Fragment', *Museum Helveticum*, 1977, 34: 40.

45 E. Bethe had already drawn the parallel, 'Die dorische Knabenliebe: ihre Ethik und ihre Idee', *Rheinisches Museum*, 1907, 62: 439–40, but it found widespread acceptance only after the Second World War. Most recently: B. Sergent, *L'Homosexualité initiatique dans l'Europe*

*ancienne*, Paris, 1986, 14–24.

46 Buffière, *Eros adolescent*, 246–9; M. Vetta, 'Il P. Oxy. 2506 fr. 77 e la poesia pederotica di Alceo', *Quaderni Urbinati di Cultura Classica*, 1982, NS 10, 7–20.

47 See Bremmer, this volume, ch. 1.

48 *Test.* 2, fr. 214 B1.

49 See Bremmer, this volume, ch. 1.

# 3

# To the limits of kinship:
## anti-incest legislation
## in the early medieval west
## (500 – 900)
### *Mayke de Jong*

Early medieval legislation strictly condemns incest. This has long
been a source of puzzlement, for today 'incest' is usually defined
in terms of close blood relationships – parents and children,
brothers and sisters, or persons fulfilling the role of parents and
the minors dependent upon them. In Western Europe in the early
Middle Ages the term had a much wider scope. Not only consanguinity but also affinity had to be taken into account before
sexual and marital proceedings were initiated. The idea of affinity
was a very complicated one, which can be illustrated by the fact
that even extra-marital relations could be included. And this was
not all: from the eighth century onwards ecclesiastical and secular
interdicts were placed on 'spiritual' relationships arising from
baptism or confirmation. Thus 'forbidden kindred' included
godparents as well as godchildren. Literal obedience to all these
prescriptions implied an extreme form of exogamy.

Curiously enough this strict legislation developed at a time when
ecclesiastical weddings were the exception rather than the rule.[1]
A Christian marriage certainly had to be monogamous and lasting,
but a church ceremony was not yet regarded as essential. Clerical
involvement turned principally on research into possible
impediments to marriage. Possibly the avoidance of incest was the
crucial matter; priestly blessings came second.

What did popes, bishops, and princes have in mind when they
formulated their wide-ranging prescriptions against incest? Recent
attempts at explanation centre upon the benefits which the church
reaped from this legislation. Priests were held to be responsible for
preventing incestuous unions; thus clerical involvement in the
battle against incest strengthened the ecclesiastical control of

marriage.[2] Furthermore, the family's grip on inheritances was loosened by the need to find a marriage partner outside of the kindred: this led to an increase in gifts to ecclesiastical institutions.[3] However, this line of thought seems to confuse cause and effect. It credits the church with a unified and well-targeted policy against kin-marriage. From the eleventh century onwards such a policy did gradually come into being. Earlier medieval churchmen made great efforts to reach agreement about the theory and practice of Christian life, but ecclesiastical mechanisms of control long remained too weak to ensure real unity. Witness to this is the haphazard way in which the legislation against incest evolved. It is hard to imagine a conscious plan to further institutional self-interest concealed under a complex of frequently contradictory prescriptions.

From the modern point of view the almost unending extension of forbidden relations seems a phenomenon which is difficult to explain. Hence the search for a 'reasonable' explanation. Institutional self-interest is often used as a portmanteau for many puzzling aspects of ecclesiastical legislation. Consequently, the cultural and intellectual environment in which the offensive against incest was mounted is ignored. Yet exactly this context poses the really pressing questions. Who supported this legislation? What was actually understood by 'incest'? What dangers ensued upon this crime? What logical systems circumscribed the interdicts? And how did they relate to other similar prescriptions?

In this chapter it will be argued that early medieval legislation about incest was not only a matter of self-interested clergy forcing an alien morality upon a newly converted and resisting laity. It was no coincidence that the real explosion of anti-incest legislation occurred not in the Christianized Roman Empire, but only within the Germanic 'successor-kingdoms'. The new rulers firmly supported clerical strictures against marriage among kinsmen. This indicates a conjunction of ecclesiastical and secular values. Cultural roots of the aversion against incest extended beyond the clerical milieu. A close examination of the sources shows too that the prescriptions covering incest were part of a finely meshed system of classification which separated licit from illicit sexual encounters. The fear of 'pollution' sustained this rigid classification: incestuous unions involved disruption of both social and religious order.

## 1 THE DEVELOPMENT OF LEGISLATION IN THE EARLY MIDDLE AGES

Early medieval opponents of incest found only little support in the Bible or in Roman tradition. Leviticus 18: 7–20 gives a long list of blood and other relations with whom a sexual relationship was out of bounds. First cousins of the same generation, however, were not included. In Roman law until the end of the fourth century union with a first cousin also remained licit.[4] As little justification for the subsequent extremely strict policy could be found in the patristic period. Ambrose and Augustine spoke out against marriage between close relatives, but their moral reflections were not codified into legal opinions.[5] Many church councils met in Gaul in the fourth and fifth centuries; and yet episcopal decisions show no evidence of intense concern over marriage between relatives.[6]

The first major extension of the circle of forbidden marriage partners occurred in the newly established Frankish kingdom. In 517 a gathering of bishops in Epaon decreed that sexual intercourse was forbidden with a brother's widow, a wife's sister, a stepmother, a first or second cousin, the widow of a paternal or maternal uncle, or stepdaughter. Such unions they considered incestuous and unworthy of the name of marriage.[7] The emphasis is on affinal kin; close blood relations go unmentioned, for incest of this sort is deemed 'too terrible to enumerate'.

If the term *sobrina* in this text indeed designates a second cousin, the limits of consanguinity now extended laterally to the sixth degree according to the Roman method of calculation. The degrees were based upon the number of 'steps' between relatives passing through the common ancestor. Within the same generation, this method of calculation places brother and sister in the second degree, first cousins in the fourth, and second cousins in the sixth.[8] In Roman law this method had served only to determine rights of inheritance, but in the early medieval kingdoms calculations of kinship were increasingly used in the fight against incest. The first ruler to do so was the Visigothic king Chindasvindus (643–53): he declared blood relations out of bounds up to the sixth degree.[9]

Such a generalized view of the matter remained exceptional in this period. In other Germanic kingdoms no attempt was yet made to delineate a formal limit within which marriage was forbidden. The Frankish bishops contented themselves with listing illicit marriage partners by category, following the principles laid down in 517 in Epaon. Nevertheless, episcopal interest in incest was clearly on the increase in the sixth and seventh centuries; it was a recurrent issue in larger and smaller Frankish ecclesiastical gatherings.[10] The silence of the councils of preceding centuries was definitely broken. In addition, royal authority also began to meddle with the question. King Childebert II decreed in 596 that marriage with one's stepmother was a capital offence; furthermore, he banned from his court all those who refused to comply with the bishops in matters of incestuous marriage.[11]

However, the real growth of the Frankish campaign against incest dates from the eighth century, when relations with Rome were strengthened by the Carolingian rulers. Papal decrees and letters began to circulate in the north; these also influenced legislation about incest. Regarding blood relations, papal views at first were stricter than Frankish legal opinion; in other respects new legislation from Rome coincided with already existing taboos. The addition of 'spiritual kinship' to the list of impediments to marriage is a case in point.

In 721 a Roman council led by Pope Gregory II forbade marriage with one's *commater*, i.e. the godmother of one's child, or with the mother of a child to whom one was godfather. This brought the papacy in line with legislation passed in Byzantium some decades earlier.[12] The remarkably quick adoption of these principles suggests that the Frankish clergy already held similar views. This is illustrated by a curious story told by an anonymous Frankish clergyman in 727. He berated the treacherous manner in which the infamous concubine Fredegund had succeeded in making herself the legal spouse of King Chilperic. During a long absence of the king she had persuaded her rival, Queen Audovera, to become godmother to her own newborn daughter. Thus the naive Audovera was suddenly transformed into the *commater* of her own husband, making any further marital relations impossible and leaving the way open to Fredegund.[13] This fabrication shows that only a few years after the Roman council of 721 the anonymous author and his public were well acquainted with the impediments arising from spiritual kinship. Had this not been the case it would have been impossible to accuse Fredegund of her crafty trick. The letters of the missionary Boniface bear further witness to this. In 735 he asked the Scottish bishop Pehthelm if it was allowed to marry a widow who was mother to one's godchild. 'All the priests in Gaul and the land of the Franks' stated that this was a grave sin, he writes.[14] This struck him as strange, for he had never heard of it before. The question must have been on his mind for he wrote on the subject to two other Anglo-Saxon clerics in the same year.[15] Evidently the missionary was as yet unacquainted with this impediment to marriage, while the continental clergy he was dealing with considered it a very grave matter.

The development of this taboo is clearly visible in Carolingian ecclesiastical and secular legislation.[16] Both baptism and confirmation generated spiritual kinship; anyone acting as 'sponsor' in these ceremonies could no longer enter upon sexual or marital relations with the child and its family. In matters of consanguinity and affinity, however, eighth- and ninth-century legislation presents a more complicated picture. Instructions from Rome initially clashed with local prescriptions; the prevailing disagreement led to the fabrication of influential forgeries. The ensuing confusion was partly caused by the parallel existence of two methods of defining kinship. The Roman system, which calculated the degree of kinship in the collateral line via the common ancestor, has already been mentioned. The 'Germanic' method used by the Franks counted only the number of generations by which kinsmen were individually separated from their common ancestor. A changeover from Roman to Germanic custom therefore signified an immediate 50 per cent reduction in the number of 'degrees'. Under Roman law first cousins were related in the fourth degree; to the Franks they were second-degree kinsmen. Terminology differed accordingly; Frankish legislation generally used terms like *generatio*, *genu*, *geniculum*, or *progenies* instead of *gradus*.[17]

In the eighth century the northern regions were confronted with strict papal guidelines. The first evidence of this comes from the flurry of letters that passed between Boniface and Rome. True enough, in 726 Pope Gregory II warned his missionary to exercise moderation towards newly converted barbarians; they could therefore contract marriages after the fourth *generatio*. But his successor would have no more of such laxity. Gregory III wrote briefly in 732 to the same Boniface that kinship extended to the seventh *generatio*; within these limits marriage was out of the question.[18]

It is staggering to reflect on the consequences of this decree for the newly converted Christians who calculated in the 'Germanic' way. Or was there some kind of misunderstanding? Could it be that the popes counted in the Roman manner and so erroneously laid an incomprehensibly heavy interdict on people who calculated kinship differently? Possibly. However, *generatio* points in another direction, because this expression does not belong to Roman law, but to the Vulgate. In the Old Testament especially it is frequently used; for example, in the Ten Commandments: 'I the Lord thy God am a jealous God, visiting the iniquity of the fathers upon the children unto the third and fourth generation of them that hate me' (Exodus 20: 5).[19] Biblical usage undoubtedly contributed to a growing preference for this term in matters regarding kinship and incest, which becomes visible in ecclesiastical and secular sources from the eighth century onwards. This shift to biblical expression reflects an important conceptual change. Precise legal phrasing was replaced by sacred language, heavy with meaning. The influential letters to Boniface conform to this pattern; not Roman law but biblical precepts and symbolic numbers seem to have inspired the papal definition of the limits of kinship.

As could have been expected, the extension of these limits to the seventh generation met with resistance, not only from those who were unable to find a suitable marriage partner, but also from clergy who had difficulty in persuading their flock to conform. In this climate a very effective forgery came into existence, known as the 'privilege' of Gregory the Great. The first traces of this document are already found in Boniface's correspondence. In 735 he requested Archbishop Nothelm of Canterbury to instigate a search for a letter from Gregory to the Anglo-Saxon missionary Augustine, a letter in which the pope was said to have permitted marriage in the third *generatio*. Boniface had become suspicious: he doubted whether the statement had been made by Gregory himself, all the more so since he could find nothing of the sort in the papal archives.[20] His mistrust is understandable, for just a short time before, in 732, he had heard from Gregory III that sexual relationships were forbidden within the limits of the seventh *generatio*. Could it be that this pope had completely ignored the opinion of his illustrious predecessor and namesake? Boniface was in an awkward position, since he was faced with people appealing to the alleged papal 'privilege' in order to contract an incestuous marriage.[21]

Nothelm's reply has not been recorded, but he too must have sought in vain. The 'privilege' was a forgery, as Boniface already suspected.[22] But his suspicion was unable to curb the influence of the document in question, as is apparent from repeated attempts to draw its sting. To this end in 743 Pope Zacharias ordered a new search of the papal archives which brought to the surface everything except the alleged Gregorian letter. Zacharias thought it likely that his predecessor had permitted a third-degree marriage for newly converted peoples, but exceptions of that kind were no longer fitting in 743. The general rule was clear, he stated; Christians were not permitted to marry if they were in any way related to each other.[23]

This by no means meant the end of the 'Gregorian privilege'. More than a century later counteraction still remained necessary. Around 850, a clever West Frankish cleric invented an exchange of letters between Gregory the Great and a certain bishop, Felix of Messina.[24] The author adapted himself admirably to his material. He has 'Felix' complain wordily about Gregory's alleged leniency. This had proved a source of great confusion for the unfortunate Felix; to the best of his belief, every one of the pope's predecessors and each council had ordered all spouses related up to the seventh degree to separate. The letter is full of an 'old boy' tone, giving the impression that the pope and the bishop were childhood friends. In other words, Felix was a confidant of the pope, and if he were not well informed, who then could claim to be? The equally fictitious answer from Gregory is crystal clear. The whole city of Rome was witness to the fact that he had made an exception exclusively for the newly converted Anglo-Saxons. Anyone else had to conform to the general rule: marriage with relatives up to the seventh *generatio* was forbidden.

This tangle of forgeries shows that the development of early medieval law against incest was a slow and tortuous process. Carolingian lawmakers agreed upon the need to destroy incest root and branch, but the limits of forbidden kinship remained vague for a long time. Conciliar decisions and royal ordinances from the first half of the ninth century generally went no further than the fourth or fifth *generatio*; only marriage between third-generation kinsmen was sufficiently close to justify separation of the culprits.[25] This rule of thumb was also maintained by ninth-century bishops in their instructions to the clergy. Bishop Haito of Basle had these 'third-degree' incestuous partners do penance and then choose another marriage partner. However, anyone married in the fourth degree (*genu*) had to remain together in chastity and to rid themselves of the stain of incest by lifelong penance.[26]

The caution shown by Haito and his colleagues arose from practical problems experienced by all bishops. For if their flocks had succeeded in obtaining annulment of practically any marriage by appealing to distant kinship, the resultant chaos would have been awesome. Clearly some did attempt to abuse the prescriptions in this way. Women even acted as sponsor at the confirmation of their own children in order to rid themselves subsequently of their husbands.[27] Incest legislation threatened to undermine the stability of Christian marriage.

The position the Carolingian clerics found themselves in was thus far from simple, and was further complicated by the need to blaze a trail through a jungle of contradictory decrees, both genuine and forged; no wonder some of them lost their way. In 842, for instance, a puzzled bishop, Humbert of Würzburg, asked counsel of the learned abbot of Fulda, Hrabanus Maurus. Which authoritative texts should be followed in view of the fact that they all contradicted each other? So many were in circulation.[28] The problem of incest was a heavy burden for the ninth-century episcopate; the bishops attacked it earnestly and longed for clear guidelines.

Yet an official consensus gradually began to emerge. The imaginary exchange of letters between Gregory and Felix must have contributed to this process; it was generally regarded as authentic, even by influential church leaders such as Hincmar of Reims.[29] And Hrabanus Maurus, who tried to steer a careful middle course in his advice to Humbert, took a much stricter line a few years later. As archbishop of Mainz he chaired a council in 847 which ordered the immediate separation of married persons related in the fourth degree. Even more important, the meeting decided in no uncertain terms that this ruling applied not only to those related by blood but also by marriage. Once man and woman had become one flesh they acquired a common circle of relatives (*parentela*).[30]

This principle was not new; for the same reason, widows of close blood relatives and sisters of the deceased wife had long been out of bounds. Carolingian legislation, however, turned this into a general rule. Kinship through marriage was placed on the same level as kinship by blood; sexual relations created a 'unity of the flesh' which annulled the distinction between the two categories. The result was that kin by marriage as well as consanguineous relatives had to be taken into account when choosing a marriage partner. Even worse, the underlying logic of this principle meant that even extra-marital relations of themselves created kinship. An 'affair' with a woman automatically excluded all her kin from consideration as legitimate marriage partners.

Around the middle of the ninth century the impressive construction of legislation against incest was almost complete. Marriage was forbidden within the degrees of kinship, up to the seventh *generatio* or 'as far as memory could go back' – which to all intents and purposes amounted to the same thing.[31] The church held on to this view until 1215, when the Fourth Lateran Council reduced the forbidden degrees to four.

Naturally one wonders to what extent such prescriptions could be realistically imposed. Did they not remain a dead letter, especially in small and isolated communities where choice of a marriage partner would be strictly limited? Obviously, the ecclesiastical guidelines were very hard to follow. In any case, the clergy were not lacking in energy at a local level. Episcopal instructions give occasional glimpses of priests operating as a kind of vice squad, making their investigations among the 'honest and God-fearing people' in order to track down incestuous marriages.[32] The growing clamour for marriages to be made public was certainly connected to the fight against incest.[33] But it must have been the higher strata of society who allowed themselves to suffer the greatest discomfort from the situation, for they had a greater degree of geographic mobility.[34] Whatever the case, the rare sources quoting actual case histories all deal with people from the upper classes.

An intriguing case is set out in the correspondence of Hincmar of Reims.[35] A certain Stephanus, count of Auvergne and royal vassal, made an unpleasant discovery after his engagement (*desponsatio*) to the daughter of his powerful colleague Regimund: a woman with whom he had previously had sexual relations turned out to be kin of his intended. He consulted his confessor who, penitential in hand, informed him that marriage with Regimund's daughter was out of the question: it would be incestuous. At first Stephanus wanted to go ahead with the marriage while submitting to a secret penance, but this proved impossible. A penance would be fruitless as long as the incestuous union continued. The count found himself in an awkward predicament. A *desponsatio* was a binding agreement; any breach of faith would unleash the full wrath of his powerful father-in-law and the latter's kin. And in fact they soon forced him to provide the girl with a dower and to make her his wife in a public ceremony. However, to safeguard his bride from the 'contamination' of incest he abstained from sexual contact with her, something that annoyed his in-laws just as much. The affair developed into a full-blown scandal, not least because Regimund lodged a complaint against his son-in-law before the synod of Touzy in 860.[36] Hincmar's report was meant to pave the way for a solution to the wretched business. If Stephanus had told the truth then the couple should separate immediately, he advised, for an incestuous union could never be qualified as a licit and indissoluble marriage.

Was this ninth-century scandal merely a veiled attempt to reject a spouse who appeared unsuitable on further consideration? Stephanus could have thought of simpler ways of accomplishing the same end. It would seem that this count took his confessor's instructions seriously and was prepared to pay a high price for his salvation. He was not alone in this.[37] And, even if he was cynically abusing the decrees against incest, this in no way implies that they remained a dead letter. On the contrary, the ability to manipulate or circumvent particular laws indicates at least some familiarity with the standards they set. If Stephanus really was anxious to rid himself of his spouse, he knew very well what he was doing – just like the mothers who sponsored their own children in confirmation. Resistance and manipulation are witnesses just as powerful to the influence of legislation as obedience to the law.

## 2 EXPLANATIONS

What was it that drove early medieval legislators to elaborate such a strict and impractical system of impediments to marriage? In the older literature three reasons were usually advanced. A marriage with kin would destroy the respect and shame owed to family members; marriages outside the kinship group encourage social solidarity since people form ties outside their own circle; in addition, incest would constitute a threat to the mother's fertility and the health of any children.[38] Respectively a moral, social, and biological justification; and since all three can be found in one form or another in the work of medieval authors, it can be said that they are based on 'the native point of view'.

In recent years some historians have ventured further, stating that the church had a lot to gain by extending the limits of forbidden kinship. The search into the antecedents of prospective partners involved the local priest and community; this guaranteed a high level of publicity, which enabled the clergy to control marital customs and thus impose the ecclesiastical model of marriage on the laity.[39] According to others anti-incest legislation was part of ecclesiastical politics on an even wider scale, embracing not only laws against incest but also against second marriages, adoption, and concubinage. The overall aim was to limit the number of licit male heirs; this would loosen the family's grip on its inheritance and lead to an increase in gifts to ecclesiastical institutions.[40] Of course an endogamous marriage was not in itself a way of obtaining licit heirs, like adoption and concubinage; but the inheriting wife's possessions would remain within the family, thus strengthening familial solidarity. This stronghold was impaired by the strict laws governing a Christian marriage; moreover, these laws made it very difficult to find a licit partner and to produce licit heirs.[41]

At this point, one may wonder whether cause and effect are not being confused. Were marriages up to the seventh *generatio* indeed forbidden in order to enable priests to stick their noses into things? Or was the priests' involvement merely a fortunate side-effect of the anti-incest laws? The latter seems more likely. The clergy could just as well have employed more direct means of controlling the laity's marital practices – for instance, a refusal to recognize any marriage not blessed by a priest. And yet in the very period in which the fight against incest gained momentum there was no obligation to marry in church. Pope Nicholas I, reminding the newly converted Bulgars in 866 of their Christian duties, pointed out that the only condition for a licit marriage was the consent of both parties; in the same letter he emphatically forbade any marriage within the kindred group.[42] This seems indeed a rather roundabout way to encourage ecclesiastical influence on marriage ceremony.

As to the economic argument, it is not clear how the church would have profited directly from a lack of legal heirs. Defence of the opposite thesis would be equally justified. In the early Middle Ages religious communities usually recruited their new members from the ranks of so-called child oblates, children offered to the service of God by their parents. If the latter were rich, they were also expected to offer a substantial gift, not infrequently consisting of the child's entire inheritance. In view of this pattern of recruitment, a reduction of the number of legal heirs would have threatened religious institutions with a serious decrease in members and wealth.[43] And child oblation was part of a larger pattern: most of the riches came into ecclesiastical hands as gifts *pro remedio animae*, for the salvation of the soul. Early medieval donation charters attempted to prevent members of the family from laying their hands on these gifts at some later date; therefore the consent of direct heirs was carefully recorded in these documents. Obviously, the absence of such heirs would have smoothed the transfer of possessions to the church. But did the clergy really feel the need to oppose second marriages, adoption, and incest to ensure a steady increase of wealth? Certainly in the early Middle Ages the need to obtain God's favour by means of pious gifts was so great that people were prepared to risk conflict with family members for the sake of spiritual welfare.[44] This flow of gifts seems to have reached its destination regardless of the legislation against incest.

It is one thing to assume that anti-incest laws contributed to clerical control of marriage practices or the growth of ecclesiastical wealth, but it is quite another to credit the early medieval church with a unified policy against incest that served to further institutional self-interest. Moreover, this does not go very far towards explaining the virtually unlimited extension of forbidden kindred. Interference in marriage practices or the undermining of family solidarity could have been assured without prohibiting marriage up to the seventh *generatio*, let alone the inclusion of extra-marital and spiritual relationships. It is precisely the extreme nature of the early medieval incest interdict that calls for a different approach.

The roots of aversion must have been very deep indeed.

It seems a foregone conclusion that this aversion was initiated and sustained by the church. Current historical opinion regards the offensive against incest as a purely clerical endeavour; the laity either complied or resisted. However, ecclesiastical involvement is only one side of the picture, albeit an important one. The main corpus of legislation stems from councils in Germanic lands and was zealously supported by secular rulers. Admittedly, the latter turned for precise instructions to the papacy, but that does not alter the fact of their commitment to a common cause.[45] Furthermore, it remains doubtful whether mere legislative command, ecclesiastical or secular, could create *ex nihilo* a strong sentiment about incest. In the words of Joseph Lynch: 'But if such a sentiment existed already, the law could channel it, reinforce it, diffuse it to new groups or areas, fix its contours, and settle disputes about its limits. The early medieval written law on the matter was basically rather a reaction than a cause.'[46]

Since most sources for the extension of forbidden kindred consist precisely of legislation, it is difficult to corroborate this sensible statement. However, some circumstantial evidence does exist. The story of Fredegond and Audovera suggests that the Franks were very likely familiar with the prohibition of marriage with spiritual kin before the Roman legislation of 721 could possibly have had any influence. The fact that by the early ninth century people had so far internalized these laws that they could use them for their own ends, or even jeopardize these same ends because of incest taboos, also indicates that clerical opinion was to a certain extent in conjunction with sentiments among the laity. And did the church indeed battle against a laity that preferred to marry within its kindred? The existence of forgeries allowing marriage beyond the third or fourth *generatio* does not warrant this conclusion. The fourth generation is very distant kin indeed; yet this was the more liberal limit which was under attack in the ninth century. When Count Stephanus turned to his confessor for advice, he hopefully mentioned the fourth generation; apparently this would have saved him from his predicament.[47] The bad news he received was that *all* relations, either by blood or (extra-marital) affinity, were out of bounds. The difference between rigorists and their opponents was one of degree only, not of principle.

There seems no reason to ascribe endogamous tendencies to the

Franks – or, for that matter, to any other of the Germanic nations. Their very method of defining kinship speaks against this. Germanic calculation of *generationes* covered a much wider range of relations than the Roman system. In other words, the perceived extent of the family was larger. This conclusion implies in no way a return to the 'Germanist' phantom of an omnipresent extended family or clan. Current research rightly stresses the importance of the nuclear family in early medieval society; none the less, the solidarity of larger kindred groups does occasionally emerge in sources, especially with regard to political alliances and feuds.[48]

It is hard to imagine that this perception had no bearing at all upon the evolution of early medieval legislation against incest. At the very least it must have been a precondition for ever-increasing ecclesiastical prohibitions, which otherwise would have made no sense at all. But possibly the cultural roots of the taboo against incest went deeper: did not clerical ideology and local tradition reinforce each other, in spite of staunch resistance against the seventh *generatio*? If taken literally, this purely symbolic number set extremely improbable limits to kinship; therefore it was often replaced by the phrase 'as far as affinity can be calculated'. Although such calculations were not always up to the standards of literal-minded rigorists, they already went very far indeed.

Another approach to the enigma of early medieval anti-incest law merits exploration. A collection of mid-ninth-century prescriptions describes the fate awaiting those who commit the sin of incest: 'From these unions are usually born blind, crippled, hunchbacked and squinting children, and others afflicted with ugly contaminations.'[49] The same was said of a married couple enjoying sexual relations on a Sunday, in Lent, or on a feast day: they could expect to bring forth a monstrous issue.[50] Sins of this sort led to a state of impurity; the sinners risked a dangerous 'pollution'.

This concept has received much attention in recent years.[51] 'Pollution' does not necessarily mean detectable dirt but rather a state of impurity, deriving from a violation of limits regarded as fundamental in a given society. These involve not only human relations but also the relationship between nature and culture, and especially that between mankind and the supernatural. Of course the way in which these limits are set varies a great deal; different cultures use their own systems of classification. But in all cases such classification serves to order conceptually the material and immaterial world in which people live; the fear of pollution functions as a means to eliminate dangerous confusion. The idea of pollution is used to delimit spheres of life that should not be united; anything placing the classification in jeopardy by escaping from it is rejected. A ritual cleansing after pollution is not simply some hygienic gesture, though water may be used. It is rather an act of restoring the order that has been disturbed. Even when the 'guilty party' has violated a fatal border without being aware of it, the restoration of order remains essential and retribution is required.

Early medieval sources testify abundantly to the polluting effect of incest – but which order was violated by this crime? With regard to the taboo on spiritual kinsmen, Joseph Lynch pointed out that this is connected to the belief that the sexual and the sacred cannot be united. Whereas physical birth was carnal and therefore sinful, the 'second birth' by baptism belonged to the sphere of the spiritual and the holy. If spiritually related persons were to have relations with each other, dangerous confusion ensued. 'Sexual acts between spiritual kin were inappropriate because they moved the participants from the realm of grace to that of fallen nature.'[52] The interpretation of this particular form of incest as a 'border violation' may shed some light on the development of early medieval incest legislation as a whole. Is it in any way valid with regard to the extreme avoidance of relations by consanguinity and affinity?

Undoubtedly the opposition between the sexual and the sacred strongly affected theory and practice in early medieval Christianity, mainly under the influence of Old Testament law.[53] The dividing line between both spheres was, for example, of great consequence for the religious cult, primarily for priests. Since they were obliged to celebrate the eucharist daily, they came into regular contact with the holy; hence they had to be in a permanent state of purity and could not marry.[54] Bishop Theodulf of Orleans (died 826) pointed this out to his clergy in answer to the question of celibacy. Continuous contact with the flesh and blood of Christ required priests, deacons, and subdeacons, unlike their Old Testament predecessors, to refrain from any form of sexual contact.[55] Even the laity was bound by prescriptions of purity. If they wished to receive communion, they first had to purify themselves by refraining from sex. Anyone ignoring these precepts ran the risk of pollution, which usually manifested itself externally by sickness, malformed children, or even death.[56]

This rigid separation of the sexual and the sacred also played an important role in early medieval incest legislation. 'Incestuous' relations included not only those between spiritual kin but also sexual contact with consecrated virgins.[57] And even unchaste clergy were spoken of in terms of *incestum*.[58] Quite clearly the concept referred to a broad spectrum of sexual relations which were experienced as defiling and shameful; this was in part related to a violation of the border between the holy and the sexual. But what about the other categories of incest, stemming from blood relationship, marriage, or extra-marital relations? A more extensive principle of classification must have governed these taboos.

Incest legislation in its full scope seems to have been connected to a notion of 'order' designed to hold in check the human bodily functions in general and sexual activities in particular. The dividing line between sexual and sacred was part of this, but the total complex of rules went much further. The basic idea was that human sexuality is by definition dangerous and disorderly, in contrast to its paradisiacal counterpart. To the church father Augustine the relationship between Adam and Eve before the Fall seemed 'without disorder' (*sine confusione*); elsewhere, he typified their union as uncorrupt and controlled, since lust played no part.[59] In other words, human sexuality can become 'ordered' only if the dangerous aspect of desire is reined in as much as possible.

Conceptions of this type can be found in detail in the early medieval penitentials.[60] Their prescriptions deal partly with the separation of the sexual and sacred, such as the rule that after childbirth women should go through a period of purification before re-entering a church; or the obligation laid on married couples to refrain from intercourse in periods of fasting and on Sundays and holy days. But in addition to all this, an attempt was made to regulate sexual behaviour itself, even when it was not in conflict with a holy place or time. This led to detailed lists of forbidden acts and attitudes. The legitimate sexual sphere was delimited in many and varied ways; sexuality was tied not only to marriage and reproduction, but also to an extremely restricted number of times and types of behaviour. This basic theme produced ever more extensive variations. On the basis of the rules contained in the early medieval penitentials, sexual relations were forbidden for more than half the year.[61]

In this context it is easier to understand the extreme extension of legislation regarding incest, for this also restricted legitimate sexuality: the number of licit partners was drastically reduced. An anonymous bishop of the eighth century spoke in a sermon on the 'inadmissible frenzy of human lust' and then proceeded to list a series of forbidden relationships based on Leviticus 18: 7–20.[62] To him the link between control of human sexuality and the fight against incest was crystal clear. Recognition of this conceptual connection is essential if the study of early medieval legislation concerning incest is to be pursued. The stronger the urge to 'tame' sexuality, the wider the circle of illicit relationships, approaching the point where this extends to the limits of kinship – or to the seventh *generatio*.

Sources testifying to the dangers of pollution inherent in incest are almost all of ecclesiastical origin. However, there are some notable exceptions. In an ordinance of 802 Charlemagne rejected out of hand any form of clemency for those who had defiled themselves by incest. They were to be severely punished in order to deter others 'so that the Christian people may be thoroughly cleansed of impurity'. The text continues: people should not attempt to defile themselves and others by entering into incestuous relationships; the emperor also required that those stubbornly persisting in incestuous unions should await trial in isolation 'so that they may not inflict impurity upon the rest of the people'.[63] This calls to mind Count Stephanus, who refused to contaminate his 'healthy' bride with the disease of incest. Obviously the pollution resulting from this crime was considered contagious. Not only those directly involved but also the whole community would thus be placed in jeopardy. The degree of contagion was sometimes interpreted in a narrow sense, sometimes in broader terms. Theodulf of Orleans expressed concern regarding the direct surroundings (*vicinitas*) of the guilty parties;[64] the Christian emperor worried about the moral integrity of all members of Christianity (*populus christianus*). Both, however, were united in their conviction that incest had to be destroyed root and branch, since God's wrath would fall not only on the guilty themselves but also on the community that had tolerated the evil in its midst.

This brings to light yet another remarkable characteristic of Carolingian legislation regarding incest: the act and its punishment were first and foremost a *public* affair. Incest was listed with murder (of kin), adultery, and heresy as an exceptionally serious and scandalous offence, which – according to current penitential practices – was punished by means of a public penance.[65] To a twentieth-century observer this seems strange, since in our society incest is completely hidden from the public gaze. Incestuous relations occur in the secret reaches of the nuclear family, so much so that it is extremely difficult to bring them to account. But the situation in the ninth century was very different. First of all, the circle of illicit partners was so large that the assistance of the local community was required when determining whether the partners-to-be were related or not. The above-mentioned imperial ordinance warns that 'no one should attempt to contract marriage before the bishops and the priests together with the elders of the people have carried out a detailed examination of any possible relationship between those intending to marry'.[66] The decision whether a marriage would be incestuous or not was therefore a public one; furthermore, the immediate social environment of the guilty parties was thus made jointly responsible. For this reason they participated in the public rituals of rejection and reconciliation to which incestuous pentitents were subjected. However, the public retribution for incest was more than anything linked to the polluting consequences attached to such a crime. Incest was 'contagious', not only for those responsible for the sinful deed but also for those in social contact with them. They too had to purify themselves of pollution. The purification – that is, the penance – thus assumed an expressly collective character.

## 3 CONCLUSION

There are no easy explanations for the extent of early medieval legislation against incest. A wide range of sources and various approaches merits exploration. Research into this intriguing field should start with an investigation of the context of well-known prescriptions. How did early medieval legislators define 'incest'? Which terminology was used in this regard, and how did clerical strictures against incest relate to other (sexual) offences? The view of anti-incest legislation as an explicit means to enhance ecclesiastical power does not seem tenable. The often haphazard evolution of legislation precludes such an assertion. The key notion of 'pollution' offers a more fruitful approach to the problem, for this leads to a better understanding of early medieval perception of incest. Both social and religious systems of order were involved; the *pollutio* affecting those guilty of incest and their vicinity was perceived as the tangible proof of a disordered relationship with God. The fear of this form of impurity drove adversaries of incest to the limits of kinship.

The question of social and religious implications of incest confronts the historian with an old problem: what was the extent of clerical influence on early medieval society? And was incest the concern of clerics only, or did they share a strong sense of taboo with the laity? Admittedly, the nature of sources often makes it impossible to grasp the sentiments of the illiterate laity. Yet a more systematic interrogation of written sources may yield some unexpected results. Anti-incest legislation certainly was no one-way street. The public nature of retribution suggests that aversion against incest had taken root beyond the clerical milieu. And the pollution affecting offenders points to a stronger source of authority than legislation alone, ecclesiastical or otherwise: namely, local tradition. The taboo on incest was part of a pollution-ridden moral system, which can be detected in penitentials, in royal ordinances, in conciliar decisions, in letters, and in liturgical texts. This system and its cultural background have not yet been mapped; the documents mentioned here constitute only the tip of an iceberg. Further research into early medieval incest legislation should take this moral system into account. If interest in these matters has been at all aroused by this chapter, it has served its purpose.

## ABBREVIATIONS

| | |
|---|---|
| AASS | Acta Sanctorum (opere Bollandistarum) |
| CCSL | Corpus christianorum, series latina |
| Mansi | J. D. Mansi, *Sacrorum conciliorum nova et amplissima collectio* |
| MGH | Monumenta Germaniae Historica |
|   Capit. | Capitularia regum Francorum |
|   Capit. episc. | Capitula episcoporum |
|   Conc. | Concilia, aevi Merovingici et aevi Carolini |
|   Epp. | Epistolae |

Epp.sel.    Epistolae selectae
Formulae    Formulae Merovingici et Carolini aevi.
LL          Leges (in-folio)
LNG         Leges nationum Germanicarum
SRM         Scriptores rerum Merovingicarum
Migne PL    J. P. Migne, *Patrologiae cursus completus* . . . *series latina*

## NOTES

For their comments on the English version of this chapter I thank Esther Cohen and Arjo Vanderjagt. The basis for this translation was laid by Michael J. Collins.

1 For the ecclesiastical wedding ceremony see esp. K. Ritzer, *Le mariage dans les églises chrétiennes du Ier au XIe sciècles*, Paris, 1970; also G. Duby, *Le Chevalier, la femme et le prêtre. Le mariage dans la France féodale*, Paris, 1981.
2 G. Duby, 'Le mariage dans la société du haut Moyen Age', in *Il matrimonio nella società altomedievale*, Vol. I, Settimane di studio XXIV, Spoleto, 1977, 28–9. G. Duby, *Medieval Marriage: Two Models from Twelfth-Century France*, Baltimore, Md, 1978, 17–20.
3 J. Goody, *The Development of the Family and Marriage in Europe*, Cambridge, 1983.
4 A. Esmein, *Le mariage en droit canonique*, Vol. I, ed. R. Génestal, Paris, 1929, 371–5.
5 J. Freisen, *Geschichte des canonischen Eherechts bis zum Verfall der Glossenlitteratur*, Paderborn, 1893, 376–7; Augustinus, *De civitate Dei*, lib. XV, ch. 16, ed. B. Dombart and A. Kalb, CCSL 48, Turnhout, 1955, 476–9.
6 Cf. C de Clercq's edition: *Concilia Galliae a. 314–506*, CCSL 148, Turnhout, 1963.
7 Council of Epaon (517) ch. 30, ed. C. de Clercq, *Concilia Galliae a. 511–695*, CCSL 148A, Turnhout, 1963, 31–2. The rest of the Merovingian conciliar decrees quoted are taken from this edition.
8 Blood relations up till the sixth degree were able to inherit; this right was also extended to the children of second cousins, kindred in the seventh degree. As part of the work of the third-century jurist Paulus this maxim found its way into the Romano-Visigothic law code: *Pauli sententiarum* IV, X, *Lex Romana Visigothorum*, ed. G. Haenel, Leipzig, 1848, 408–9.
9 *Lex Visigothorum*, III, 5: 1, ed. K. Zeumer, MGH LNG I, 159; as a possible precedent, see the council of Toledo (527) ch. 5, Migne PL 84, cols 336–7.
10 Council of Orleans (511) ch. 18, 9–10; council of Orleans (538) ch. 11, 18; council of Paris (614) ch. 16, 280; council of Clichy (626–7) ch. 10, 293.
11 *Childeberti secundi decretio*, ch. 2, ed. A Boretius, MGH Capit. I no. 7,

15; cf. the decree of the council of Clichy quoted above.

12 Council of Rome (721) ch. 4, Mansi XII, 261; in this regard J. H. Lynch, *Godparents and Kinship in Early Medieval Europe*, Princeton, NJ, 1986, 234–7.

13 *Liber historiae Francorum*, ch. 31, ed. B. Krusch, MGH SRM II, 292–3.

14 Bonifatius, *Epistolae*, ed. M. Tangl, Berlin, 1916 (MGH Epp. sel. 1), no. 32, 56. All letters quoted from this edition.

15 Ibid., no. 33, 57–8 (to Nothelm of Canterbury) and no. 34, 59 (to Abbot Duddo); here this opinion is ascribed to the 'Romani'.

16 Cf. Lynch, *Godparents and Kinship*, 243–57.

17 This terminology is less abstract than the Roman; it refers to the human body, divided into the head (the ancestor) and limbs (*genu* or *geniculum* means 'knee', or, in a more general sense, 'joint'). As well as this, the term *gradus* was occasionally used in combination with *generatio*; compare Pope Zacharias in his argument at the Roman council of 743, ed. A. Werminghoff, MGH Conc. II-1, l. 15 (*gradus*) and 20, ll. 11–12 (*generatio*).

18 Bonifatius, *Epistolae*, no. 26, 45; no. 28, 51.

19 Cf. B. Fischer OSB, *Novae concordantiae Bibliorum sacrorum, iuxta Vulgatam versionem critice editam*, Stuttgart, 1977.

20 Bonifatius, *Epistolae*, no. 33, 57.

21 Ibid., no. 50, 83–4.

22 Bede included this text in his *Historia ecclesiastica gentis Anglorum*, lib. I, ch. 27, 5, ed. B. Colgrave and R. A. B. Mynors, Oxford, 1969, 84–6. It is part of what is known as the *Libellus Responsionum*, at present regarded as the work of Gregory the Great, with the exception of the text in question concerning the marriage of blood relations; this seems to be an interpolation. See in this regard P. Meyvaert, 'Bede's text of the *Libellus Responsionum* of Gregory the Great to Augustine of Canterbury', in *England before the Conquest. Studies in primary sources presented to Dorothy Whitelock*, ed. P. Clemoes and K. Hughes, Cambridge, 1971, 15–33; S. Brechter, *Die Quellen zur Angelsachsenmission Gregors des Grossen*, Munster, 1941, 74–81.

23 Council of Rome (743), ch. 15, ed. A. Werminghoff, MGH Conc. II-1, 19–21. In 800 in a letter to the Bavarian bishops Pope Leo III referred once more to the fruitless search made by his predecessor Zacharias in the Rome archives, and he confirmed that the letter could not be found: Leo III, *Epistolae*, no. 5, ed. K. Hampe, MGH Epp. V, 62.

24 *Decretales Pseudo-Isidorianae et capitula Angilramni*, ed. P. Hinschius, Leipzig, 1863, 747–53.

25 Decree of Compiègne (757) chs 1–3, ed. A. Boretius, MGH Capit. I, no. 15, 37–8; decree of Verberie (758–68) ch. 1, ibid., no. 16, 40. The council of Mainz (813) ch. 54, ed. A. Werminghoff, MGH Conc. II-1, 273, however, ordered separation in the fourth degree, and the *Capitulare missorum generale* (813) ch. 6, ed. A. Boretius MGH Capit. I, no. 83, 162 extended its interdict to the sixth *generatio*.

26 Haito of Basle, *Capitula* (803-23) ch. 21, ed. P. Brommer, MGH Capit. episc. I, 217.

27 Council of Chalon (813) ch. 31, ed. A. Werminghoff, MGH Conc. II-1, 279.

28 Hrabanus Maurus, *Epistolae*, no. 29, ed. E. Dümmler, MGH Epp V, 444-8; cf. also no. 31 (*ann.* 842), 457-8 to Hatto of Fulda, and no. 56 (*ann.* 853-6), 511-12, to Heribald of Autun.

29 Benedictus Levita, *Capitularia spuria*, ch. 75, MGH LL Vol. II, add. IV, 151; Hincmar of Reims, *Epistolae*, no. 136, ed. E. Perels, MGH Epp. VII, 96; in his life of Gregory the Great, Johannes Diaconus also refers to the exchange of letters in question: *Vita s. Gregorii papae*, lib. II, ch. 4, AASS Mart. II, 153.

30 Council of Mainz (847) ch. 30, ed. W. Hartmann, MGH Conc. III, 175-6. This text consists of elements originating in the decrees of two councils held in 713, one in Mainz (ch. 54, ed. A. Werminghoff, MGH Conc. II-1, 273) and the other in Chalon (ch. 29, ibid., 279). In this regard see Esmein, *Le mariage en droit canonique*, Vol. I, pp. 414-20.

31 Council of Worms (868) ch. 32, Mansi XV, col. 875 (= Nicholas I, *Epistolae*, no. 156, ed. E. Perels, MGH Epp. VI, 672-3, l. 34).

32 Theodulf of Orleans, *Capitulare* II, ch. II-2, ed. P. Brommer, MGH Capit. episc. I, 139-40; Haito of Basle, *Capitula*, ch. 21, ibid., 217; council of Mainz, (847) ch. 28, ed. W. Hartmann, MGH Conc. III, 175. cf. also the less well-known council of Friuli (797) ch. 8, ed. A. Werminghoff, MGH Conc. II, 1, 192. In this regard see A. M. Koeniger, *Die Sendgerichte in Deutschland*, Munich, 1907, 11-57.

33 *Capitulare missorum generale* (802) ch. 35, ed. A. Boretius, MGH Capit. I, no. 33, 98; Benedictus Levita, *Capitularia spuria*, lib. III, ch. 179, MGH LL II, 2, 113. cf. also *Concilium Baiuwaricum* ch. 12, ed. A. Werminghoff, MGH Conc. II, 1, 53.

34 C. B. Bouchard, 'Consanguinity and noble marriages in the tenth and eleventh centuries', *Speculum*, 1981, 56: 268-87; J. M. Van Winter, 'The imperial aristocracy in the tenth and the beginning of the eleventh centuries', *Byzantium and the Low Countries in the Tenth Century. Aspects of Art and History in the Ottonian Era*, Herne, 1985, 22-7. Regarding the geographical mobility of the Frankish aristocracy, see R. Hennébique, 'Structures familiales au IXe siècle: en groupe familiale de l'aristocratie francque', *Revue historique*, 1981, 265: 289-333.

35 Hincmar of Reims, *Epistolae*, no. 136, ed. E. Perels, MGH Epp. VIII, 1: 87-107, esp. 89-90. On this subject see G. Fransen, 'La lettre de Hincmar de Reims au sujet du mariage d'Etienne. Une relecture', in R. Lievens *et al.* (eds), *Pascua Mediaevalia*, Louvain, 1983, 133-46. The letter was addressed to the bishops Radulfus of Bourges and Frotharius of Bordeaux.

36 Hincmar, *Epistolae*, no. 136, 95.

37 See below, n. 49.

38 G. Oesterlé, 'Consanguinité', *Dictionnaire de droit canonique*, Vol. IV,

1949, 232–48, esp. 240–1.

39 Duby, *Il matrimonio* . . ., 28–9; Duby, *Medieval Marriage*, 17–20.

40 Goody, *Development*, 46, 59, 95, 103–56.

41 Ibid., 44–5.

42 Nicholas I, *Epistolae*, no. 99, chs 2–3, ed. E. Perels, MGH Epp. VI, 569–70.

43 See M. de Jong, *In Samuel's Image. Child Oblation in the Early Medieval West* (forthcoming with Brill, Leiden). A similar criticism is voiced by D. Herlihy, *Medieval Households*, Cambridge, Mass., 1985, 13. His alternative explanation, however, is not very convincing; the legislation entailed an attempt on the clergy's part to diminish the concentration of marriageable women in the households of the rich and powerful. The interdict on marriage between relatives would have encouraged the circulation of women in the community (cf. 61–2). The early medieval church as marriage bureau before the fact? Also critical of Goody's thesis is J A. Brundage in his recent synthesis, *Law, Sex and Christian Society in Medieval Europe*, Chicago/London, 1987, 606–7, on the grounds that the effectiveness of ecclesiastical legislation remains doubtful. The latter author's treatment of early medieval anti-incest legislation, however, does not yield any new points of view.

44 G. Duby, *La société au XIe et XIIe siècles dans la région Mâconnaise*, Paris, 1961, 53–7; Ph. Jobert, *La notion de donation: convergences, 630–750*, Paris, 1977, 219–25.

45 Cf. Lynch, *Godparents and Kinship*, 238–41, about the co-operation between Pope Gregory II and the Longobardian king Luitprand; furthermore, *Codex Carolinus*, lib. III, ch. 22, ed. W. Gundlach, MGH Epp. III, 485, 61–2.

46 Lynch, *Godparents and Kinship*, 260.

47 Hincmar of Reims, *Epistolae*, no. 136, ed. E. Perels, MGH Epp. VIII, 1: 87: 'et audieram, quod a quarto genu et in reliquum pertinentes sibi copulari valerent'.

48 For a discussion of early medieval kinship, see P. Guichard, 'De l'Antiquité au Moyen Age: Famille large et famille étroite', *Cahiers d'Histoire*, 1979, 24: 45–60; A. C. Murray, *Germanic Kinship Structures. Studies in Law and Society in Antiquity and the Early Middle Ages*, Toronto, 1983, esp. 161–81, 216–24. A survey of recent scholarship is provided by J. P. Cuvillier's contribution to the *Histoire de la famille*, Vol. I, ed. A. Burguière *et al.*, Paris, 1986, 318–27.

49 Benedictus Levita, *Capitularia spuria*, lib. III, ch. 179, MGH LL II, 2: 113. In this collection incest is forbidden up till the seventh *generatio*: ibid., add. IV, ch. 75, 151.

50 See below, n. 56.

51 A fundamental study is that of Mary Douglas, *Purity and Danger. An Analysis of the Concept of Pollution and Taboo*, London, 1966, as also other publications of hers: *Natural Symbols. Explorations in Cosmology*, Harmondsworth, 1973, and 'Pollution', in *Implicit Meanings. Essays in Anthropology*, London, 1975. See further: R. Parker, *Miasma. Pollution*

*and Purification in Greek Religion*, Oxford, 1983; Th. C. W. Oudemans and A. P. M. H. Lardinois, *Tragic Ambiguity. Anthropology, Philosophy and Sophocles' Antigone*, Leiden, 1987.

52 Lynch, *Godparents and Kinship*, 276.

53 Ibid., 261–4; John Bugge, *Virginitas: An Essay in the History of a Medieval Ideal*, The Hague, 1975.

54 R. Kottje, 'Das Aufkommen der täglichen Eucharistiefeier in der Westkirche und die Zölibatsforderung', *Zeitschrift für Kirchengeschichte*, 1971, 82: 218–28.

55 Theodulf of Orleans, *Capitulare* II, chs 1–8, ed. P. Brommer, MGH Capit. episc. I, 152.

56 See, for instance, *Vita Liutbirgae*, ed. O. Menzel, Leipzig, 1937, ch. 33, 39; Thietmar of Merseburg, *Chronicon*, ed. W. Trillmich, Darmstadt, 1957, lib. I, chs 24–5, 26–8; Ekkehard of St Gall, *Casus Sancti Galli*, ed. H. Haefele, Darmstadt, 1980, ch. 30, 70–2.

57 *Pippini regis capitulare* (754–5), ed. A. Boretius, MGH Capit. I, no. 13, 31; *Capitulare missorum generale* (802) ch. 3, ibid., no. 33, 97; see also Lynch, *Godparents and Kinship*, 276–7.

58 Bonifatius, *Epistolae*, no. 50, MGH Epp. sel. I, 82, ll. 26–7.

59 Augustinus, *De civitate Dei*, lib. XIV, chs 21–4, CCSL 48, 443–8; Augustinus, *De nuptiis et concupiscentia*, ed. C. F. Urba and J. Zycha, CSEL 42, Vienna, 1902, lib. I, ch. 6, 216–7 and lib. XXII, ch. 37, 291; in the latter text one reads the phrase 'in paradiso . . . esset sine confusione commixtio'. On this, Bugge, *Virginitas*, 24–9.

60 P. J. Payer, *Sex and the Penitentials. The Development of a Sexual Code, 550–1150*, Toronto, 1984.

61 J. L. Flandrin, *Un temps pour embrasser. Aux origines de la morale sexuelle occidentale (VIe–XIe siècle)*, Paris, 1983, 8–40.

62 *Alloquutio sacerdotum de coniugiis inlicitis ad plebem*, ed. L. Machielsen, 'Fragments patristiques non-identifiés du ms. Vat. Pal. 577', *Sacris Erudiri*, 1961, 12: 534: 'Clamat ecce Deus noster et humanae libidinis inlicitam rabiem praevidens contestatur.'

63 *Capitulare missorum generale* (802) chs 33 and 37–8, ed. A. Boretius, MGH Capit. I, no. 33, 97–8.

64 Theodulf of Orleans, *Capitulare* II, ch. II, 2, ed. P. Brommer, MGH Capit. episc. I, 154: 'Et episcopi hoc ipsum extirpare satagant, ne tanto flagitii scelere et illi polluantur et pereant et alii eorum vicinitate omnipotentis dei iram incurrant.'

65 B. Poschmann, *Die abendländische Kirchenbusse im frühen Mittelalter*, Breslau, 1930, 128.

66 *Capitulare missorum generale*, ch. 33, 97 (see above, n. 63).

# 4

## A bridle for lust:
### representations of sexual morality in Dutch children's portraits of the seventeenth century

*Jan Baptist Bedaux*

## INTRODUCTION

In contemporary discussions about upbringing and educational psychology we find instances of animal behaviour that are used to corroborate theories regarding human conduct. This way of reasoning already occurs in writings from antiquity, and it should not surprise us that this argument affected subsequent educational views. There is, for example, a group of seventeenth-century children's portraits depicting metaphors that may be related directly to these writings, and which should be looked upon as arguments *ad oculos* to support views on education current at the time.

After a fairly general treatment of visualization in consequence of these theories, I shall deal with the children's portraits in greater detail, and focus on the sexual aspect afterwards. I shall finish with a brief epilogue on iconology, the research method employed in this chapter, which has cast so much light on Dutch paintings of the sixteenth and seventeenth centuries.

In 1651 Theodoor van Thulden painted the portrait of Josina Copes-Schade van Westrum and her offspring (Plate 3). The mother shows her children, who are faced with the choice between good and evil, the arduous road to the Temple of Virtue, perched on a mountain. One of the Latin inscriptions in the painting refers to this road as the origin of eternal life. The lure of evil is embodied in the statuary on the left. These statues represent the inseparable trio Bacchus, Venus, and Cupid, who, according to the inscription on the pedestal, mislead naïve mankind. What is less readily apparent in this painting is that its representation was also determined by a personification from the *Iconologia*, a manual written by the Italian Cesare Ripa. This publication filled the need for illustrated books, allegories, and visualized general truths. It was intended for literary and visual artists as well as for 'lovers of erudition and true sciences', as we may read in the introduction to the Dutch edition, published by Dirck Pieterszoon Pers in 1644. The representations in the *Iconologia* were ordered alphabetically, the very reason why this handbook was much sought after by designers of allegories like van Thulden, who was indebted to Ripa for his personification of '*huysbestieringe*' or '*oeconomia*' (household economy; Plate 2). This personification is represented as a woman adorned with an olive wreath who holds a pair of compasses in her left hand and a wand in her right. She can also be recognized by the ship's rudder next to her. Since the mother in our picture has only been equipped with the rudder of this personification (which she holds in her left hand), we may conclude that the painter or his client meant to emphasize a particular aspect of household economy, namely the education of children. After all, according to Ripa, a rudder represents 'the concern and supervision a Father [and, by implication, the mother] ought to behave with respect to his children in order that they do not stray from the path of Virtue into the Sea of childish sensualities, in which effort children should be guided with all diligence and assiduity'.

## THEORIES

This moral lesson, as represented here by van Thulden, is specifically related to the feelings of lust in a child – passions which it must learn to bridle under the guidance of its parents. This aspect of education should be considered within the context of contemporary pedagogical theory, which to a great extent took its inspiration from classical sources. A major source of inspiration turned out to be *De liberis educandis* by the Greek Plutarch (c. AD 46–120), a treatise on education which was frequently reprinted, translated, and adapted from the fifteenth century onwards. It had a tremendous impact on pedagogical literature, and presumably on educational practice too.

Plutarch's theory derives from Aristotle (384–322 BC), who stated that *natural aptitude* (nature) must always be improved by *rules* that can be taught (education) and which must constantly be

61

*practised* (exercise). Only a combination of nature, education, and exercise guarantees a successful upbringing. Plutarch illustrated and clarified this by means of a number of educational metaphors. The central metaphor is the one of Lycurgus, king and legendary legislator of Sparta. He propounded the thesis that only through training and discipline might one achieve a successful education. In order to visualize this proposition he took two dogs, gave them a pot of food and released a hare at the same time. One of the dogs immediately chased the hare and retrieved it, while the other fell upon its food. When bystanders wanted to know what this was all about, Lycurgus explained that he had raised the dogs, which had come from the same kennel, in different ways. One of them had been raised as a hound, while the other, through lack of discipline, had degenerated into voracity. Lycurgus' metaphor enjoyed immense popularity at the time. It appears in numerous educational treatises as well as in other writings dealing with learning processes. This makes it all the more puzzling why depictions of this parable are almost completely absent from the visual arts. In the whole of European painting only one example is known of a visualization of this metaphor. This is the *Lycurgus* by Caesar van Everdingen, commissioned by the corporation of the city of Alkmaar around 1600 (Plate 4). The painting served as a decoration on the Prince's Chamber in the Alkmaar city hall, and should be considered in connection with the controversial education of the later stadholder-king, William III.

## EMBLEMATIC REPRESENTATIONS

In other variants, the training of dogs did occur in the visual arts, particularly in seventeenth-century portraiture and genre painting we frequently come across the attribute of the well-behaved dog that sits up and begs (Plates 5 and 6). This iconographical tradition originated directly from Plutarch's treatise as a self-evident translation of this text into a compact visual image that fitted in with contemporary practice. Thus the anecdotal dog from Lycurgus was transformed into a standard attribute. That this process of condensation did indeed occur in this way may well be demonstrated by means of an emblematic contribution to an *album amicorum* from the end of the sixteenth century (Plate 7). The two little dogs in the icon, the pictorial component of the emblem, bear witness to what education (*doctrina*) and exercise (*usus*) may achieve. Thus, in this emblem, education and exercise, the two components from the Aristotelian triad which make up the emblem's motto, are immediately related to the trained dogs.

Another instance of this variant, which is of greater interest because of its wide dissemination, occurs in the *Houwelyck* ('Marriage'), Jacob Cats's noted manual of behaviour, from 1625 (Plate 8). It appears in the engraving that accompanies the poem 'Maeghde-Wapen' ('Maiden's Arms') in which the author compares the young virgin to a flower in bud. The latter has to be treated with utmost care in order that the delicate plant will still be unspoilt when it blooms. The poem as a whole may be regarded as a warning against physical love, which even in its most innocent form may stain the social reputation of the girl. In this poem, Cats relates the requirement of chastity to two behavioural characteristics, namely '*eenvoudicheyt*' (simplicity) and '*leersucht*' (docility). In Cats, simplicity refers to the avoidance of evil in general, and docility to the acquisition of those aspects that make a decent and honourable citizen. Below the motto '*Lateat dum pateat*' ('*Let it be hidden until it opens*') in the engraving accompanying this poem, we find two young virgins on either side of a lozenge-shaped coat of arms. The latter contains an ornamental vase as well as a tulip surrounded by a swarm of bees – an image of the virgin besieged by suitors. The attributes of the girl on the right, who personifies simplicity, are a pigeon and a lamb. The lamb in particular recurs time and again in children's portraits – with or without attributes contrasting with this age-old symbol of innocence. The other girl figures as Docility. Apart from her sewing things, her attributes are a parrot as well as a dog that sits up.

The parrot, too, appears in children's portraits as an example of docility. It recurs in the same sense in Cats's emblem book *Proteus* under the motto '*Dwanck leert sanck*' ('Discipline teaches speech'). If someone aspires to honour, it is imperative, according to Cats, that this person be subject to severe discipline from childhood. In the *Iconologia*, too, it is a young virgin with a parrot who personifies docility. Ripa, referring to the Greek physician Galen, states that she must be depicted as a young girl, because it is the young child which is best suited to learn. According to the medical views current at the time this was due to the condition of

63

the brain, which in a young person was supposed to be soft and tender because of its great humidity. Hence the child is highly susceptible to impressions and does not have much difficulty practising the things it has been taught. But just as the child easily applies itself to the path of virtue, so can it learn evil. And this cannot be undone at a more advanced age because of the altered physical condition. It is for this reason that the child from its early childhood may only be exposed to virtuous and socially acceptable behaviour.

Plutarch lavishly illustrated his treatise with additional metaphors, all of which, however, are variations on the above-mentioned *ars-natura* theme – a theme that lent itself to endless variation throughout the sixteenth and seventeenth centuries. Consequently, in educational literature a long series of metaphors came into being which served to clarify the theoretical pedagogical point of view that had emerged from the nature-education-exercise triad. Now, it is these metaphors that we find visualized in numerous sixteenth- and seventeenth-century portraits of children, shown with or without their parents.

## CHILDREN'S PORTRAITS

If a painter wished to communicate the sitter's good breeding, he might choose from disciplined dogs, trained finches, talking parrots, or other tamed animals, trained trees, or plants, and all sorts of fruits. Ill breeding, on the other hand, was generally symbolized by means of nature run wild, like crooked trees, thistles, and thorns. Such accessories have a fairly general significance that is restricted to an educational ideal which in the paintings themselves is hardly, if at all, specified. To us, who live in an age of entirely different ethics, these symbols consequently tend to remain obscure. Our situation is quite unlike that of the contemporary beholder, who automatically related these accessories to the educational ideals that reigned supreme at the time. Sexuality, on the other hand, is an educational aspect that is specifically referred to. It is visualized by means of the so-called bridle metaphor that also appears in Plutarch, at that particular point where he warns the educator not to loosen the reins when the children are growing up. Especially then it is of the utmost importance, Plutarch argues, 'to bridle the vicious lusts of children with great care and under close guidance, as their early age makes them highly susceptible to stimuli and easily inclined to indulge in all sorts of carnal desires. Hence they need a sharp curb.'

## SEXUALITY

The bridle or rein was a well-known attribute of Temperantia, or Moderation. It occurs, for example, in the pseudo-emblematic coat of arms in Cats's *'Vryster-Wapen'* ('The spinster's coat of arms') (Plate 9) preceding the chapter *'Vryster'* ('Spinster'), which is part of Cats's *'Houwelyck'* ('Marriage'; Plate 8). In *'Vryster-Wapen'*, the author gave expression to the ideal of chastity on behalf of the unmarried virgin. *'Una via est'* ('There is only one way') reads the motto of the coat of arms that contains a hand holding a bunch of grapes by the stem. The bunch of grapes symbolizes the maiden's virginity, the stem stands for marriage. The hand belongs to the man who may make a maid his own only through marriage. This metaphor derives from the custom of grasping a bunch of grapes by the stem in order to prevent the grapes from losing their bloom. The same applies to the unmarried girl. If she is possessed otherwise than through marriage she will lose her virginity – and this will inevitably be a blot on her social reputation. It is within this sexual context that we should interpret the bridle which serves as an attribute of the girl on the left, who, according to the inscription, personifies *'sedicheit'* (modesty). The relationship between the bridle and the curbing of sexuality occurs also in a series of children's portraits. The portraits in question are those in which a child with a stick or a whip, but usually with a bridle, curbs a goat – an animal traditionally associated with lust and wanton behaviour (Plates 10–12). The striking fact that it is especially boys who are depicted with bridle and goat, may bear directly on the presumption that women, by nature, are much more moderate than men. For this reason it was thought that boys (more so than girls with their all but innate sense of shame) needed severe discipline to help them check their natural passions. That girls were by no means entirely safeguarded against such feelings of lust, however, may appear from a girl's portrait by J. G. Cuyp (Plate 13). In this painting, the bridling of carnal appetites is represented as a cat – the pre-eminent symbol of lust – which the girl holds back from the object of its greed, a fish. Cuyp contrasted this scene with a couple indulging in pastoral love-play at the back of the garden.

Educational theory gave first priority to learning to restrain one's passions. This is what every education should be based on, if we are to believe a highly popular work entitled *Den schat der gesontheyt* ('The treasure of health'). This seventeenth-century medical vade-mecum was written by the renowned Dordrecht physician Johan van Beverwijck in co-operation with his friend Jacob Cats. In the second part, which deals with the question of how a child should be brought up until it is seven years of age, van Beverwijck asserts that it is crucial that the child's emerging desires be nipped in the bud. In education, van Beverwijck reasons with Aristotle; it is the physical development that has first priority in order that the appetitive element of the soul may function at its best. Only if this condition is fulfilled can the appetitive element wholly serve and obey reason. Therefore, the physician concludes, human perfection is based on the moderation of one's carnal appetites, as moderation is the instrument which makes passion obedient to reason. In addition, it is through moderation, van Beverwijck goes on to say, that man becomes pious and blessed. His final conclusion stresses that with children, passion first and foremost needs to be restrained, otherwise it will get the upper hand by sheer force of habit.

## EPILOGUE

We owe a great deal of what we know about seventeenth-century children's portraits to iconological research as carried out by art historians from the early 1960s onwards. Iconological research has been brought to bear on several fields in art history, as, for example, seventeenth-century painting – particularly genre painting and portraiture. To avoid a distorted view of this scientific method, it should be borne in mind that here I have merely focused on a single aspect of children's portraits, namely the above-mentioned accessories. These include all sorts of staffage with which a painting may be filled in and enlivened. The ascription of meanings to such accessories is therefore just one facet of this research method. Iconology, however, aims at an integral interpretation of the image, an interpretation which also takes into account the ways in which formal and intrinsic elements are related.

This branch of science was introduced in the 1920s by the so-

called Warburg school, with Erwin Panofsky as its main representative. But it was only during the 1960s that iconology gained
currency among researchers of seventeenth-century Dutch painting. The reason for this delay was that as late as the 1960s, many
scholars continued to approach this type of painting in traditional
nineteenth-century fashion, that is, as if this type of painting were
merely concerned with faithfully rendering reality. The persistence
of this view is primarily due to the assumption that a great
number of those pictures are indeed realistic, or were at any rate
meant to be so. This is not invalidated by our knowledge that
paintings were generally composed in the studio and that the
figures occurring in genre paintings are usually types. However
this may be, artists, in accordance with contemporary art-
theoretical views, must have intended more than a mere registra-
tion of reality in quite a few cases. With respect to this 'more',
we may think of the addition of specific ideas or moral lessons as
in the pictures discussed above. Hence the occasional use of the
term pseudo-realism, which implies that realism serves as a bearer
of intentional symbolism. Now, it is the task of the iconologist to
try to distil such meanings from this pseudo-realism. No easy task,
since it is the very realism which frequently hides the symbolism
from the researcher's eye.

If we proceed to assess the results of iconological enquiry, we
may safely state that it has contributed to no small extent to socio-
cultural historiography. Slowly but surely, the pictures have been
released from their art-for-art's-sake isolation, and have been put
as much as possible into the socio-cultural context within which
they ought to be considered.

A major obstacle to this research method has undoubtedly been
the fact that the iconologists in many cases could not fall back on
the indispensable researches by historians – a predicament which
compelled them to create this socio-cultural context themselves.
One of the reasons why the iconologists have often played the
historian's role against their will was that it carried them away to
some extent from their own discipline. It is hardly surprising,
therefore, that iconology has sometimes become synonymous with
socio-cultural history. The changes that have taken place in the
study of history in the past few years, including the conspicuous
rise of the socio-cultural approach, will unmistakably affect the
iconologist's position. Iconologists will be able to shift their

researches increasingly towards their own branch of science, which will improve the level of their research, and will enable them to accomplish new tasks and meet fresh challenges.

## BIBLIOGRAPHY

J. B. Bedaux, 'Beelden van "leersucht" en tucht. Opvoedingsmetaforen in de Nederlandse schilderkunst van de zeventiende eeuw', *Nederlands Kunsthistorisch Jaarboek*, 1983, 33: 49–74.

J. B. Bedaux, 'Discipline for Innocence. Metaphors for education in Dutch seventeenth-century painting', in Mary Anne Stevens and Christopher Brown (eds) *Images of the World; Dutch genre painting in its historical context*, London, 1989.

Johan van Beverwyck, *Schat der Gesontheydt*, 2 vols, Dordrecht, 1640–2.

Jacob Cats, *Alle de wercken*, 2 vols, Utrecht, 1700.

Cesare Ripa, *Iconologia of uytbeeldingen des verstands*, introd. Jochen Becker, Soest, 1971: reprint of the edition by D. P. Pers, Amsterdam, 1644.

E. de Jongh (introduction), J. B. Bedaux, P. Hecht, J. Stumpel, *et al.*, *Tot Lering en Vermaak: Betekenissen van Hollandse genrevoorstellingen uit de zeventiende eeuw*, Amsterdam, 1976.

# 5

## The woman on a swing and the sensuous voyeur:
### passion and voyeurism in French rococo

*Mirjam Westen*

The voyeur motif, the theme of the sly or otherwise active curious spectator, is popular in the French rococo art of the eighteenth century (*c.* 1720–70). The voyeur, typically of the male sex, hidden behind curtains, doors, or bushes, is looking at a female. She is shown in such a way that the observer of the picture also sees the source of the excitements. The titillation of the voyeur is obvious. We will concentrate here on a beautiful example of the theme, Jean Honoré Fragonard's painting *The Swing*, from 1767 (Plate 14). First, a description of the work and its origin will be given. Then I will discuss the meaning of the painting. Finally, the position of the woman portrayed will be considered: an analysis of the erotic female image.

### THE SWING

A young woman on a swing is depicted in the middle of the picture, surrounded by the luxuriant green of rose-bushes and trees. At the bottom, behind her, a man sitting in the shadow keeps the movement going by means of two ropes attached to the swing. The swinging movement is pictured at the moment when the swing has reached its highest point. This is emphasized by the woman leaning backwards, her skirts billowing and her left leg stretched. One shoe has slipped off her foot, perhaps intentionally, and is flying high in the air. To the left of the woman, at the bottom, a man is hidden in the rose-bushes in such a way, half-lying, half-sitting, that he can peep under the billowing skirts and at her spread legs. He is depicted in an excited pose. The upper part of his body and his opened right hand are turned towards the spectator. His stretched left arm, with a hat in his hand, and his head askance, emphasize the direction of his gaze. Both his eyes and the woman's are clearly visible. She gazes at him, he at what is hidden under her skirts.

He is, in fact, not the only one watching her. Below the woman, one of two cupids on a dolphin-like object is facing her. About the middle of the painting, on the left side, an *amour silencieux* in profile, seated on a pedestal, is also watching the woman, with forefinger on his lips. It seems as if he is telling the excited participants in this happening (from which the man in the shadow seems to be excluded) to be silent about what is going on. A little dog is visible at the bottom right of the picture. His open mouth suggests that he is disobeying the command for silence.

## ORIGIN

Approximately in 1767, the Frenchman Collé mentions in his diary the story of the painter Doyen who was said to have been approached by a baron with a commission to paint his portrait. The baron specified a number of details of the picture. 'I would like you', as he is said to have put it, 'to paint Madame' (and he showed his mistress) 'sitting on a swing which is put in motion by a bishop. You will depict me in such a position that I am able to see the legs of this beautiful girl, especially if you want to brighten up your painting a bit more.' Doyen, adding that slippers flying through the air would not be unbecoming in such a picture, rejected the commission, however, ('so inconsistent with my usual style') and sent the baron to Fragonard.[1]

At that moment, 1767,[2] Fragonard ('the cherub of erotic painting') was a successful artist. Up to 1765, he painted mostly biblical and mythological scenes, landscapes, and portraits, but from 1765 on he depicted mainly genre-like *scènes d'amour*. In the same year, he carried out the commission of the baron, identified in the nineteenth century as Baron de Saint-Julien, but confined himself to painting only one slipper flying in the air and portraying a layman instead of a bishop.[3] He even seems to have made copies.[4] In 1782, the engraver de Launay contributed to the distribution on a larger scale. His prints show the scene mirrorwise. With the caption *Les Hazards heureux de l'escarpolette* ('The pleasant risks of the swing'), de Launay once more emphasized the possibilities that swinging offers to voyeuristic looks. The swing is one of the many types of painting of the French rococo, in which the theme of love, lasciviousness, and passion is visualized. Nonsense, jest, and sarcasm play an important part in the reproduction of amorous, impassioned, and erotic relations between men and women. Many an artist was inspired by theatrical performances and literature in the reproduction of this on paintings, engravings and illustrations.

Adultery, intrigue, so-called '(un)lucky accidents' whereby parts of the female body are exposed, the *désordre* (disarray)[5] of clothes and/or the interior of a room are frequent, but above all the languorous male gaze: these are characteristic themes, symbols, and motifs in the *scènes d'amour*.

## MEANING

The motif of the voyeur is combined in art with other elements. In this example the elements are the amourette, the swing, and the surrounding scenery. These elements have been represented in art for centuries. Fragonard's depiction is by no means exceptional. With the help of the iconographic method reference is often made in art history to the pictorial tradition of symbols and motifs in order to decipher the meaning. However, meanings cannot be reduced exclusively to observable aspects, nor can they be squeezed into a certain pictorial tradition. In order to discover the meanings that were attributed to the swing, it is important for scholars to explore profoundly, among other things, the reception of the picture. So far, however, little research has been carried out along these lines. By relating the surrounding scenery, the amourette, and the swing to the pictorial tradition in art history, I merely wish to indicate the meanings *The Swing* might have had.

### 1 Garden of Desires

An amorous scene situated in rural surroundings or in a garden has a long tradition in European art. In literature this is even one of the oldest themes. Inspired by, among others, Vergilius' *Bucolica*, it is the representation of an ideal, carefree nature in which shepherds are enjoying lavish fruit and peace and love. Since the thirteenth century the literary pastoral genre had been mixed with the courtly, chivalrous style. In this new literary blend eroticism gradually was freed from the rigid and conventional dogmas of courtly love.[6] Since the Renaissance in literature and in art, nature has been depicted as the ideal opportunity for the upper classes to withdraw from the world into intimate private surroundings.

The pictorial tradition of the garden of love, influenced by the literary imagination, goes back to the late Middle Ages, according to art historian Elise Goodman, and is 'a backdrop or stage-setting for the activities of the society that inhabited it . . . to which they withdrew for intimate conversation and dalliance'.[7] To Hauser, it is obvious that in the eighteenth century, the age of gallantry, the pastoral genre reaches the high point of its development. The upper classes live in artificial communities with rigid rules. One rule in the game of love is gallantry, which, like the pastoral scene, had been a form of play in the earliest examples of erotic art.[8] The poetic and Arcadian landscapes in Watteau's *fêtes galantes* provide an ideal setting for love and courtship.

Therefore, the relation between nature and love in *The Swing* by Fragonard is by no means exceptional. The rose-bushes could even be called standard. A mere knowledge of the tradition, however, does not make the effect of Fragonard's representation of nature clearer or easier to understand. What could be the effect of his luxuriant foliage and freakish branches? This collage-like, rural scenery is far too dense according to Wentzel ('one cannot hang a swing for adults in such a dense wood'), the spatial proportions with regard to the figures unclear and unrealistic, but 'full of poetry and loving charm'. Posner also noted that there is hardly any space to swing in. He thinks that with this reproduction of nature the artist wants 'to establish a mood of tremendous excitement by means of the dense twisting and turning of trees and bushes, and by the sparkling activity of leaves shimmering silver in the blue-green atmosphere of what at first seems a forest glade. . . . Fragonard must have recognized that an image of nature's luxuriance and fertility would make an appropriate context for his amorous swinging scene too. Furthermore, the density and thickness of nature's growth seem to screen the figures and suggest a secret place for this curious lovers' tryst.'[9]

Enclosing the swing in the surrounding nature guarantees an intimacy. The voyeur sees something which others (the person sitting in the shade, for instance) cannot see. His refuge in the bushes makes him think that he is the only one who can see something without himself being noticed. The scenery intensifies the effect of the watching and spying, inherent in a voyeuristic gaze.[10]

Amourettes have appeared in art since the Renaissance. They are usually interpreted as references to love. They are either part of a mythological scene, or are a remnant of it, and represent in genre painting, for example, a last reference to the mythological love lyrics. In eighteenth-century rococo, they are indispensable as decoration and/or allegory of love. The sculptured group, on the right beneath the swing, consists of two cupids riding a dolphin across the waves. In classical mythology, Cupid-ridden dolphins pull the water-cart of Venus, the goddess of love.[11] The sculpture on the left of the picture is a copy of the *amour silencieux* by the sculptor Falconet.[12] The silencing gesture of this Amor, in particular, contributes to the effect of intimate seclusion compelling secrecy. The *amour silencieux* as such refers not to love and passion, but to the intrigue preceding the voyeuristic gaze. Both sculptures emphasize the voyeuristic look by the (glancing) direction of their heads.

## 2 Irresolution

There is an unquestionably large quantity of depictions of swings in eighteenth-century rococo art. Artists like Watteau, Lancret, and Pater use this motif several times in their works. Wentzel traces the swing motif back to Greek antiquity and does not see it again until the seventeenth-century emblem books. The motif, a woman on a swing pushed by a man, refers among other things to the irresolution and capriciousness of a woman in love.[13]

The subject in eighteenth-century rococo paintings is also generally a woman on a swing, pushed by a man. But does this motif still refer to the above-mentioned interpretation? In his iconographic survey of the swing motif in rococo art, Wentzel merely comments that a rural game, innocent or presented as such, suited an excursion by courtiers into the 'simple life'. He adds that 'in fact the participants of the scene depicted are not as naive as they are supposed to be in the painting'. He is reticent about such a possible interpretation of eighteenth-century swing representations.[14] On the basis of seventeenth-century emblem books and the caption of a print 'Women's fickleness in matters of the heart after Watteau's *Swing*', Posner dares to call this one of the most popular associations with the eighteenth-century motif. This also explains, at least to him, why it is always a woman and never a man who is on the swing.[15] As Posner relativizes his remarks, in the eighteenth century not all swings were associated with the capriciousness of women, but were all indeed associated with romantic or erotic feelings. 'Assuming the associations people had in those days with the swing, the scene gets a remarkable psychological colouring. We feel the delightful excitement of the early stages of love: invitation and flirtation will be followed by the playful irresolution of the young girl's heart.' Posner attaches two more metaphorical meanings to the swing: 'The passivity of the woman on the swing and the controlling of the starting and proceeding movement of the swing by the man make a natural metaphor for traditional courting.' Apart from the natural metaphorical meaning, he distinguishes an erotic metaphorical meaning: 'swinging puts the body into a rhythmic action'. The swing as depicted by Fragonard, combined with other symbols, gives this painting an intense erotic tension, according to Posner.[16]

### 3 Seeing and wanting to be seen

The presence of an overseeing 'eye' in the form of a Peeping Tom completes and reinforces the effect of the 'retrousse', in this case the uncovering of a part of the body because of the billowing of the skirts. The swinging woman seems to be aware of his presence and even flirts with him by losing her slipper, the fetish *par excellence*. The furtiveness of the peeping eye, in *The Swing* (the silencing gesture, the hiding under the bushes) is a pretended game. In fact it is a 'consciously manipulated accident'.[17]

The woman knows she is being peeped at, her expression suggests 'wanting to be seen'. The 'wanting to be seen' and the 'wanting to see' have been expressed in one picture by Fragonard. As far as I know, Fuchs is one of the first to distinguish the sex-specific assignment of *'sehen wollen'* and *'gesehen werden wollen'* in the visual arts. For him it is certainly resolved in the natural division of roles, which assigns sexual activity to the man and passivity to the woman, so that 'wanting to see' often suits the man and the woman is quite keen on showing herself when she wants to be seen.[18] In the *scènes d'amour* seeing and wanting to be seen are represented as an amusing game, in which all participants seem to profit equally. The desire to see (male role) reinforces the desire to be seen (female role) and emphasizes the female beauty. The desire to be seen reinforces, affirms, and legitimizes the desire to see. Key notions in this game are refinement and complication, in order for the game to be varied. The calculated uncovering of the female body for the eyes of strangers is the central theme. In that sense the representation of the voyeur motif in art confirms the sex-specific character of voyeurism: it is predominantly the female body that is shown to the peeping glance of the male.

The subtlety of these scenes is enhanced, according to Fuchs, when the artist incriminates the peeped-at woman. 'Of course she pretends again and again to be unaware of her surroundings, and in the mean time she constantly assumes piquant poses, so as to prevent the voyeur from missing anything.' Fuchs is not only referring to the male spectator in the picture, but also to the male spectator of the picture, the artist in particular. 'When the artist portrays the opportunity enabling the peeper (of course women peep as well) to enjoy watching at his ease the charms of the intimate gathering . . . he illustrates the construction "oh, would it not be exciting if I were in this situation [. . .]."'[19] Apart from the "retrousse" of clothes, the voyeuristic look is provoked by the tension of "the occasion, the coincidence of the moment." Fragonard has depicted a moment in which the female body is suddenly and very briefly shown. This moment indicates also the end of the revelation: the swing and the skirts are on the verge of coming down again.' Who knows whether this moment will be repeated, as Starobinski puts it rhetorically.[20]

## 4 The Female Image

The depiction of a voyeur is a frequent motif in French eighteenth-century *scènes d'amour*, inspired mainly by contemporary plays and literature. The sleeping Diana has become a sleeping coquettish lady in modern clothes; Zeus a gallant lifting her skirts with his walking-stick. The handling of the enema, a phallic symbol *par excellence*, creates a marvellous situation for the male voyeur to gaze, hidden behind a curtain or glass. When women are taking a bath, the spectators can only just be kept outside the door.

A number of art historians have already indicated that the depiction of the voyeur motif in art has increased statistically since the sixteenth century. Mittig gives a few explanations for the increasing interest in this motif in art. He points out the greater importance attached to visuality from the sixteenth century as well as the 'pragmatization' of human contacts caused by capitalist developments.[21] In due course, people tend to get more and more acquaintances whom they know only slightly. Contact is restricted to partial aspects of the other. A parallel can be drawn between this tendency of the growing impersonality of human contacts and the characteristics of voyeurism: anonymity and narrowing contact merely to the visual. Many authors assert this, referring to the increasing separation between private housing and public streets, the division of living space into rooms which are separated according to their function (a separate bedroom, kitchen, etc.) and the decrease in daily physical proximity. They form the basis for a personal intimate atmosphere. This intimate atmosphere is the object of voyeurism. The voyeur enjoys the distance between himself and that which he is looking at as a commodity of which he can deprive others as well as a protection against having to be involved in things. The developments sketched here shed doubt on the validity of Fuchs's statement that the 'inquisitive erotic look' was always and everywhere considered immoral. The erotic look, the voyeuristic look, has never been an anthropological, historical constant: voyeuristic behaviour is determined by changing social circumstances. Is the sex-specific assignment of (male) watching and (female) being watched socially determined as well?

According to a number of feminist art historians, the sex-specific assignment of seeing and (wanting) to be seen is an important principle, in particular within the analysis of erotic female images in art. What counts is not only the position of the persons in the picture, but also the position of the spectators of the picture. The analysis usually concentrates on the relation between the female personage and the position of the man as spectator in the picture. The title of Hess and Nochlin's book, *Woman as Sex Object*, is characteristic of the feminist point of view, developed since the 1970s, of the female personage who is exposed to the male look. The book denounces the stereotyped and sexist character of female images in erotic art, and interprets it as the object, the projection of the male look, lust, and sexuality.[22] In *Ways of Seeing*, Berger contributes to popularizing this criticism. He points to the fact that the assignment of male watching and female being watched are socially determined. Because of the limited space that the woman is allowed under the male wing, she is forced to keep an eye on herself all the time. The way women manifest themselves socially is the historical result of the ingenuity that they have had to develop in order to be able to live under such patronizing, restricted circumstances. Men act and women appear. Men look at women. Women regard themselves as creatures who are looked at.[23] This aspect is particularly clearly expressed in nude painting, according to Berger.

Mulvey, who analysed the erotic female image in film, also emphasizes the social definition of watching and (wanting) to be watched. In a world determined by sexual inequality, the wish to watch is subdivided into active male watching and passive female wanting to be watched. In the exhibitionistic role attributed to women, they are watched and exposed at the same time. Bryson, basing himself on Mulvey's text, finds confirmation of the sex-specific watching in *The Swing* by Fragonard: 'Woman as the Image, Man as bearer of the Look'.

The spectator of the picture can identify himself with the male voyeur in the picture: 'The male within the painting acts as a surrogate for the male viewer, to whose sexuality the image is exclusively addressed'.[24] They all denounce the stereotyped and sexist character of the female images in the erotically biased art, and characterize this image as the object, the projection of the male look, lust, and sexuality. When, in addition to the woman, the man has been depicted as well, this may be used as a 'substitute' for the male spectator. Many authors argue that the male look, men's watching, confirm the power of men over women: (male) watching and (female, the female image) being watched express the sex-specific, dichotomous impressions of sexuality. According to this view, male sexuality is represented as active, spontaneous, genital, object-directed; female sexuality as passive, available, and reacting to male sexuality. Watching is active, male; being watched is passive, female.

The sex-specific division of watching and being watched is inherent in the social balance of power between men and women.

The assignment as such is based on conceptions of sexuality, femininity, and masculinity, which are changeable, in my opinion, and not determined by biological differences between men and women, as Fuchs thinks.

I have already quoted a few art historians on the subject of the painting *The Swing* who interpret the woman on the swing in this way. According to Posner, *The Swing* expresses sex-specific behaviour with respect to courting: the woman on the swing is passive, she is put and kept in motion by the man (active, control). Besides, she is the object of the male look. Through this objectivization, the man projects his desire. The female image is the spectacle on which he projects his narcissistic fantasies. The female image connotes 'body and nature, i.e. passive, available, accessible and powerless', according to Parker and Pollock.[25] In and by male projection, femininity is reproduced in an idealized way in art; according to many female and some male critics this is in direct contrast to reality.

The way in which women's sexual pleasure is idealized (in literature) contrasts sharply with the way in which the eighteenth-century morals, for instance, misjudge this female pleasure, as Gutwirth puts it. Swiderski considers in literature the cultivated beauty of the woman as a compensation for her subordinate social position, by means of which the male author tries to relieve his bad conscience.[26] As we saw with Posner, *The Swing* shows the relation between the male viewer of the picture and the female image in it. The imbalance of power between the sexes is inherent in this relation. When female images are analysed in this way the female image is, in other words, reduced to the conditions on which the picture has been made. The female image is considered as the result of the imbalance of power. The meaning of the female image is reduced to the working of the picture: it is determined and established by the male look.

During the 1980s these approaches to the (erotic) female image in art have been subject of increasing criticism. The basic principle for this criticism was the notion that meanings cannot be seen as mere reflections of already existing meanings, balances of power and/or ideologies, and that meanings simply cannot be 'read' from pictures.

In her article, 'Women, representation and the image', Cowie criticizes the way in which the homogeneous content in or meaning of a picture is assumed, which many authors, as it were, read from the picture. Meanings are not intrinsic to the picture but are effected by the meaning-giving process, the reception. Another point of her criticism concerns the way in which the balance of power between the sexes is related to the meaning-giving process.

Feminist analyses do not depart from the idea that the balance of power as such is reflected in the meaning-giving process: the ideologies, in which the social relation is expressed, influence the meaning-giving process. When the male spectator looks at the female image, the power of men over women is confirmed at an ideological level. This line of reasoning runs the risk, according to Cowie: of the meaning-giving process being seen as an effect (reflection, mirroring, reproduction) of already existing meanings. Meaning-giving processes do not reflect ideologies, they are part of the production of meanings themselves.[27]

The remarks about femininity and masculinity are also open to criticism. In his article 'The domain of the sexual', Mort says that the categories masculinity and femininity are complex constructions. The relations female-passive and male-active cannot be applied just like that as 'monolithical units' in investigations for conceptions of sexuality.[28] Neither categorizing the erotic female image as the projection of the male desirous glance, nor taking this female image as a delusion disguising the (correctly ascertained) bad social position of women, contributes to answering the question of the meanings that were attached to the *scènes d'amour* in the eighteenth century.

Returning to the picture of *The Swing*, I would like to say that the female person cannot be reduced to a tame sheep in the analysis, to a passive object of the active male look. As in so many French eighteenth-century *scènes d'amour*, she gets attention, she is admired, looked at, and moreover languorously desired. In this role she is, as Mulvey puts it so strikingly, watched and gloriously exposed: the appearance of the female personage is 'streamlined' on visual and erotic charisma. One might say that she connotes 'wanting to be seen'.[29] Examination is needed to determine whether, and to what extent, female sexuality has been encouraged by these *scènes d'amour* and disciplined at the same time.[30]

Finally, a remark about the role of the man. A possible meaning of the male personage seems to be being at the mercy of the wanting to be seen of the female personage. He has, so to speak, shown himself as an admirer on his knees and looks appealingly upwards at her or rather at what is beneath her skirts. He has been caught by, or is at the mercy of, his voyeuristic looks. Especially his being at the woman's mercy is ridiculed in *The Swing*. Perhaps as early as the eighteenth century, may this have been considered a criticism of, or an ironic comment on, the male leering voyeuristic looks?[31]

## NOTES

This chapter is a slightly revised version of 'Who knows whether this moment will repeat itself? Viewing pleasure in the French rococo', which appeared in *Lover, literatuuroverzicht voor de vrouwenbeweging*, January 1986, pp. 14–21.

1 Collé, *Journal et Mémoires*, Paris, 1868, III, 165; Fragonard was born in Grasse in 1732 and died in 1806. From 1746 he was an apprentice with Chardon and Boucher respectively, from 1753 at the Ecole des Elèves Protégés, under the direction of Charles van Loo in Paris. He stayed in Italy several times for a number of years, particularly in Rome (1756–61 and 1773–4).
2 Edmund and Jules Goncourt, *L'art du XVIIIième siècle*, Paris, 1910, III, 243.
3 Edmund and Jules Goncourt (1910) (reprint 'Fragonard', chapter from *Gazette des Beaux Arts*, 1985) and Ralph Nevill, 'Jean Honoré Fragonard', *Burlington Art Magazine*, 1903, 3: 52–6, erroneously date the painting in 1766 and 1765 respectively. Investigation has shown that Collé's diary was written in 1767. Because *Les Hazards* is found in the collection of Baron Saint-Julien at the end of the eighteenth century, it is generally assumed that he was the patron. Depicting nuns and clergymen in erotic and pornographic engravings and paintings was by no means unusual. About the relation between spirituality and erotic literature see Barry Ivker, 'John Cleland and the Marquis d'Argens: eroticism and natural morality in the mid-eighteenth century English and French fiction', *Mosaic*, 1975, 8: 141–8. Ivker interprets their presence in 'libertine' literature as an indication of the impossibility of aiming at the Christian ideal of celibacy and monogamy, and as a possibility of mocking certain clergymen, or religion in general (144). I also assume that their presence can add to an increasing erotic tension: under their supervising eye the 'forbidden' is ignored. Or the clergy cannot control itself.
4 According to Nevill (1903), a replica with a blue instead of a pink dress is in the possession of Baron de Rothschild. The original, under the title *The Swing*, is part of the Wallace Collection. Nevill regrets that 'the little lady of the Escarpolette must of necessity swing her

dainty rose-coloured lingerie' in England 'before a public which by nature and training is unsympathetic towards irresponsible and unfettered frivolity' (56). The copper-plate of this painting was destroyed by the customs; initially, the painting was refused admission to England (5); Virgile Josz, *Fragonard, moeurs du XVIIIe siècle*, Paris, 1901. Josz mentions three replicas: 'celle du baron de Saint-Julien passée en dernier lieu de M. de Mornay chez Sir Richard Wallace: une Escarpolette figure dans la collection d'Edmund de Rothschild et une plus petite appartient à M. le duc de Polignac' (98).

5  *Désordre* is, for instance, the disordered condition of bedclothes, a fallen chair or table, an unfastened blouse or trousers.

6  Quote from Warren Roberts, *Morality and Social Class in 18th Century French Literature and Painting*, Toronto, 1974, 114.

7  Elise Goodman, 'Rubens conversation à la mode. Garden of leisure, fashion and gallantry', *Art Bulletin*, 1982, 64: 247–59.

8  Arnold Hauser, *Sociale geschiedenis van de kunst*, Nijmegen, 1975, 345.

9  Peter Gorsen, 'Von der Darstellung des Nackten zur "aphrodisischen Aktkunst"', Anfänge des "Sexismus" und seiner Kritik in der frühbürgerlichen Aufklärung', in G. Nabakowski, H. Sander, and P. Gorsen, *Frauen in der Kunst*, Frankfurt am Main, 1980, 2: 91–102; Hans Wentzel, 'Jean Honoré Fragonard's "Schaukel"'. Bemerkungen zur Ikonographie der Schaukel in der Bildenden Kunst', *Wallraf-Richartz, Jahrbuch*, 1964: 24: 187–218; Donald Posner, 'The swinging woman of Watteau and Fragonard', *Art Bulletin*, 1982, 64: 75–88; Norman Bryson, *Word and Image, French painting and the Ancien Régime*, Cambridge, 1981, 96.

10  The suggested intimacy, in my opinion, is also intensified by the (rather) small size of the painting.

11  Posner, 'The swinging woman', 84.

12  Identified by Wentzel, 'Jean Honoré Fragonard's "Schaukel"', 109. Falconet exhibited this sculpture in the Salon in 1755. In the same year he made a marble replica at the request of Madame de Pompadour.

13  Wentzel, 'Jean Honoré Fragonard's "Schaukel"', 198, explains the quantity as follows: Frederick II of Prussia owns a large collection of paintings by Watteau, Lancret, and Pater (who all depicted numerous swinging women). Other kings and monarchs try to imitate him. 'Kein Wunder also', says the author, 'daß auch das Schaukelmotiv sich über die Pariser Malerschule der 1. Hälfte des 18. Jahrhunderts hinaus verbreitete.' Other meanings that Wentzel mentions are: financial insecurity, symbol of childhood or idleness (nineteenth century), and, as symbol of one of the four elements, air (193).

14  Wentzel, 'Jean Honoré Fragonard's "Schaukel"', 78–9, 210.

15  Posner, 'The swinging woman', 76. He refers to the following poem: 'Au Jeu d'Escarpolette, Acis voit sa Bergère/Prendré d'un Ait dispos, ses innocens Ebas/Il l'excite, il l'anime, il l'aide de ses bras;/Trop content de la voir encore plus legère//Pour dresser une Agnes à l'Effort qu'elle a pris/Tel un galant adroit met tout l'art en

usage:/Mais bientôt il la trouve à son gré trop volage;/Du fruit de ses leçons, il n'est point d'autre prix.' From J. Fürstenberg, *La gravure originale dans l'illustration du livre français au XVIIIe siècle*, Hamburg, 1975, 151.

16 Posner, 'The swinging woman', 78, 79, and 88.

17 Gorsen, 'Von der Darstellung . . .', 98.

18 Eduard Fuchs, *Illustrierte Sittengeschichte. Zweiter Band. Die Galante Zeit*, Munich, 1910, 201–2; Eduard Fuchs, *Geschichte der erotischen Kunst. Erster Band. Das Zeitgeschichtliche Problem. Dritter Band. Das Individuelle Problem II*, Berlin, 77, 64, 67; in my opinion, the *retrousse* effect is reflected more strongly in engravings. The contract between clothed (black/dark) and unclothed or showing underclothing (white/light) is stronger than painted contrasts of colour (in *The Swing*, for instance). It is often used in pictures of *Glückliche Unfälle*, in which the happiness applies to the male; for example, in the case of a woman who has fallen from a donkey or a see-saw in such a way that the lower part of her body is uncovered.

19 Fuchs, *Geschichte der erotischen Kunst*, (n. 18), 116.

20 Jean Starobinski, *L'invention de la liberté, 1700–1789*, Geneva, 1964, 76. See, for example, Fragonard's *Le Verrou* and *Le Baiser à la dérobée*, cf. Michael Fried, *Absorption and Theatricality, Painting and Beholder in the Age of Diderot*, Berkeley, Calif., 1980, 138.

21 Hans-Ernst Mittig, 'Erotik bei Rubens', in Renate Berger, *Der Garten der Lüste. Zur Deutung des Erotischen und Sexuelles bei Künstlern und ihren Interpreten*, Cologne, 1985, 48–88.

22 Thomas Hess and Linda Nochlin, *Woman as Sex Object. Studies in Erotic Art 1730–1970*, London, 1973.

23 John Berger, *Ways of Seeing*, London, 1972, 46–7.

24 Laura Mulvey, 'Visuelle Lust und narratives Kino', in C. Nabakowski, *Frauen in der Kunst*, Frankfurt am Main, 1980, 30–47; Bryson, *Word and Image*, 98–9.

25 Rozsika Parker and Griselda Pollock, *Old Mistresses: Women, Art and Ideology*, London, 1981, 116, 132; see also Berger, *Ways of Seeing*.

26 Madelyn Gutwirth, *Madame de Staël, Novelist. The Emergence of the Artist as Woman*, Urbana, Ill., 78, 163; Marie-Laure Swiderski, 'La condition de la femme française au XVIIIe siècle d'après les romans', in Paul Fritz and Richard Morton, *Woman in the 18th Century*, Toronto, 1976, 105–27; Klaus Theweleit, *Männerphantasien. I. Frauen, Fluten, Körper, Geschichte*, Reinbeck bei Hamburg, 1980, 336.

27 Elizabeth Cowie, 'Women, representation and the image', *Screen Education*, Summer 1977, 23, 15–23.

28 Frank Mort, 'The domain of the sexual', *Screen Education*, Autumn 1980, 36: 69–85. Also Lucy Bland, 'The domain of the sexual: a response', *Screen Education*, Summer 1981, 39: 56–69.

29 Mulvey, 'Visuelle Lust', 30–47. Mulvey's basic assumption that the desirous look is by definition male, and thus condemnable, has been undermined in the last few years within women's studies because of the analysis and the formulation of women's viewing pleasure. See

*Scopohilia, het genot van het kijken*, symposium volume, Tilburg, January 1986 and the special issue 'Scopohilia, kijkgenot', of the *Tijdschrift voor Vrouwenstudies*, 27, vol. 7, no. 3, 1986.

30 Theweleit, *Männerphantasien*, does not interpret the eroticized and idealized beauty of women in female images as compensation for, but as a function in, the disciplinary process of female sexuality, which serves in turn as a strategic part of the process of monogamy.

31 The question of the role of the male patron is outside the scope of this article, but will certainly be dealt with in a subsequent study of the reception of French eighteenth-century *scènes d'amour*. What need made the baron ask to have himself portrayed in this voyeuristic pose? I assume that the baron's desire was roused by seeing himself in this pose with his mistress. It will be necessary to examine to what extent this depiction can be interpreted as a part of the narcissistic ego of the baron.

# 6

## Venus Minsieke Gasthuis:
### sexual beliefs in
### eighteenth-century Holland
#### Herman Roodenburg

## 1 INTRODUCTION

In 1794, the Dutch author Cornelia Lubbertina van der Weyde published her novel *Henry–Louize*. The book contains a remarkable passage. Louize lives with an extremely pious aunt, 'Tante Bedilziek' ('Aunt Meddlesome'). However, one day she finds a number of letters and books which show her aunt's piety in a new and surprising light.[1] Among the books are erotic novels such as *De Amsterdamsche Lichtmis*, *De Haagsche Lichtmis*, and *De Leydsche Student*.[2] Louize also finds two sex manuals, translated from the French. One of these books is *Venus Minsieke Gasthuis*, which was first published in Dutch in Amsterdam[3] in 1687. The French edition had been published two years earlier in the same city.[4] The author had concealed his identity behind a pseudonym. Later, he turned out to be the French physician Nicolas Venette (1633–98), professor of anatomy and surgery at La Rochelle.[5]

Louize did not hold with books of this nature; she considered them unsuitable for 'a decent eye'. They should be avoided by respectable people and clearly her aunt was not one of them.

Louize's harsh judgement differs greatly from the carefully considered opinion given by Pierre Bayle on the publication of Venette's sex manual. According to Bayle, the author had really gone quite far; perhaps it would have been better if he had written it in Latin. Bayle also thought the book's tenor rather lax on occasion. But all this was more than compensated for by the fact that the author provided his readers with an enormous amount of information. Unlike Louize, Bayle did not see it as an immoral book. In fact, the opposite was true; although he believed it was dangerous, he also saw that it would be extremely useful for many readers.[6]

It seems to me that we should see Louize's reaction in terms of the 'civilizing campaign' which had got under way in the late eighteenth-century republic.[7] A number of sex manuals appeared in this period but they are more covert in tone; people wrote less openly about sexuality. A prime example is the other sex manual Louize discovered, *De natuurkundige beschouwing van de man en de vrouw in den huwelijken staat*. This treatise, written by the French surgeon M. de Lignac, appeared in Dutch in 1782. It was reprinted in 1785.[8] Louize is clearly more lenient in her judgement of this book; it was unsuitable for women but it could be useful reading for men.


## 2 INTERPRETATION

Little is known about sexual attitudes in the republic. Research into moral tracts, medical treatises, and other sources, along the lines of that done in other countries, has hardly begun in the Netherlands.[9] Nor has much attention been given to Venette's remarkable book.[10] Yet, in spite of its 650 pages, this book was extremely popular. It was reprinted no fewer than ten times between 1687 and 1781, while a second Dutch translation appeared in 1728 which was reprinted in 1767. Apparently, the eleventh reprint, in 1781, did not sell particularly well, because in 1797 the remaindered copies were given a face-lift in the form of a new title page and put back on the market. However, that was the end of the *Minsieke Gasthuis*.[11]

Venette was not only widely read in the republic. He was also popular in Germany.[12] In France his work continued to be reprinted not only during the eighteenth but also throughout the nineteenth and even in the twentieth centuries. The final edition appeared in 1955.[13] Venette reached a much smaller audience in Britain and the United States as his book had to compete with a no less widely read sex manual, *Aristotle's Masterpiece*, which was published in London in 1684.[14] It is striking that the publication of the first two sex manuals occurred in the 1680s, both in Europe and in the United States. It is not easy to find an explanation for this. Seeing the lack of real precursors,[15] we can assume that up until this particular decade information on sexual matters was passed on verbally. If we are to believe Johan de Brune, this information was far from crude. In 1644 he wrote:

> As a rule, our menfolk are so honeyed with all kinds of untimely dalliance that they have no need of Aretino when they come to pay the conjugal duty owed to their brides; and the weaker sex were often so practised and artful that on the first night of their wedding they hardly learnt anything new . . .. I mean to say . . . that generally they had already learnt so much that (and here my pen falters) they are not entirely unacquainted with the means through which two people enrich the world with a third.[16]

In the following sections I will go into a number of ideas and concepts in *Minsieke Gasthuis*. Precisely because this book was so widely read, it should be possible to infer something of sexual attitudes in the eighteenth century republic. In doing so, we will discover little about the lower classes as Venette's readers must have been primarily well-to-do; a readership with enough education to follow his more technical discourses and his numerous erudite allusions.

Family historians have sometimes reached sweeping conclusions on sexual intercourse in earlier centuries. In this respect, Lawrence Stone's work on early modern England is interesting. According to Stone, various phases in the sexual attitudes of the elite can be discerned. Until the end of the sixteenth century a measure of tolerance towards sexuality existed. Thereafter, roughly between 1570 and 1670, under the influence of Puritanism, followed a period of sexual repression which in its turn was succeeded by a new period of permissiveness, even of licence, which lasted until the end of the eighteenth century.[17]

The two periods of tolerance were by no means identical. Behind Stone's phasing lies his conviction, primarily borrowed from Max Weber, that the Western European family underwent a complex process of individualization. From the end of the seventeenth century, women and children acquired a more independent position within the family while, at the same time, affective bonds between the family members strengthened. This 'rise of affective individualism', as Stone calls this process, would eventually result in the western nuclear family we know today. For our purposes, it is important that from the end of the seventeenth century, the increased affective bonds between men and women were expressed in a greater space for sexual pleasure.[18]

This evolutionary perspective has been widely criticized. According to Alan Macfarlane, Stone has twisted or simply ignored the historical evidence which does not fit into his scheme of things. He gives numerous examples to support this criticism.[9] Stone also handles Venette's work in a remarkable manner.

Stone probably found the book less tolerant than he had expected for an eighteenth-century publication. In any case, he classifies it as 'neither very illuminating in detail, nor very positive in its attitude towards sexuality'. He had found the same attitudes in *Aristotle's Masterpiece*. In order to hold fast to his notion of a tolerant eighteenth century, Stone concludes that the readers probably did not take much notice of this negative attitude.[20] A surprising conclusion considering the immense popularity of both sex manuals. One wonders why people actually bought the book in the first place.

In order to avoid the trap of drawing conclusions based on unilinear models borrowed from sociology, it would seem sensible and preferable to approach Venette's book from a more contextual standpoint. In doing so, another social science, cultural anthropology, would be more useful than sociology. An anthropologically oriented approach, as argued by historian Natalie Davis, can form a valuable counterbalance to 'evolutionary schemes'. In models of this kind, the strange and surprising (e.g. early popular culture) are all too quickly pushed aside as marginal phenomena, whereas anthropology has shown us that it is precisely these phenomena which can give us deeper insight into other cultures.[21]

The medical literature of early modern Europe contains numerous data which appear strange and surprising to people today. In recent years, French research into the history of sexuality in particular has used these sources to great advantage.[22] This chapter is the result of similar research. However, anthropology can also be useful in another way. Davis praises anthropologists for 'their interesting ways of interpreting symbolic behaviour'. She refers to the work of Victor Turner and Clifford Geertz[23] in particular. Their insights have been used only sparingly in French research. And yet, as I hope to prove, such insights can be fruitful. Obviously, the approach chosen here is not without risks, if only because Venette was a Frenchman and not a Dutchman. The question immediately arises: is it possible to draw conclusions about sexual attitudes in the Dutch Republic from a French sex manual? However popular *Minsieke Gasthuis* may have been, we will, of course, have to keep in mind that Venette sometimes wrote about subjects that were of little interest to people in the republic.[24] It is also possible that Venette's views were comparatively personal, and not shared by a great majority of people. For these reasons, I have placed Venette's ideas in their context as far as possible by consulting medical and other treatises from the republic itself, and by using recent historical research into the history of sexuality.

## 3 VENETTE'S MEDICAL IDEAS

Like those of most physicians of his day, Venette's ideas were based to a great extent on the works of Hippocrates and Galen. For example, his treatise is dominated by Hippocrates' humoral pathology: the science of the four bodily fluids – blood, mucus, white bile, and black bile. Based on these four fluids, four temperaments were distinguished: the sanguine, the phlegmatic, the choleric, and the melancholic.

At the same time, most physicians adhered to Galen's science of pneumata, or three spirits: the animal, the vital, and the natural spirits. Venette quotes one of Galen's cases. A number of men had been to bed with a woman so often that their brains had shrivelled to the size of a fist.[25] This may sound like a tall story today, but Venette and his contemporaries did not see it that way. They, too, were convinced that sperm was extracted from the whole body, and from the brain in particular. For it is from the brain that animal spirits flow to the sexual organs and, as a result, too much sex could impair the brain.

Another of Galen's theories was also current in the seventeenth and eighteenth centuries. It was believed that not only men but also women had a seminal emission during orgasm. Up until the sixteenth century, doctors had accepted Aristotle's theory that a woman's only contribution to conception came in the form of menstrual blood. If sperm entered the womb, a fermentation process took place and this process produced an embryo about forty days later. From the sixteenth century onwards, doctors were more inclined towards Galen's theory. They came to believe in the existence of both male and female sperm. The difference between the two theories was great. In contrast to Aristotle, Galen assigned women an active role in procreation: an orgasm, a seminal emission, was vital.[26] Venette shared his opinion.

Obviously, Hippocrates and Galen are not the only physicians cited by Venette. He also mentions contemporaries such as Harvey and Ruysch. But their role remains limited, while Swammerdam and Leeuwenhoek are absent altogether. There is no trace in Venette's work of the incipient discussion between ovists and animalculists. And in 1772, de Lignac rightly remarks that Venette's work has become dated in some respects although 'this is less the writer's fault than that of the time he lived in'.[27]

## 4 HOW WOMEN WERE SEEN

Although Venette believed that a woman had a seminal emission, that she made her own, independent contribution to procreation, at the same time women remained creatures who were clearly inferior, both physically and mentally, to men. Venette's low opinion of women is apparent in the whole book. It is obvious from the very beginning when he deals with the sexual organs. Here, he sings the praises of the penis: 'there are no temptations or enchantments to compare.'[28] In comparison to his colleagues, Venette was relatively moderate in his praises.[29] However, he describes male sperm as much stronger and richer in spirits than the watery, womanly sperm. Nor does the latter taste as good. Once, when he was dissecting a young girl's corpse, her sperm had splashed in his face and without thinking he licked his lips. It was, according to Venette, tasteless, insipid, and at the same time rather sharp.[30]

To Venette it was self-evident that the womb hungered for male sperm. Like other physicians of his day, he was convinced that during coitus the womb tilted itself in the direction of the penis in order to suck out the sperm and in this way satisfy 'her salaciousness'.[31] The womb was insatiable, or so Venette believed; 'Neither hell, nor fire, nor the earth devour as voraciously as this organ.'[32] He is quoting a medieval proverb here.[33] His opinion was shared by most contemporaries. Venette also associated hysteria with the womb. If the womb did not receive male sperm and the female sperm accumulated, then it would rot and drive women to frenzy. This concept can also be found in Galen. Hysteria was primarily a disease afflicting unmarried women: spinsters, widows, and nuns.[34] According to Venette, the nuns of Loudun suffered from this affliction.[35] Women themselves shared this belief. Isabella de Moerloose, a clergyman's widow who published a remarkable autobiography in 1695, was convinced that if female sperm did not bear fruit it would rot and 'being rotten would bear vermin which devour the womb'.[36]

Essentially, the sexual insatiability of women was based on the female temperament. After all, with their excess of blood and mucus, they were much more vaporous than men. They possessed much more sperm. Moreover, men were in a position to lose excess sperm in nocturnal emissions. Therefore, to a much greater degree than men, women were tormented by an excess of sperm, sperm they could get rid of only during coitus.[37] Venette is, however, true to his time in that he no longer bases women's inferiority on theological grounds. From the sixteenth century this inferiority was increasingly anchored in nature.[38]

## 5 SEXUAL PLEASURE

What was so scandalous about Venette's work? Why did he hide behind a pseudonym and have his book published in Amsterdam? Why would Bayle have preferred the book to have been published in Latin, and why did Louize see no difference between *Minsieke Gasthuis* and three erotic novels?

In all probability, the book's offensiveness lay in the extensive attention Venette gave to sexual pleasure. His only precursor in this was the French physician Ambroise Paré (1517–90), and his work had caused a scandal.[39] Venette was the first doctor who again accorded sexual pleasure an important role. He was even convinced that 'mutual embraces' – and by that he meant coitus – 'are the knots of love in marriage, and that they truly determine the well-being thereof'.[40]

This emphasis on pleasure disappears again at the end of the eighteenth century when, more often than not, the contrary was asserted: if sexuality predominates, then the marriage will be endangered.[41]

Venette's extensive attention to pleasure is already apparent in his treatment of the sexual organs. He indicates the erogenous zones, calling the clitoris 'the fire or the passion of love'; it is the 'seat' of 'female lustfulness'. Nature placed there the 'throne of her wantonness and salaciousness', 'just as it has done at the top of the shaft of the man'.[42]

Many of the questions Venette asked himself and particularly the gratifying way he answered them will also have been cause for controversy. He ruminated on 'what measure', in other words what temperament, 'a man must have in order to be enormously lusty'. He asked the same question about women. De Lignac had been irritated by the latter question in particular.[43] Venette also posed questions such as: who is more 'lusty', the man or the woman? And which party had most pleasure in bed? He also paid extensive attention to aphrodisiacs. According to de Lignac, whatever Venette might claim, this chapter was downright 'poison for the young'.[44] The chapters in which Venette elaborated on how many times a man and woman could have intercourse in one night and which positions they could assume when doing so will also have been received with mixed feelings.

A chapter in which Venette eulogized virginity may seem rather hard to place in the book's context. But elsewhere it appears that we should not take all this glorification too seriously because Venette provides tips on how a deflowered woman can pass as a virgin on her wedding night. She has to insert two or three small balls of congealed lamb's blood in the mouth of the womb before retiring. During intercourse she will shed blood and her brand-new husband will be quite satisfied. Venette also admits that he hesitated for a long time before giving this advice (which, by the way, is mentioned in *Fanny Hill*). But what is more important, he asks himself, the fact that in a moment of weakness a woman allowed herself to be seduced, or the 'harmony of families and the man's peace of mind'?[45]

## 6 ADVICE AND RULES FOR COITUS

Although Venette goes into the role and means of sexual pleasure at great length, at the same time he realizes that the 'bliss of love' also causes problems for a lot of people. Therefore, he proffers a string of practical advice and attempts to combat numerous

91

superstitions. He also gives clear pointers on what is and what is not allowed in bed; for him there were also limits to pleasure. One of the most important problems was the bride's virginity, a subject on which doctors often wrote at great length. This is not really surprising as during marriage negotiations not only the dowry but also the virginal state of the bride was often taken into consideration.[46] In France, people still talk about 'le petit capital'.[47] However, Venette warns that it is extremely difficult to determine whether a woman is still a virgin. After all, the hymen can be torn in various ways; for example, by 'mounting a horse in the Italian manner'.[48] And even a woman who is breast-feeding can still be a virgin.[49] Bayle actually praised Venette for making the latter point.[50]

Venette gives detailed advice on the best age for marriage: after 25 for men and after 20 for women. If they enter the married state earlier there is a risk of the man's seed being too low in animal spirits, while the woman could be too narrow internally. Such a union would in all likelihood produce only girls or children who are too small and too weak.[51] These ideas were probably widespread in the republic. The family historian Donald Haks recorded the case of a 16-year-old boy who had begotten a child with a young girl. The boy believed that 'through his tender years no child could come of it'.[52] Venette also notes that men lose their fertility around their 65th and women around their 50th year. Obviously, there are exceptions. The bailiff of Vianen appears to have been famous for fathering a child at 90. The overlord stood godparent at the baptism.[53]

Sexual intercourse during menstruation is strongly discouraged by Venette, even though the woman is more 'in love' than normal because of the spirits and the blood that flow to her genitals. The man has to bear with her, but he must not give in to her. Children begotten during menstruation would either die young or 'languish' all their lives, a belief which was shared by most theologians and doctors.[54]

Sex during pregnancy was also condemned by Venette although he admitted opinions were divided on this point. However, Venette warns that the 'forceful movements' during coitus could damage the foetus, while menstruation, which according to Venette would start again, could smother the child.[55] It was advisable to wait twenty days after the birth. The man would have to take responsibility for this period since Venette is convinced, as he notes elsewhere, that no sooner has the woman given birth than 'she begins to attack her husband once again . . . she comes time and again to an incessant fury and never says it is enough'.[56]

Some seasons are more suitable than others for sexual intercourse. This has to do with the temperaments. Because of their hot and dry temperament, the sun's heat exhausts men so much that they are unable to perform their daily tasks in the season 'wherein men must labour hard'. The opposite is true for women with their cold and vaporous temperament. As men become increasingly lethargic, the women become increasingly heated: 'It is at this time . . . that their careless nakedness suggests they are dying of lust to quench the fire that Nature has ignited in their bosom.' Winter is bad for both sexes. And autumn is not a particularly suitable time either. The best season is spring when temperature and temperament are in harmony. Again, the danger is that men and women will go to bed together too often, resulting in foolish or clumsy offspring.[57]

Venette even gives pointers on the time of day. The best time is four or five hours after the noon meal or four or five hours after the evening meal. By this time, most of the food has been digested and, thanks to the food, the body is full of warmth and animal spirits.[58] Venette would appear to prefer the second option, the period after the evening meal, because in his subsequent chapter he ponders on 'How often a man may unite with his wife in one night'.

A lot of fairy-tales are told about this subject, Venette warns. And indeed, the jokes of the Hague lawyer Aernout van Overbeke (1632–74) concern various men who have miraculous scores. One of them could even 'sit up' fifteen times in one night.[59] But five times is the highest possible number, Venette insists. If a man tries a sixth time, he will only emit rather watery seed or even blood 'like that of a fowl which has just had its throat cut'. This had happened to one of Venette's acquaintances. This man had been to bed with two whores fives times in one afternoon and during his sixth attempt he had lost no less than two ounces of blood.[60]

Here again Venette points out the insatiability of women. The men become exhausted just as the women become passionate. Besides the ever-hungry womb, Venette also attributes this to the division of labour in bed. After all, it is the man 'who does all the work himself during a mutual embrace' while the woman 'does nothing more than suffer the impressions the man gives her'; she is made only 'to receive'.[61] Thus, a woman has absolutely no excuse for refusing her husband her owed duty. Even if she is ill, love is a better medicine than many a herb.[62]

In the chapter on 'If a man may kiss his wife from behind when there are obstacles to prevent him doing this from in front', Venette goes into the various positions for coitus. Again, he lashes out at women. The twelve 'postures' invented by the whore Cyrene and used by the Emperor Tiberius to decorate the walls of his apartments 'do show us women know all the twists of love much better than we'. Compared to women, Venette opines, men are mere novices in bed.[63] To Venette, the only permissible positions are those whereby the man's seed is properly received and at the same time the male sense of honour is not injured. Standing or sitting positions, therefore, are rejected as the sperm is not properly absorbed by the womb. The same applies for the position in which the woman lies on top. This position is all the worse because the man, 'who according to the laws of nature must have dominance over the woman and who is master over all the animals', would be 'cowardly' if he gave in to his wife in this manner, if he shared with her 'the wantonness of an unchaste love'. If children are born of such a union, then they are 'dwarves, cripples, hunchbacks, cross-eyed or imbeciles'.[64] De Lignac agreed with Venette. He, too, was convinced that immoderate love produced only deformed children. He warned of 'that great crowd of unfortunate creatures whose wasted and misshapen limbs bear witness to the unchasteness of their parents'.[65]

In certain circumstances Venette considers permissible the position in which the woman is approached from behind – 'more canino' as it was called by the casuists. From the fourteenth century onwards, some theologians had not been totally opposed to this position, even though the laity, as Brantôme notes, were sometimes highly indignant about this.[66] Venette did not think this position was wrong because the womb could catch the sperm properly. Moreover, if a woman was so 'fat' that the man couldn't get close enough, shouldn't the man better 'serve' her from behind rather than let things end in divorce?[67] This position was also preferable when the woman was heavily pregnant and the man could not control his lust. After all, in this position the foetus would not be affected.[68] After coitus it was advisable for the woman to remain lying down for a while 'to preserve the precious pledge' that had just been entrusted to her.[69] In this way, the male seed would not flow away and it would mingle better with the female seed. It was common advice.[70]

## 7 ON CORDING AND OTHER MAGIC

Besides providing all kinds of rules and advice, Venette also wanted to dispel a number of fears connected to sexuality. Thus, he combats the belief in incubi and succubi, evil spirits that lie either on top of or underneath a person.[71] I will not go into this in depth as in all probability this kind of demonological superstition was no longer common in the eighteenth-century republic, although it may still have been current among the lower classes. Isabella de Moerloose tells a story about some people in late seventeenth-century Ghent who still believed in incubi and succubi. A young girl was caught in the act with a man and it was believed she had been seduced by an incubus. Isabella had other ideas; it was more likely a sneak-thief or a student.[72]

Venette has the same sceptical approach. Incubi and succubi do not exist, he assures his readers, they are merely the products of human imagination. They are the nightmares of men and women with impure thoughts. A second superstition combated by Venette is the so-called 'knotting of the *nestel* ('cord')'. Other physicians, such as Paré, had already attempted this.[73] To make a man impotent, it was believed, during his wedding someone had to tie a number of knots in a piece of string or a belt while mumbling some words, preferably at the moment bride and groom joined hands. The *'nestel'* is an old word for penis. Thus, there need be little doubt about the symbolism. If this knotting was carried out, then the newly wed husband would be unable to do anything in bed, at least not with his own wife. The spell would be broken only if the man urinated through his wife's wedding ring. Other antidotes were smearing the bedroom door with wolves' grease or hanging roosters' testicles on the bed-end.[74]

It is difficult to say how far this superstition was still current in the eighteenth-century republic. Martin Guerre, the French farmer who was the subject of a whole book by Natalie Davis,[75] was said to have been impotent for more than eight years after a cord had been knotted. This was also mentioned by Cats who incorporated Martin Guerre's adventures in his *Trouringh*.[76] Indications that this belief existed not only in France but also in the republic are to be found in Daniel Jongtys's *Tooneel der jalouzyen* and in the work of Johan van Beverwijck.[77] Folklorists later found traces of the superstition in Groningen, Limburg, and Flanders.[78] It is unclear to what extent this belief was current among the eighteenth-century elite.

## 8 ON WINE MARKS, BIRTH MARKS, AND MONSTERS

One belief which we know was definitely current among the eighteenth-century elite was in the so-called maternal imagination. People believed that abnormalities in the foetus (wine marks, birth marks, and also deformities) were caused by the pregnant mother's imagination. It was, for example, possible that during the pregnancy the mother had had a sudden desire for strawberries, a desire that she had been unable to satisfy. Her child would subsequently be born with marks the shape and size of strawberries. It was also possible that the pregnant mother had been badly frightened by a deformed man or woman. The result would be a child with the same deformities. In all these cases, people said, the cause was maternal imagination.[79] We find examples of this as early as the Middle Ages, but many cases are recorded in the medical literature of the seventeenth and eighteenth centuries.

One of the most remarkable cases is recorded by the English physician James Blondel (1665–1734) He tells the story of a woman who was so eager to give birth on the feast of the Epiphany that she was brought to bed of three boys, two white and one black.[80] In fact, Blondel, along with, for example, von Haller, was one of the few doctors in the eighteenth century who tried to combat this kind of belief. Most of their colleagues, including those in the republic, were convinced that maternal imagination influenced the foetus.[81] The surgeon Job van Meek'ren, a student of Tulp's, reports a distressing case that occurred in Amsterdam in 1643. A pregnant woman had been badly frightened by a dead man who had just had his head crushed by the counter-weights on the Reguliers Bridge. The blow was so hard that his 'brains . . .

spattered out of his skull'. The result was predictable: the pregnant woman's child was born with a misshapen head. The case of a woman in Deventer is a lot more cheerful. During her pregnancy she consumed more than a thousand herrings. What happened? The child was barely breathing before it was calling loudly for herring.[82]

This kind of conviction was widespread in the republic. Cats goes into the subject at length in his *Houwelijck*. He warned pregnant mothers in detail.[83] The cases recorded by the Leiden physician Willem Mylius are particularly interesting. His notes show clearly how great the fear of strong or unpleasant impressions was among pregnant women.

In 1713, he recorded the following case. When she was three months pregnant, the wife of Nicolaas N., a weaver on the Cellebroersgracht in Leiden, had been shown 'the painting of a child with two heads, three arms and four legs'. This panel was 'carried by common, strange folk, through street and alleyway, to be viewed for money'. In December of that year, the woman was brought to bed of a deformed daughter. The child, which died a few days later, had a swelling on her loins as large as a 'wheaten bun'. When the woman told Mylius about the panel he was certain that the swelling enclosed a second head. Therefore, he called in the help of a doctor, Pieter Hollebeek, and a surgeon, Barent Schepers. When the swelling was opened they discovered it did indeed contain a 'lump of brains'.[84] This case provided Mylius with the opportunity of reporting a monster he had once seen at the Leiderdorp fair. It was a 35-year-old man 'who had hanging from his breastbone a second head with black hair, terrible to look upon, having deep sunk eyes with closed lids, a nose and mouth and black beard, incapable of movement other than that it could be moved up and down with the hands'.[85] It is possible that Mylius is describing the 'Monstre double, qui est un des plus remarquables en ce genre', which according to Hartsoeker was exhibited in the Hague at the beginning of the eighteenth century.[86]

In 1700, another woman, the wife of a Leiden butcher, gave birth to a 'monster'. The indefatigable Mylius – he had followed the lectures of Ruysch – asked the father if he could see the dead child. This was allowed. But when he tried to remove the monster for dissection, offering the father recompense, this was refused 'very gruffly'. The butcher made it quite clear that 'neither the flesh of his flesh, nor the blood of his blood' was on sale. However, Mylius was not to be discouraged. He knew the man had to go to the Meat hall next morning so, accompanied by a painter to draw the child, he made his way to the house when the husband had left. The woman then told him what had happened before the birth.

It appeared that when the woman was two months pregnant, the butcher had slaughtered a cow in calf. First, he had cut away the womb 'to throw to the dogs'. But he had become curious and had opened the womb only to find a two-headed calf. It could all have ended well, the woman said, if her husband had not been so foolish as to tell her all about it when they went to bed. The next morning she had secretly slipped out of bed – 'himself lying snoring in a deep sleep' – and she had examined the calf closely. At that moment she had not felt a thing but now she knew better. However, she would not allow Mylius to remove the child either, for fear of her husband.[87] Even more distressing was the case of a baker's wife in 1714. This woman had borne 'a terrible monster'. What had happened? When she was three weeks pregnant, her husband, 'being surly and hasty by nature', had beaten to death a cat which had tried to steal bread. The beast's eyes 'stared in a terrible way from its head which he had crushed and the innards hung from its body'. Exactly the same way her own child had come into the world.[88]

Fortunately, not all distressing confrontations ended this way. Mylius records the case of his own wife. A woman had come to fetch the doctor to a sick person in her neighbourhood. He was not at home so his wife answered the door. She was terribly shocked as the woman had no nose, only a triangular cavity where it should have been. His wife was now convinced she would bear a nose-less child. But it all turned out well for she was brought to bed of a perfectly healthy daughter.[89]

Mylius was certainly not the only doctor who saw a link between maternal imagination and abnormalities in the foetus. Midwives such as Catharina Schrader, surgeons like Job van Meek'ren and Tamme Visscher, and professors such as Boerhaave were convinced of the connection.[90] An Amsterdam report dated 1798 even suggested putting a stop to 'the wanderings of lunatics and frightful persons'; looking upon them was dangerous, especially for pregnant women.[91] The anthropologist Arnold van Gennep has pointed out the ever-recurring pattern of rites which accompany the various changes in status in the human life-cycle, such as birth, betrothal, marriage, and death. He also saw pregnancy as such a change in status.[92] These passages, or liminal zones, as he and other anthropologists have emphasized, are considered ambiguous.[93] They are a simultaneous source of care and danger. This ambiguous attitude would seem to emerge in the exceptionally widespread belief in the powers of maternal imagination. People were fascinated by the womb, by that mysterious female organ, and by the close and very fragile bonds between mother and child. Pregnant women were, therefore, surrounded by care and concern. At the same time, people were convinced those same bonds could also damage the child, that the mother could even bear a 'monster'. The period of pregnancy in particular must have been a terribly fearful time for mothers. A sudden confrontation with a deformed person – and there were more than enough deformities to be seen in the streets – was enough to fill them with fear. Unfortunately, Venette's opinion on these convictions is unclear. He intended to go into this point in a sequel to his book but this was never published.[94] However, he does mention the consequences of maternal imagination, not in the context of pregnancy, but during coitus itself.[95] Here, in fact, he makes a contribution to early forensic medicine.[96] Some doctors, such as Paré, believed that the likeness of children to their parents was determined by maternal imagination during intercourse. Venette rejects this idea but Cats definitely saw a connection. In the various treatises on the subject, a specific case is often quoted which is attributed to Hippocrates. Cats also includes this story. When a woman was accused of adultery because she had borne a very comely child whereas both she and her husband were ugly, Hippocrates visited the house. In the woman's bedroom he found a beautiful portrait of a child. To him the whole matter was clear. He called the people into the house and had the baby fetched, and, indeed, the likeness was remarkable.[97] Thus, Cats advised his readers to think about a beautiful child or the portrait of such a child during coitus. Similar notions are also to be found in the work of the French physician Claude Quillet, whose *Callipédie* went into a number of editions in the republic.[98] A book on the 'art of producing comely children', by the Swiss physician Andreas

Jungman, was also published in 1791. Jungman also advised his readers to hang up a painting 'that is as comely as you would wish your own children to be'.[99] But, at the same time, Cats was equally convinced that women could bear a deformed child if they thought about a misshapen animal or 'monster' during intercourse. Nowadays, we are inclined to ridicule these fears of producing a deformed child, certainly in cases where theologians or doctors cautioned that they were the result of too much or 'deviant' sex. Yet, as we have seen, these fears were current among the whole population. Thus, it would seem sensible to take them seriously. In all probability, they were a remnant of earlier sexual attitudes. In spit of the extensive attention Venette gives to sexual pleasure, both he and his readers continued to fear the birth of 'monsters' as a result of maternal imagination.

## 9 ON HERMAPHRODITES

Finally, Venette's writing on hermaphrodites are of interest. There were quite a few known cases in his day. Venette himself wrote: 'Indeed, hardly five years pass than we hear of some hermaphrodites, who in the past were thought to be evil portents and monsters, and who today are considered a very uncommon matter.'[100] Venette differentiates five types, which he subsequently classifies in either the male or the female sex. It was unthinkable for hermaphrodites to fall outside either classification; the idea was simply too threatening. One of the types is interesting. It concerns those women who possess an exceptionally large clitoris, women 'whose clitoris', Venette writes, 'is much bigger and much longer than that of others, and through which they deceive the common folk who have no great knowledge of the parts they are made of'.[101] It is these hermaphrodites, Venette opines, who are called 'tribades' by the Greeks and 'ribaudes' by the French. Their clitoris is so large that with it they can pleasure other women. This concept of female homosexuality was also current in the republic. A famous case, that of Hendrika Verschuur, is recorded by Nicolaas Tulp.[102]

In fact, most treatises on hermaphrodites discuss tribadism or female homosexuality. Venette and his colleagues are silent on the subject of sodomy, male homosexuality. However openly Venette may have written on sexuality, he did not touch on this subject at all. Doctors clearly considered sodomy far worse than tribadism.

This distinction was also made by judicial authorities. Tribades received lighter punishments than sodomites. This is definitely true of eighteenth-century Holland. Whereas elsewhere a number of women were drowned or burnt,[103] as far as we know this never took place in the republic. However, quite a large number of men were executed in the eighteenth century.[104]

Various explanations have been offered for this greater leniency towards tribades. They did not engage in anal sex; sodomites did. Anality, animality, and sin formed three closely interlinked concepts in Christian thinking.[105] Another explanation was that sodomites wasted seed Nature had intended for procreation.[106] This explanation is also plausible. To Isabella de Moerloose, coitus interruptus was as bad as sodomy, 'the sleeping, or rather the playing, of men with men'. To her, both practices were a 'ridicule of procreation'.[107] However, there is yet a third, more medical explanation possible. After all, a tribade with her large clitoris was a deviation of nature. Tribades were born with their inclination and were an interesting anatomical phenomenon for doctors and surgeons. This did not apply to sodomites. Besides this, women were more quickly forgiven their sexual impulses than men. They were closer to nature, were more governed by nature, than men. In short, while sodomites consciously committed mortal sin, this was not the case, or to a lesser extent, with tribades. The responsibility for their actions was sought in nature and that could, in part, account for their lighter punishments.

## 10 CONCLUSION

Using Venette's sex manual, I have tried to discover something about sexual attitudes in the eighteenth-century republic, at least among the elite. According to Stone, Venette was not particularly enlightening as regards sexual details. Nor had he a very positive approach to sexuality. Stone concludes, therefore, that the eighteenth-century public, to him so very tolerant, can hardly have taken Venette's advice seriously.

However, the question is whether Stone has classified Venette's book correctly. Seen from the 1970s, Venette's advice does not make a particularly liberal impression. But compared to earlier medical and theological advice in the republic – we need think only of Cats – Venette's book was very detailed indeed. Moreover, Venette's belief that sexual intercourse was the mainstay of all affection within marriage would have been unacceptable to Cats. It is precisely in his details and in his re-evaluation of sexuality within marriage that Venette's work differs from earlier advice. It is not without reason that Bayle believed the book should have been published in Latin.

Admittedly, a fair number of negative aspects can be found in *Minsieke Gasthuis*. Venette's tolerance extends only to heterosexuals. Male homosexuality is ignored totally while female homosexuality is seen as a pitiful deviation of nature. *Minsieke Gasthuis* is also negative about women in general; the idea of their sexual insatiability dominates. In all these ways Venette's attitudes hardly differ from the notions behind Aernout van Overbeke's jokes.

A look at the 'strange' and 'surprising' provided further remarkable results. In the traditional medical history of sexuality, the eighteenth century obtains as the age of ovists and animalculists, of their ideological conflict which would be decided in the former's favour only in the nineteenth century. This classification may have applied for scholarly members of universities but not for the general public of that time. As we have seen, their sexual knowledge was still based on the notions of Hippocrates and Galen. Even more remarkable was the belief in maternal imagination. If Venette's sex manual made anything clear, it is that our ancestors in the eighteenth and perhaps in the nineteenth centuries held totally different ideas about the body from those we have today. The extensive attention given to Hippocrates' humoral pathology and Galen's pneumata is an indication. The concepts of the insatiability of the womb and the sensitivity of this organ to outside influences, to us so remarkable, shows that ideas about the female body differed as radically. It would be interesting to discover to what extent this concept, which was considered self-evident at the time, was inextricably interwoven with the numerous theological and moral discussions about women.

## NOTES

This chapter was first published in *Documentatieblad werkgroep achttiende eeuw* 1985, 17: 119–141.

1 C. L. van der Weyde, *Henry en Louize, Eene Nederlandsche geschiedenis*, in

*gemeenzaame brieven*, Leiden, 1794, II, 301–2.

2 Probably *De Leidsche Straatschender, of de Roekeloose Student*, published in 1683, cf. *De Amsterdamse Lichtmis, of zoldaat van fortuin*, ed. B. Pol, Muiderberg, 1983, 35.

3 *Venus/Minsieke Gasthuis,/Waer in beschreven worden/De bedryven der Liefde/in den staet des houwelijks,/Met de natuurlijke eygenschappen der Man-/nen en Vrouwen, hare siekten, oirsaken/en genesingen./* Door I.V.E. Medicinae Doctor./t'Amsterdam/by Timotheus ten Hoorn, Boekverkooper, in de Nes,/in't Sinnebeelt, 1687.8°. Hereafter cited as VMG.

4 *Biographie Universelle, ancienne et moderne*, ed. J. F. Michaud, Graz, 1966–70, XLIII, 111–13.

5 Ibid.

6 P. Bayle, *Oeuvres diverses*, La Haye, 1737, I, 675–6.

7 B. Kruithof, 'De deugdzame natie. Het burgerlijk beschavingsoffensief van de Maatschappij tot Nut van't Algemeen', *Geschiedenis van opvoeding en onderwijs. Inleiding, bronnen, onderzoek*, ed. B. Kruithof *et al.* Nijmegen, 1982, 363–77.

8 (M. de Lignac), *Natuurkundige beschouwing van de man en de vrouw in den huwelijken staat*, Amsterdam and Leiden, 1785².

9 But see E. de Jongh, 'Erotica in vogelperspectief. De dubbelzinnigheid van een reeks 17de eeuwse genrevoorstellingen', *Simiolus*, 1968–9, 1: 22–72; D. Haks, *Huwelijk en gezin in Holland in de 17de en 18de eeuw. Processtukken en moralisten over aspecten van het laat 17de-en 18de-eeuwse gezinsleven*, Assen, 1982; H. Roodenburg, 'The autobiography of Isabella de Moerloose. Sex, childrearing and popular belief in seventeenth-century Holland', *Journal of Social History* 1985, 18: 517–540; R. Dekker and H. Roodenburg, 'Humor in de zeventiende eeuw. Opvoeding, huwelijk en seksualiteit in de moppen van Aernout van Overbeke', *Tijdschrift voor Sociale Geschiedenis*, 1984, 35: 243–66; for the history of sodomy in the Dutch republic, see esp. Th. van der Meer, *De wesentlijke sonde van sodomie en andere vuyligheeden. Sodomietenvervolgingen in Amsterdam, 1730–1811*, Amsterdam, 1984; for some important recent research (the original article was finished in 1984), see: *Documentatieblad Werkgroep Achttiende Eeuw*, 1985, 17; *Soete Minne, Helsche Boosheit. Seksuele voorstellingen in Nederland, 1300–1850*, ed. G. Hekma and H. Roodenburg, Nijmegen, 1988; and R. Dekker and L. van de Pol, *The Tradition of Female Transvestism in Early Modern Europe*, London 1989.

10 But see: A. Geyl, 'Historische kantteekeningen', *Nederlandsch Tijdschrift voor verloskunde en gynaecologie*, 1895, 4: 257–9, 264–272; J. G. de Lint, 'Venus Minsieke Gasthuis', *Nederlandsch Tijdschrift voor verloskunde en gynaecologie*, 1916, 25: 273–81; H. F. Wijnman, 'Venus Minsieke Gasthuis', *Beschavings- en zedengeschiedenis van Nederland*, ed. H. Lewandowski and P. J. van Dranen, Amsterdam, 1933, 280–4.

11 For the various editions, translations, and reprints in the Republic, see: Wijnman, passim.

12 Ibid., 283: Th. Tarczylo, *Sexe et liberté au siècle des Lumières*, Paris, 1983, 301.

13 Y. Knibiehler and C. Fouquet, *La femme et les médecins. Analyse historique*, Paris, 1983, 315, n. 111.

14 About this book, see for England: J. Blackman, 'Popular theories of generation. The evolution of Aristotle's work. The study of an anachronism', in *Health Care and Popular Medicine in Nineteenth Century England*, ed. J. Woodward and D. Richards, London, 1977, 56–88; R. Thompson, *Unfit for Modern Ears*, London, 1979, 162–8; P.-G Boucé, 'Some sexual beliefs and myths in eighteenth-century Britain', in *Sexuality in Eighteenth-Century Britain*, ed. P.-G. Boucé, Manchester, 1982, 28–46; for Venette in England, cf. R. Porter, 'Spreading carnal knowledge or selling dirt cheap? Nicolas Venette's *Tableau de l'Amour Conjugal* in eighteenth-century England', *Journal of European Studies*, 1984, 14: 233–55 and ' "The Secrets of Generation display'd": Aristotle's Masterpiece in Eighteenth-century England', *Eighteenth-Century Life* 1985, 9: 1–21; for *Aristotle's Masterpiece* in the United States, see O. T. Beall, 'Aristotle's Masterpiece in America. A landmark in the folklore of medicine', *The William and Mary Quarterly*, 1963, 20: 207–22; V. C. Bullough, 'An early American sex manual, or, Aristotle Who?', in *Sex, Society and History*, ed. V. C. Bullough, New York, 1976, 93–103.

15 The French surgeon Ambroise Paré in his *De la génération* also gave some sexual advice. However, his book was only published as part of his *Oeuvres*.

16 J. de Brune de Jonge, *Wetsteen der vernuften oft beqaam middel om van alle voorvallende zaken aardighlik te leeren spreken*, Amsterdam, 1644, 'Aen den leser'; also cited by de Jongh, 'Erotica', 53, n. 70.

17 L. Stone, *The Family, Sex and Marriage in England, 1500–1800*, London, 1977, 545.

18 Ibid., 543–5, 643–8.

19 Cf. his review in *History and Theory*, 1979, 18: 103–26, esp. 106; for another critical review, see E. P. Thompson in *New Society*, 8 September 1977.

20 Stone, *The Family, Sex and Marriage*, 494 ff.

21 N. Z. Davis, 'The possibilities of the past', *Journal of Interdisciplinary History*, 1981, 12: 267–75; cf. H. Medick, ' "Missionaries in the Rowing Boat"? Ethnographical Ways of Knowing as a Challenge to Social History', *Comp. Stud. Soc. Hist.*, 1987, 29: 76–98; see also the interview with Carlo Ginzburg: 'Über Archive, Marlene Dietrich und die Lust an der Geschichte. Carlo Ginzburg im Gespräch mit Adriano Sofri', in C. Ginzburg, *Spurensicherungen. Über verborgene Geschichte, Kunst und Soziales Gedächtnis*, Berlin, 1983, 22–3.

22 See, for example, the studies by Darmon, mentioned in notes 24 and 29, and Knibiehler and Fouquet, mentioned in n. 13.

23 Davis, 'The possibilities of the past', 267.

24 The *'congrès'*, for example – sexual intercourse in the presence of witnesses, if a woman had summoned her husband before a church court because of his impotence – was unknown in the Dutch republic. See: VMG, 543–9; on such trials see P. Darmon, *Le tribunal de l'impuissance. Virilité et défaillances conjugales dans l'Ancienne France*, Paris,

1979, esp. 207–31, and E. Fischer-Homberger, *Medizin vor Gericht. Gerichtsmedizin von der Renaissance bis zur Aufklärung*, Berne, 1983, 191. For an echo of such trials in a fascinating collection of seventeenth-century jokes, see Dekker and Roodenburg, 'Humor', 257.

25 VMG, 292.
26 J.-L. Flandrin, 'Homme et femme dans le lit conjugal', in J.-L. Flandrin, *Le sexe et l'occident. Évolution des attitudes et des comportements*, Paris, 1981, esp. 131–2.
27 De Lignac, *Natuurkundige*, I, 'Bericht'.
28 Ibid., 3; cf. Boucé, 'Some sexual beliefs', 32.
29 P. Darmon, *Le mythe de la procréation à l'âge baroque*, Paris, 1977, 15–18.
30 VMG 366.
31 Ibid., 27, 28.
32 Ibid., 177.
33 Darmon, *Mythe*, 26.
34 Cf. Knibiehler and Fouquet, *La femme et les médecins*, 74.
35 VMG, 182.
36 Roodenburg, 'Autobiography', 531.
37 VMG, 182–3.
38 Cf. Knibiehler and Fouquet, *La femme et les médecins*, 74.
39 Ibid., 131, 156–7, 311, n. 36.
40 VMG, 147.
41 De Lignac, *Natuurkundige*, II, 141–3; H. G. van Breugel, *De geordende en gelukkige huishouding, aangewezen en aangepreezen in agt leerreedenen*, Dordrecht, 1794, 59–60; A. P. Z. Loosjes, *De man in de vier tijdperken zijns levens*, Haarlem, 1809, 226–7; A. P. Z. Loosjes, *De vrouw in de vier tijdperken haars levens*, Haarlem, 1809, 225–7. With thanks to Marja van Tilburg.
42 VMG, 19.
43 De Lignac, *Natuurkundige*, I, 37.
44 Ibid., 84.
45 VMG, 104, 108–9.
46 Haks, 'Huwelijk', 97, 107; cf. Stone, *The Family, Sex and Marriage*, 636.
47 Boucé, 'Some sexual beliefs', 33.
48 VMG, 93.
49 Ibid., 100; for such problems in general, see Fischer-Homberger, *Medizin vor Gericht*, 210–22.
50 Bayle, *Oeuvres diverses*, 675.
51 VMG, 118–30, 472 ff.
52 Haks, 'Huwelijk', 82.
53 VMG, 158.
54 Ibid., 150–1; cf. Boucé, 'Some sexual beliefs', 36; J.-L. Flandrin, 'La vie sexuelle des gens mariés dans l'ancienne société', *Communications*, 1982, 35: 106; Roodenburg, 'Autobiography', 528–9.
55 VMG, 132–3.
56 Ibid., 146–7, 151–2.
57 Ibid., 191–3.

58 Ibid., 197.
59 Dekker and Roodenburg, 'Humor', 258.
60 VMG, 217–18.
61 Ibid., 125, 148; cf. Flandrin, 'Vie sexuelle', 105; M. Delon, 'La prétexte anatomique', *Dix-huitième siècle. Revue annuelle*, 1980, 12: 39.
62 VMG, 149–50.
63 Ibid., 260–1.
64 Ibid., 262–3; cf. Flandrin, 'Vie sexuelle', 107.
65 De Lignac, *Natuurkundige*, I, 4.
66 Flandrin, 'Vie sexuelle', 107.
67 VMG, 264–7; for a joke on a 'very fat nobleman' who 'because of his fatness' could not do 'his things', see Dekker and Roodenburg, 'Humor', 26.
68 VMG, 266.
69 Ibid., 202.
70 Cf. Darmon, *Mythe*, 142; Darmon, Paré, and Quillet.
71 VMG, 610–41.
72 Roodenburg, 'Autobiography', 521–2.
73 Fischer-Homberger, *Medizin vor Gericht*, 147.
74 VMG, 577.
75 N. Z. Davis, *The Return of Martin Guerre*, Cambridge, Mass., 1983.
76 J. Cats, '''s Werelts begin, midden, eynde, besloten in den trouringh, met de proef-steen van den selven', in his *Alle de wercken, so oude als nieuwe*, Amsterdam, 1655, 162.
77 D. Jongtys, *Tooneel der jalouzyen, waarop vertoont werden veel treurige gevallen, wonderlijke geschiedenissen, schrikkelijke en wreede uitwerkselen der jaloersheid*, Amsterdam, 1699², I, 666–83. Jongtys mentions Bodin, Delrio, Montaigne, Sanchez, and Sennert.
78 K. ter Laan, *Groninger Volksleven*, Groningen, 1961, II, 108; for a case in 1697: J. G(rauwels), 'Verering van S. Benedictus', *Limburg*, 1966, 45: 117–8; A. de Cock, *Volksgeneeskunde in Vlaanderen*, Ghent, 1891, 219n. With thanks to Ton Dekker.
79 H. W. Roodenburg, 'The maternal imagination. The fears of pregnant women in seventeenth-century Holland', *Journal of Social History* 1988, 21.
80 Cited by Darmon, *Mythe*, 172.
81 For cases in France, see E. Fischer-Homberger, *Krankheit Frau und andere Arbeiten zur Medizingeschichte der Frau*, Berne, 1979, 106–29, esp. 118–27.
82 J. van Meek'ren, *Heel-en geneeskonstige aenmerkkingen*, Amsterdam, 1668, 437–9; T. Visscher, *Heelkonstige aenmerkingen*, Amsterdam, 1696, 262.
83 J. Cats, 'Houwelick, dat is, het gansche beleyt des echten-staets', 157.
84 W. Mylius, *Bijgelovige overblyfzelen, onder geneeskundige oeffeningen by de Hollanderen bespeurd en nagedacht*, ms. UB Amsterdam, ff. 33–6.
85 Ibid., f. 36.
86 N. Hartsoeker, *Suite des conjectures physiques*, Amsterdam, 1708, 132.
87 Mylius, *Bijgelovige*, ff. 30–32v.
88 Ibid., ff. 37v.–38v.

89  Ibid., ff. 40v.–41v.

90  For Catharina Schrader, see M. J. van Lieburg, 'Het "Memoryboeck" als medisch-historische bron', in *C. G. Schrader's Memoryboeck van de vrouwens. Het notitieboek van een Friese vroedvrouw, 1693–1745*, ed. M. J. van Lieburg, Amsterdam, 1984, 33; for Boerhaave, see Stokvis, *Het verzien*, 30.

91  *Rapporten, strekkende als bylaagen tot de verzameling van stukken, betrekkelyk de aanstelling eener commissie van geneeskundig toevoorzicht te Amsterdam*, Amsterdam, 1798, 'vijfde stuk', 79.

92  A. van Gennep, *Rites de passage*, Paris, 1909, ch. 4.

93  M. Douglas, *Purity and Danger. An Analysis of the Concepts of Pollution and Taboo*, London, 1966; V. W. Turner, 'Betwixt and between. The liminal period in rites de passage', in his *The Forest of Symbols. Aspects of Ndembu Ritual*, Ithaca, NY, 1967, 93–111; E. Leach, *Culture and Communication. The Logic By Which Symbols are Connected*, Cambridge, 1976, 33–6.

94  VMG, 654.

95  Ibid., 470–96.

96  Cf. Fischer-Homberger, 'Krankheit Frau', 118.

97  Cats, 'Houwelick', 157.

98  J. J. V. M. de Vet, 'Het "Huwelyks Mintafereel"', een leerdicht van Claude Quillet (1602–1661) in de achttiende eeuw', *Documentatieblad* (n.g.), 51–66.

99  A. Jungman, *De kunst om schoone kinderen te teelen. Alles behalven gekheid. Een handboek voor jonge echtelieden*, Amsterdam, 1791, 71.

100  VMG, 585.

101  Ibid., 586.

102  N. Tulp, *De drie boecken der medicijnsche aenmerkingen*, Amsterdam, 1650, 244 ff.

103  L. Crompton, 'The myth of lesbian impunity. Capital laws from 1270 to 1791', *Historical perspectives on Homosexuality*, ed. S. J. Licata and R. P. Petersen, *Journal of Homosexuality*, 1980–1, 6, 1/2.

104  According to Boon seventy men in the Dutch republic received a death sentence: L. J. Boon, 'Het jaar waarin iedere jongen een meisje nam. De sodomietenvervolgingen in Holland in 1730', *Groniek*, 1980, 66: 14–17.

105  A. N. Gilbert, 'Conceptions of homosexuality and sodomy in Western history', *Historical Perspectives*, ed. Licata and Petersen, 66.

106  A. H. Huussen jr, 'Strafrechtelijke vervolging van sodomie in de Republiek', *Spiegel Historiael*, 1982, 11: 551.

107  Roodenburg, 'Autobiography', 530.

# De Sade, a pessimistic libertine

*Arnold Heumakers*

On 20 February 1781 the Marquis de Sade (1740–1814) wrote a letter to his wife, ending with a plaintive passage, in which this short sentence keeps recurring: *Je suis un libertin*. The letter was written in the château of Vincennes, where in 1781 de Sade had already been a prisoner for four years. In the letter he discusses in detail some of the 'affaires' that led to his imprisonment.[1] He does not want to cover anything up: 'Yes, I admit I am a libertine and in that area I have imagined everything that can be imagined. But I have absolutely not acted out everything that I imagined nor do I intend to. I am a libertine, but I am not a criminal or a murderer.'[2]

It was clear to everyone in the eighteenth century what de Sade meant by 'libertine', even without hearing the details of the letter. A libertine was lax in his morals, a debauched man, a gay dog. The 1727 edition of Furetière's *Dictionnaire* associates libertinism with '*débauche, désordre, dérèglement des moeurs*' and Diderot and d'Alembert's *Encyclopédie* speaks of '*l'habitude de céder à l'instinct qui nous porte aux plaisirs des sens*'.[3] Except perhaps for bigoted extremists, these definitions meant something other than crime or murder: de Sade's confession was meant as an excuse as well as a protest against the injustice to which he had fallen victim – at least, in his own eyes.

The idea of libertinism acquires a completely different meaning in the novels, stories, and treatises written by de Sade in prison, from which he was released only in 1790 thanks to the French Revolution. In *Justine ou les malheurs de la vertu* and *Les cent vingt journées de Sodome*, crime, by preference in the shape of murder and destruction, has become the essence of all lust for the libertines, as is demonstrated by their actions. The pages of these novels are littered with the mutilated and abused bodies of their victims. But that is only one aspect. In his books de Sade not only displayed libertinism as a violent perversion, but he also invented its philosophical justification. In addition to practice, his libertinism becomes an ideology, the expression, in all its horrible sombreness, of an original and fascinating view of the world, unparalleled in the history of libertinism.

In itself, the combination of libertinism and philosophy was nothing new.[4] In the eighteenth century libertinism was above all understood as moral dissoluteness, but in previous centuries the concept implied various meanings and the association with lust and sensuality had not always been its most important characteristic. In origin, the word 'libertine' is derived from the Latin *libertinus*, 'freedman'. In the course of the sixteenth century it was used for the first time, amongst others by Calvin, to denounce a fiercely opposed protestant sect in the Southern Lowlands. Later on, those people were called libertines who deviated from the ruling moral and religious precepts. For example, in the first half of the seventeenth century those scholars were known as libertines who met in Paris in the 'Académie putéane': critical sceptics such as Gassendi, La Mothe le Vayer, and Naudé. No sign of sexual or other dissipations there! These scholars lived modestly, were law-abiding and showed their libertinism only by questioning the current religious and scientific dogmas.

Yet for the opponents, the combination of impiety and debauchery remained self-evident, even though positive proof was missing. Without the force of religion, the maintenance of strict morals was considered unthinkable. Why would people restrain their egoism and passions if no God existed to be answered to in the hereafter? In the eighteenth century, the philosophers of the Enlightenment, who in many ways can be considered as the spiritual heirs of the 'erudite' libertines of the previous century, would think up many answers to this question. Surely, without religion morality was still possible – an insight voiced first by Pierre Bayle, to the horror of the majority of his contemporaries. In his *Pensées diverses sur la comète* (1682) he was principally concerned to distinguish between atheism and immorality. Afterwards, the meaning of libertinism developed more and more exclusively in the direction of dissoluteness, purely moral and sexual candour.

Bayle made his distinction less for the libertines than to expose the hypocrisy of traditional religion, which claimed for itself the monopoly of virtue. For the libertines in his definition he had no appreciation whatsoever. And Bayle knew his subject, as his century had known plenty of libertines of the worst sort, such as the young noblemen around the poet Théophile de Viau, against whom proceedings had been started in 1623 at the instigation of the Jesuits. The second half of the seventeenth century had known worldly minded epicureans, some of whom de Sade mentions in his *Idée sur les romans*, such as Ninon de Lenclos, Marion de Lorme, Sévigné, La Fare, Chaulieu, and Saint-Evremond.[5] Their libertinism expressed itself in an elegant form, connected with *esprit* and a feeling for decorum. The drinking bouts, obscenities, and blasphemies of Théophile and his friends were replaced by an intellectual subtlety, in which, nevertheless, the *voluptas* of epicureanism was unreservedly expressed in a purely physical way.

It was this idea of libertinism that was widely spread in the eighteenth century, especially among the nobility of *la cour et la ville*. The court set the example, the city followed. Admittedly, during the last years of Louis XIV, piety and devotion, at least outwardly, were mandatory, but this changed immediately after the death of the king in 1714. The years of the regency of the Duke of Orleans are still notorious for their loose morals and religious liberality, and this situation hardly changed under Louis XV.[6] Naturally, it was only a small elite which moved in the *monde*, as it was characteristically called. In the memoirs and correspondence of that period we can read what happened, but the best analyses of what was enacted in this 'world' can be found in the novels (often called libertine) of authors such as Crébillon *fils*, Duclos, Dorat, Louvet de Couvray, and Choderlos de Laclos.

The protagonist of these novels usually cares for only two things, success and pleasure. In Crébillon's *Les égarements du coeur et de l'esprit*, love is described as *'une sorte de commerce ou l'on s'engageait'*.[7] In Duclos's *Les confessions du comte xxx* the protagonist observes that the most important aspect of love was *'augmenter la liste'*.[8] Each seduction is literally and figuratively a conquest, which must enlarge self-esteem and prestige in the *monde*. In its most radical and cynical consequences, this idea is elaborated in Laclos's masterpiece *Les liaisons dangereuses*, which, none the less, can also be interpreted as a moral rejection of mundane libertinism. To a certain extent the same can be said of the novels of Crébillon *fils* and Duclos: their subtle analysis of the *monde* clearly shows the emptiness which the pursuit of pleasure and success diffuses. These novels suggest a strong feeling of disillusion which takes its revenge in the usually virtuous denouements. Laclos also makes known the moralistic intention of his novel by letting his most libertine protagonists, Valmont and the Marchioness de Merteuil, come to a bad end.[9]

In subsequent times, the critique of mundane libertinism has only increased. According to some historians, it even explained the French Revolution: the financial problems which gave rise to the riots in 1789 were, they suggest, caused by the costly dissipations of Louis XV. During the revolution the real or supposed debauchery of nobility and clergy was fully emphasized; better propaganda for the revolution was hardly imaginable. With a little goodwill one could see an echo of this in the view of the frivolity of the past which was developed by some contra-revolutionary authors. For example, Joseph de Maistre saw in the revolution, in addition to all the 'perniciousness' it represented, also a deserved penalty of God for the degeneration of the privileged classes before 1789.[10]

Naturally, these rejections, be they of the revolutionary or the contra-revolutionary side, do not give a trustworthy picture of the nature and scale of libertinism during the *ancien régime*. They do show, however, what was thought of the former elite after the outbreak of the revolution. A similar negative view of nobility, court, and clergy can be found in the numerous pamphlets and *libelles* circulating in the literary underworld of the *ancien régime*. In anonymous treatises, such as *Les fastes de Louis XV* and *Les amours de Charlot et Toinette* (i.e. the later Charles X and Marie-Antoinette) the ruling regime was painted in the most lurid colours.[11] The current refrain of these pamphlets is: king, nobility, and clergy can do what they want, but the common citizen, groaning under a despotic yoke, is powerless, has no rights and, on top of this, has to foot the bill.

The vicissitudes of the Marquis de Sade demonstrate that this picture is in need of some correction, at least regarding the impunity of the elite. Although in his books de Sade shows the same picture of decadence and corruption as the 'underground' pamphlets, he is living proof that the nobility could not always get away with it. On the other hand, we may doubt whether he is a

very solid witness for the defence. The story of his (real) libertinism and his contacts with the authorities and the law is
complicated, even somewhat bizarre, although certainly not an
unusual course of events under the *ancien régime*. After the revolution de Sade pretended to have been locked up in the Bastille for
his enlightened ideas or his revolutionary sympathies, but even at
that time few people believed him. Already in 1793–4 J. A.
Dulaure had published a list of noblemen in which de Sade is
pictured as a 'feudal' monster of the calibre of Gilles de Retz.
Dulaure gets especially worked up about the fact that de Sade now
paraded his imprisonment in the Bastille, whereas this really was
only a favour; in his view, de Sade had deserved the death
penalty. It was only his blue blood that had saved the marquis –
convincing proof, according to Dulaure, that in the case of the
*privilégiés* the *ancien régime* always measured by two standards.[12]

Dulaure was not completely wrong. In 1772 the parliament of
Aix had condemned de Sade to death for sodomy and attempted
poisoning – a verdict quashed in 1778 thanks to the activities of
his family and in-laws, who had also saved him from the police on
earlier occasions. It can therefore hardly be denied that de Sade
profited from his social position. On the other hand, he also owed
his prolonged confinement to his family. After the death sentence
of 1772 de Sade's mother-in-law, the Présidente de Montreuil,
decided to take the law into her own hands. She managed to
acquire a *lettre de cachet*, which helped to imprison her recalcitrant
son-in-law in Vincennes and, finally, in the Bastille after the
annulment of his death sentence. In this way Madame de
Montreuil hoped to prevent a further injuring of the family
reputation – a hope only partially fulfilled, as it was in prison that
de Sade wrote the books that render his name so sinister even
today.

De Sade started to write in prison to afford a safety valve to his
clipped passions. His correspondence suggests that his confinement
brought him to the threshold of madness. To his wife he wrote in
connection with his enforced sexual abstinence: 'You fired my
head, you let me form spectres which I shall have to realize.'[13]
On paper these 'spectres' took on the shape of Justine, Juliette,
and all the other libertines and victims that populate his literary
universe.

There must, however, have been another motive too – revenge. Revenge on the world of the *ancien régime* that had excluded him, although as a nobleman he should have been entitled to all the privileges of the elite in a class society. In his novels de Sade caricatured these privileges. It is hardly chance that in his *Les cent vingt journées de Sodome* four wealthy and powerful authorities – a duke, a bishop, a president of a parliament, and a banker – retire to the castle of Silling in order to organize an orgy. It seems as if de Sade wants to say: look at the elite that has expelled me! Of these authorities, de Sade aimed especially at the judiciary. The parliament of Aix, which had sentenced him to death in 1772, is repeatedly attacked and its judges appear invariably to be far greater criminals than the poor devils condemned to the wheel or the gallows. With satisfaction Curval confesses in *Les cent vingt journées de Sodome* that as a member of parliament he had voted hundreds of times to have innocent people hanged, and that he felt a lustful tickle deep inside him every time he committed that small injustice.[14]

Yet de Sade's complaint against this kind of injustice cannot be compared with the accusations of despotism and arbitrariness raised by other victims of the ruling system, such as Mirabeau and Linguet.[15] With de Sade there is always so much ambivalence that the whole effect of his protest is already undermined in advance. His exposure of injustice always involves a reversal of values, which perversely legitimates this injustice – by an appeal not to jurisprudence but to nature. To that end de Sade has developed a complete cosmology of evil, a kind of anti-theodicy, with in its centre a 'criminal' nature, to which all actions and events in the universe have been made subservient.

This philosophical dimension of libertinism can be found in the theories, often all too long-winded, which de Sade's heroes are wont to develop in between the more practical demonstrations of their ideas, as his novels are a curious mixture of philosophy and pornography. A similar structure can already be found in a more hidden tradition of libertine literature. Both Crébillon *fils* and Duclos were part of the establishment with their novels: Crébillon even rose to the office of royal censor thanks to the intercession of Madame de Pompadour, and Duclos was secretary of the Académie française from 1775. In their novels not one indecent word is spoken, the eroticism remains hidden under a veil of elegance, and the behaviour of the heroes is a code only fully understood by the initiates of the *monde*. On the other hand, the libertine tradition to which de Sade reverted is a considerably coarser genre that can in no way be associated with the establishment but, rather, belongs to the literary underworld of the *ancien régime*, like the pamphlets and *libelles* mentioned earlier.

In the *Histoire de Juliette* de Sade gives a few examples of this openly pornographic literature. In the library of the libertine monk Claude, Juliette and Clairwil find Gervaise de la Touche's *Portier des Chartreux*, probably the biggest erotic bestseller of the eighteenth century, Mirabeau's *L'éducation de Laure*, and, finally, the notorious *Thérèse philosophe*, ascribed by de Sade (but probably wrongly) to the Marquis d'Argens. This last, a book which alternates pornographic scenes with philosophical passages, is the most appreciated: it is 'the only one that combines lust and blasphemy in a pleasant way and . . . gives an idea what an immoral book can be'.[16]

The philosophy preached in *Thérèse philosophe*[17] is not de Sade's own, but looks more like naturalism *à la* Spinoza. God and nature are represented as identical, the universe is a mechanistic whole, and man is a being whose every movement is determined by nature. Consequently, the distinction between good and evil is fictitious. From the point of view of God everything is good, but man calls good or evil only what does or does not fit in with his own self-interest. Traditional ethics can be thrown overboard and nobody needs to feel restrained by any precept whatever in the satisfaction of his lusts. Considering the good character of nature, nothing should stand in the way of a free and happy society. Unfortunately, as the Abbé T. (one of the author's mouthpieces in this book) warns, not all people are able to live according to these insights. That is why truth is only suitable for a small elite, which is free to do whatever it wants in secret, as it possesses sufficient brains and 'harmonious' passions. Religion can be left intact for the stupid and brutish masses, as under no circumstances should libertinism endanger the ruling social order – a point repeatedly stressed by the author of *Thérèse philosophe*.

However primitive, this philosophical message is part of the Enlightenment and resembles in a number of ways the views of the more radical *philosophes* such as Lamettrie, Holbach, Helvétius, or Diderot, who have been also consulted by de Sade. In a letter of 1783 he even offers himself as a 'martyr', if necessary, for Holbach's *Système de la nature*. In a footnote in *Juliette*, Lamettrie, Helvétius, and Montesquieu are mentioned with approval.[18] De Sade's only criticism of these great minds is the lack of consequence in their thinking. The mention of Montesquieu may cause surprise, as his deism cannot possibly have been to the taste of the atheistic marquis, but de Sade probably wanted to honour the cultural relativism of the author of *De l'esprit des lois*. As regards the other *philosophes*, full appreciation is more likely, as is the case with Holbach and Diderot.

All these intellectuals believed in a strictly materialistic cosmology, in which there was no place for a creating God, and in their writings they proved to be fierce combatants of the Christian 'superstition' (in this capacity, Voltaire is quoted more than once with approval by de Sade). Their moral philosophy was, at least in principle, just as naturalistic as the one in *Thérèse philosophe*, and in Lamettrie we can indeed find an egoistic hedonism that treats with indifference all other ethical precepts. All kinds of sexual practices, which tradition considered to be unnatural, were justified by him precisely for this reason. Diderot acted in the same way in some of his most daring texts, which were never published during his lifetime; for example, in *Rêve de d'Alembert* he defended homosexuality and masturbation, whereas in the amusing *Supplément au voyage de Bougainville* he warmly recommended promiscuity, incest, and adultery.[19]

Nevertheless, there are clear limits set to the relationship of de Sade with the *philosophes*, as Lamettrie and Diderot undoubtedly would have rejected his ideas. Admittedly, in their boldest writings they explored a number of highly unorthodox consequences of their philosophy, but they certainly did not want to replace the prevailing moral system by such extremism. With the exception of Lamettrie, they were often highly rigid, if not outright puritanical, regarding the social significance of the moral system. The latter attitude is even typical for Holbach, who preached the ethics of social utility, in which the individual had to adapt his self-interest to the interest of society in every respect. He shows the ultimate consequence of this idea in his *Morale universelle*, where he anathematizes all sexual eccentricities. Finally, it looks as if in his *Système de la nature* Holbach wanted beforehand to deny any identification of his own ideas with de Sade's oeuvre: 'What would be the fate of a book that nowadays mentioned that the sun is not luminous at all, that parricide is legitimate, that theft is permitted, that adultery is no crime at all? It would need little thought to realize the error of these ideas, and the whole of mankind would turn out against them; people would laugh at the madness of the author, and his book and his name would soon be known only for their ridiculous nonsense.'[20] This passage must have momentarily escaped de Sade, when he so generously offered to be a martyr for Holbach's *Système*.

De Sade's cosmology is stamped by a radical anti-morality without compromises, in which evil is good and good evil. This reversal of traditional values originates in nature itself. De Sade represents the universe as a gigantic mechanism of moving particles, that continues to exist by the grace of destruction. One could say that the doubting of the benignant intentions of nature, which the 1775 earthquake of Lisbon caused for some *philosophes*, is running away to the other extreme in de Sade: earthquakes, eruptions of volcanoes, floods, epidemics, and other catastrophes are the means *par excellence* by which nature pursues its ends. Destruction is the universal law of nature and this law is also valid for mankind, as man is also a natural phenomenon. Destruction is man's natural imperative, as his passions teach him abundantly clearly: de Sade describes sexual passion in a mechanistic terminology as an affection which reaches its maximal effect only when the partner is destroyed, preferably in the most horrible manner. De Sade defends his eroticism of destruction with the argument that it is not really ruination: in his materialistic universe death is not an irreparable rupture, only a change of shape. In the *Dialogue entre un prêtre et un moribond*, as far as is known the first text written in prison by de Sade, we can read: 'Today man, tomorrow worm, the day after tomorrow a fly – surely, this still is life?'[21]

To keep the movement going, nature needs a balance between good and evil: 'a completely virtuous universe could not exist for a minute; the wise hand of nature lets order be born from disorder and, without disorder, it would come to nothing: that is the way of the profound balance that keeps the stars in their course, that suspends them in the immense plains of space, that makes them move in a regular way. Only because of evil does it succeed in performing good; only because of crimes can it exist, and everything would break down if only virtue ruled on earth.'[22] The criminality of de Sade's libertines, then, finds its *raison d'être* in what we could call a cosmic Malthusianism, to which de Sade was inspired by Holbach and eighteenth-century biologists, such as Buffon and Robinet.[23]

In de Sade's work, the theory of natural balance between good and evil (which led Buffon to defend the utility of hunting and Robinet even that of human murderousness) leads to a rigorous dichotomy of mankind into victims and libertines. The first category betrays itself by its devotion to traditional values. De Sade considered Christianity with its altruistic morals an obvious device of the poor and weak to manipulate the rich and strong. In his view virtue was based on simple self-interest, although this is not realized by virtuous people: they sincerely believe in their own morality and religion – a belief that automatically marks them as victims. On the other hand, the libertine has shaken off all prejudice and superstition. Due to the *flambeau de la philosophie* he has acquired an understanding of the true – criminal – nature of the universe and he lives accordingly: without any scruples he satisfies all his lusts and he finds the highest satisfaction in crimes.

Together de Sade's libertines constitute an elite defined by philosophy and conduct, a new aristocracy. This aristocracy is not necessarily identical with the nobility of the *ancien régime*, even though we have seen that in de Sade's novels many aristocrats and authorities form part of the libertine elite. But a similar libertinism can be found among highwaymen and counterfeiters: libertines can exist *outside* and *above* orderly society. The libertine elite cannot be defined in social terms: in principle anyone can become part of the elite, even those who in the first instance belong to the victims: those who are willing to accept the libertine principles prove *ipso facto* that they have transcended the status of victim.

De Sade's ideas are well illustrated by the dialogues of *La philosophie dans le boudoir* which constitute a complete course in libertinism, showing how a young, complaisant girl is incited by a few advanced libertines to assault her virtuous mother. But the best-known pupil in de Sade's oeuvre is of course Juliette, who – in the more than a thousand pages of her life story – succeeds in working her way up from being a poor orphan to becoming a powerful and wealthy woman, who knows herself assured of a secure position in the corrupt *ancien régime*. She owes everything to carefully following the advice of those libertines who cross her path. Saint-Fond tells her what libertinism is. First of all, one has to forswear religion, as a libertine is by definition an atheist. Then one has to despise the '*conventions sociales*'. And finally and most important, one has to contract the '*habitude du crime*', a habit acquired only by practising the libertine tenets: what good works are for pious Christians crime is for the authentic libertine.[24]

It is of course absolutely necessary to look respectable in order to be able to commit crimes with impunity. The necessity for a double standard of morals, which we already saw in *Thérèse philosophe*, is even more urgent in de Sade's novels. Not for nothing do libertines choose remote estates, inaccessible castles, and subterranean vaults for their most uninhibited orgies. In addition, they love to indulge in Utopian fantasies, in which they as the elite openly and without the façade of virtue and convention can practise their sexual regime; preferably they would expand their secret practice to the whole of society, as the various blueprints for a perverted class society in *Juliette* show.

In his *La philosophie dans le boudoir* de Sade also sketched a programme for an egalitarian state ruled by lust, in which everybody has become a libertine, forced by the government if necessary. In the Utopia of this book de Sade addresses his compatriots who had just liberated themselves from the old monarchical regime by a bloody revolution (the book appeared in 1795). But according to de Sade something else needs to be done before France will be really free. The libertinism that he recommends to the French is explicitly defined by the concept of liberation. Seemingly, this applies to all the kinds of libertinism that occur in his novels. Irrespective of the number of victims, for the libertine elite libertinism constitutes a philosophy of freedom and liberation – liberation from the shackles of a tyrannical religion and an unnatural morality, and by this means nature's original rights can be restored. De Sade's heroes usually make it clear that they think in the same way. They feel themselves to be like gods on earth in their orgies and wallow in their power and the blood of their victims.

In this respect de Sade continues a tendency already present in earlier forms of libertinism, which also concentrated on emancipation and autonomy in spiritual and ethical respects. De Sade simply shows the most radical consequences of this tendency: man

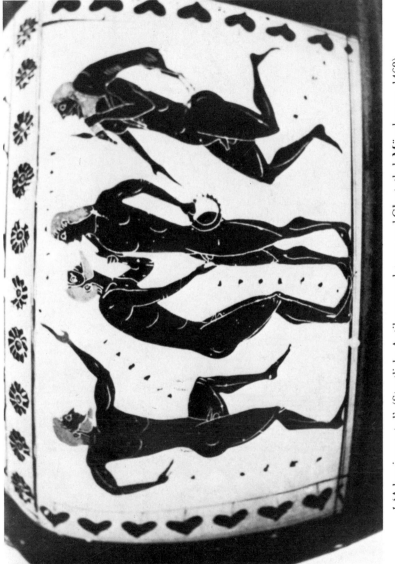

1 'A boy is courted', (Staatliche Antikensammlungen und Glyptothek München no. 1468).

*2* Personification of the 'Huysbestieringe' from Cesare
Ripa, *Iconologia* . . ., (Amsterdam, 1644).

3  Theodoor van Thulden, *Portrait of Josina Copes-Schade van Westrum and Her Children* (Noortbrabants Museum, 's Hertogenbosch).

4 Caesar Bovetius van Everdingen, *Lycurgus demonstrates the Consequences of Education* (Stedelijk Museum, Alkmaar).

5 Ludolf de Jongh, *Portrait of a Little Boy*, 1661 (The Virginia Museum of Fine Arts, Richmond, Virginia).

*6* Michiel van Mussher, *Family Portrait* (whereabouts unknown).

DOCTRINA ET VSV.

Jo: Matthæg Vacker

7 Contribution of J. M. Vacker in the *Album Amicorum Abraham Ortelius*, 1584 (Pembroke College Library, Cambridge).

*8 Maeghde-Wapen* from Jacob Cats, *Houwelyck*, (Haarlem, 1642).

*9 Vryster-Wapen* from Jacob Cats, *Houwelyck,* (Haarlem, 1642).

*10* J. G. Cuyp, *Portrait of a Boy* (whereabouts unknown).

*11* J. A. Rotius, *Portrait of a Boy* (whereabouts unknown).

*12* J. G. Cuyp, *Portrait of Four Children with Goat* (whereabouts unknown).

*13* J. G. Cuyp, *Portrait of a Little Girl playing with Cat and Fish* (private collection).

*14* Jean-Honoré Fragonard, *The Swing*, 1767 (reproduced by permission of the Trustees, The Wallace Collection, London).

*15 Tonë, c.* 1968 (with thanks to Gjelosh Tomja Bikaj).

16 *Stana with Her Sister Vukosava.* Portrait drawn on the basis of photos (with thanks to Borka Cerovic).

changes into god on earth. Later, the apologists for the marquis also put his oeuvre in this context. In 1909 Apollinaire called de Sade 'cet esprit le plus libre qui ait encore existé', Robert Desnos considered him the first manifestation in philosophy and literature of the 'esprit moderne', and the surrealists worshipped de Sade as one of their most eminent predecessors because of his rebellious qualities, his aggressive atheism, his literary extremism, and his apologetics for sexuality.[25]

However, this emphasis on the 'liberating' character of de Sade's work does not do his philosophy full justice, as liberation is only one side of the picture. The other side, unexpectedly, shows a tragic dimension to the cosmology that de Sade has constructed with so much pent-up rage. The liberation that has made the libertines gods in their own eyes appears to be an illusion, as de Sade has not refused to face the extreme consequences of his own philosophy. Already in his very first texts, libertines realize the limited nature of their crimes: their imagination always leads them to expect many more possibilities than they can fulfil. In Les cent vingt journées de Sodome, Curval regrets that he cannot attack the sun in order to put the world on fire. 'That would really be a crime', he exclaims, 'something completely different from those small excesses which only cause a few people to be changed into lumps of earth at the end of the year.'[26] In his later work, de Sade assigned a very special meaning within the context of his philosophy to this desire for excessive, in reality unfeasible, crimes. The restriction that vexes the libertine now acquires a theoretical basis, which originates from nature, like criminality itself. Just as they are physically unable to abuse the sun, so they cannot go against the intentions of nature whatever crimes they may think up. The libertine suddenly realizes his imprisonment in nature; he is a will-less part of the great mechanism that entirely transcends his individual powers.

In the libertine we notice here a curious distinction between, on the one hand, reason and imagination and, on the other, his (sexual) passions. With the latter he is chained to nature, as his reason shows him. In order to escape these chains, the libertine tries to rationalize his lust. It is not the sexual act, but the idea of crime that gives him his most intense orgasm. The apatheia is now seen as the highest ideal: apathy regarding every ethical impulse and also regarding purely physical affections. The most experienced libertines in de Sade's universe prove to be fanatical believers in a perverted 'stoicism' that guarantees them the highest pleasures.[27]

In the end, though, these are all subterfuges: every crime, be it committed from blind lust or stoical distance, conforms to the order of nature, to whom every destruction is of use. Even a return to virtue would be of no avail, since it leaves nature indifferent whether someone sacrifices or is sacrificed himself: it is only interested in the sheer fact of destruction. In this process the role of the individual is totally unimportant. It is therefore hardly surprising that in *La nouvelle Justine* and *Juliette* de Sade inspires his libertines with the desire to strike at nature itself as the ultimate crime. At this point, however, the libertine encounters a border impossible to be crossed. 'The impossibility to hurt nature is the biggest vexation of man', is the contention of the monk Jerôme. And Madame d'Esterval laments: 'I would like to disturb its plans, obstruct its course, arrest the course of the stars, overturn the globes that are floating in space, destroy what serves it, elevate what impedes it, in short I would like to strike at all its works by interrupting all its great effects – but I am without power to do it.' For that reason Bressac concludes: 'Let us revenge ourselves on what is offered to us, and let us multiply our atrocities, as we cannot improve upon them.[28] In their impotence the libertines prefer quantity above quality and they curse the almighty nature no less than they did the Christian God for the limits that are set to them.

In this way de Sade has made clear that his libertinism ultimately does not constitute a road to freedom but a circular course without any prospects: hardly by chance the only route a prisoner can cover in his cell.

## NOTES

All quotations of de Sade himself derive from the *Oeuvres complètes*, cited as *O.C.*, published in sixteen volumes in Paris by Editions Têtes de Feuilles, 1973; this edition is identical with that of the Cercle du Livre Précieux, 1962–4.

1 For more detailed biographical data see Gilbert Lely, *Vie du marquis de Sade*, *O.C.*, I–II.
2 *O.C.*, XII, 276.

3 Quoted in Andrzej Siemek, *La recherche morale et esthétique dans le roman de Crébillon fils*, Oxford, 1981, 34–5.
4 On the history of libertinage see, for example, J. S. Spink, *French Free-thought from Gassendi to Voltaire*, London, 1960; Antoine Adam, *Les Libertins au XVII siècle*, Paris, 1964; Gerhard Schneider, *Der Libertin. Zur Geistes- und Sozialgeschichte des Buergertums im 16. und 17. Jahrhundert*, Stuttgart, 1970; Peter Nagy, *Libertinage et révolution*, Paris, 1975.
5 *O.C.*, X, 10.
6 Cf. G. Chaussinand-Nogaret, *La noblesse au XVIIIe siècle. De la féodalité aux lumières*, Paris, 1976; Jean Mayer, *La vie quotidienne en France au temps de la Régence*, Paris, 1979.
7 *Romanciers du XVIIIe siècle*, t. II, Bibliothèque de la Pleiade, Paris, 1965, 15.
8 Ibid., 240.
9 Cf. Roger Vailland, *Laclos par lui-meme*, Paris, 1958; Peter Brooks, *The Novel of Worldliness*, Princeton, NJ, 1969; Marie-Hélène Huet, 'Roman libertin et réaction aristocratique', *Dix-huitième Siècle*, 1972, 4: 129–42.
10 Joseph de Maistre, *Considérations sur la France*, Brussels, 1844, 128–30 (originally published in 1796).
11 Cf. Robert Darnton, *The Literary Underground of the Old Regime*, Cambridge, Mass., 1982.
12 Françoise Laugaa-Traut, *Lectures de Sade*, Paris, 1973, 22–6.
13 *O.C.*, XII, 397.
14 *O.C.*, XIII, 164.
15 Mirabeau, *Essai sur les lettres de cachet et les prisons d'état* (1782); Linguet, *Mémoires sur la Bastille* (1783).
16 *O.C.*, VIII, 442 f. See also Barry Ivker, 'Towards a definition of libertinism in 18th-century French fiction', *Studies on Voltaire and the eighteenth century*, 1970, 73: 199–218; Barry Ivker, 'On the darker side of the Enlightenment: a comparison of the literary techniques of Sade and Restif', *Studies on Voltaire and the eighteenth century*, 1971, 79: 219–39.
17 The original edition probably appeared in 1748, but there are many reprints, most recently in the series *Les classiques interdites*, Paris, 1979.
18 *O.C.*, XII, 418; VIII, 171.
19 Cf. Jean Leduc, 'Les sources de l'athéisme et de l'immoralisme du marquis de Sade', *Studies on Voltaire and the eighteenth century*, 1969, 68: 9–65.
20 Ibid., 19.
21 *O.C.*, XIV, 62 f.
22 *O.C.*, VIII, 168 f.
23 Jean Deprun, 'Sade et la philosophie biologique de son temps', in *Le Marquis de Sade*, Centre Aixois d'études et de recherches sur le dix-huitième siècle, Paris, 1968, 189–205.
24 *O.C.*, VIII, 329 f.
25 Laugaa-Traut, *Lectures*, 179–208; Maurice Nadeau, *Histoire du surréalisme*, Paris, 1964, 34.

26 *O.C.*, XIII, 165.
27 *O.C.*, VIII, 271, 173, 463 f.
28 *O.C.*, VI, 339; VII, 229.

# 8

# Sexual morality and the meaning of prostitution in *fin-de-siècle* Vienna

*Karin J. Jušek*

## INTRODUCTION

The image of Vienna as a breeding-ground for modern ideas, a melting-pot of different peoples and their opposing interests, as a city that despite its size and the seriousness of its problems merrily waltzed to its downfall, is popular and widespread. The intellectual and artistic achievements in Vienna during the *belle époque* (1890–1914) have received considerable scientific attention. The political problems, the social differences, the nationality question, and the virulent anti-Semitism have also been studied in detail. However, there has been remarkably little interest in the sexual morality and the sexual experiences of the 'moderns'. And this despite the fact that 'the sexual question' was a topic of much debate at the time. From Vienna sexology received major impulses (Breuer, Krafft-Ebing, and of course Freud). The first German-language pornographic novel, *Josefine Mutzenbacher. Die Geschichte einer wienerischen Dirne von ihr selbst erzählt*, appeared here in 1905. In short, this is an interesting topic which has as yet received little attention – reason enough for an inquiry into this phenomenon.

This study on sexuality addresses three 'layers of reality'. First of all the ideas about sexuality and sexual urges and the use, in particular the importance, of social norms. Which ideas about sexuality were supported by whom in the German-language area? (For this part of the study I have included the discussion held within the entire German speaking area in Europe, which functioned as one cultural entity, rather than limit myself to Austria only.) Was there criticism on a dominant theory? Who were the critics? What were their arguments?

123

KARIN J. JUŠEK

Secondly I will address the attempts by the state to regulate and control the sexual behaviour of its subjects. I have focused on the activities of the vice squad and on the court cases dealing with indecency, vice, and obscenity as the most important instruments of the state for maintaining and protecting law and order and moral standards. What policy did the vice squad carry out? Which ideas formed the basis of this policy? How were the regulations applied?

Finally I will pay attention to the informal organization of sexuality. Were there erotic dilemmas? Which rules applied for starting sexual relationships? What did they mean for those involved, and what influence did they have on the relations between the sexes?

# 1 IDEAS ABOUT SEXUALITY

From the second half of the nineteenth century onward the number of publications about sexuality and everything relating to it, like hygiene, genetics, etc., rapidly increased. The human sex drive turned out to be an unlimited source of fantasies, which became the bases of many theories about 'its true nature'. There were lively discussions about it by the medical profession, psychologists, lawyers, criminologists, economists, historians, politicians, theologians, and feminists. The ideas that were discussed, supported, or rejected were rather diverse in nature, but had a common denominator: sexuality was seen as a primitive natural force that was hard to control, which manifested itself in fundamentally different ways in men and women. Male sexuality was active, female sexuality passive. These notions were surrounded by scientific pretence, although they were based on such fantasies as that which ascribed passivity to the ovum and activity to the sperm. Freud too would later use the concepts of active/male and passive/female sexuality, although there are some indications in his early work that he considered the possibility of a female libido as active as the male's.[1]

Only in intellectual and artistic circles does one sometimes encounter the idea that the primitive sexual drive, once freed from the tight bonds of morality, could lead to something positive. The other participants in the discussion agreed that sexuality should be controlled for the sake of civilization. There was, however,

124

widespread disagreement on how this grip on sexuality, which was seen as a dire necessity, should be acquired.

The most popular theory assumed that male sexuality, active as it was by nature, needed to be satisfied. This was not necessarily a problem, because female sexuality was perceived as its complement, so that, at least in theory, no sexual frustration could exist. The problem was that at the level of civilization thus far acquired in the western world the monogamous marriage was seen as the only viable social basis. And this monogamous marriage restricted male sexuality to a degree that was, in some sense, considered undesirable by the proponents of this theory. The dilemma facing them – what was good for civilization was bad for the satisfaction of the male sexual urge – was solved by defending prostitution as a legitimate outlet for male sexuality. A consequence of the solution thus created was that the theory of passive female sexuality had to be modified in order to explain the existence of prostitutes. There must be women with sexual needs and urges who were also prepared to satisfy or indulge in them, which would almost automatically bring them to prostitution. Explaining the existence of prostitutes through their basically rejectable sexual behaviour had the advantage that there was no need to further examine the origins of prostitution, unlike the feminists who kept dragging in the power relations between the sexes, and unlike the social democrats who focused on economic circumstances. Women should therefore be judged on the basis of their sexual behaviour. They thus acquired a *Geschlechtsehre*, an honour, which, depending on their behaviour, could be taken away from them. In this manner women could be divided into two categories: the good/respectable woman without sexual needs and the bad/disreputable woman with sexual needs she wished to satisfy. That this categorization was in the interest of women is explained by the German economist Kapff:

> If in fact men were judged on the basis of their sexual conduct in the same manner as girls, the consequence of their disreputable status would be that no girl could marry any man who had lost his honour through a natural sexual encounter. In that case, the unmarried woman, for whose protection and in whose favour this paragraph is included in the social code of honour, would insist on the abolition of this practice in the shortest possible time.[2]

Having a *Geschlechtsehre* was not only an advantage for women; the state also had a major interest in controlling the sexual liberties of women – the respectable ones, that is.

If a society existed that gave equal rights and liberties to both sexes and which would no longer ostracize and treat those girls who, like men, wish to engage in sexual practice to their hearts' content as fallen women, even then men would not marry such girls, but merely use them as mistresses and girls for pleasure. The number of marriages and births would decline, the number of illegitimate children would increase, and the foundation of the state would thus be undermined.[3]

Important in the categorization of women is the aspect of class. The division line between good and bad coincided, both in theory and in practice, with existing class lines. Middle-class women were sexually passive; they basically wanted children. Lower-class women, however, were sexually active and knew neither shame nor restraint. This theoretical legitimation of double standards met with severe criticism from the start, despite its enormous popularity at the end of the nineteenth century.

### Criticism

Not everyone in the medical profession agreed that prostitution was a necessary outlet for male sexuality. There were prominent doctors who plainly stated that the efforts to legitimize and/or legalize prostitution were only in the interest of men. In 1897 Dr Arnold Dodel, professor at Zurich University, wrote in a report on the effects and benefits of medical examinations for prostitutes:

Only a radical change in the sense of social and economic equality of the sexes would bring about any improvement in these aspects of sexuality. Only then will the 'natural' institution of marriage cease to be a protection of privileged prostitution sanctioned by law, as is currently often the case.[4]

Dr Albert Eulenberg, professor at Berlin University, when asked for advice on the same matter, pointed out that medical examinations for prostitutes

were concocted only in the interests of men, and would function only to guarantee this interested section of society a maximum of convenience and an – unfounded – sense of security when using this wonderful institution.[5]

The Roman Catholic church was particularly fierce in its debate of the issue. Acceptance of extra-marital sex – prostitution or otherwise – could lead only to the general and inevitable degeneration of society. Theories condoning or even legitimizing extra-marital sex should be forcefully resisted. The church doctrine on sexual needs was certainly not unambiguous. Sometimes the church warned emphatically against the immoral behaviour of men that led girls astray,[6] sometimes the female sex was more inclined towards immorality because of 'a more passionate nature'.[7] In general the Catholic church was egalitarian in the control of sexual behaviour. The primitive sex drive could occur in both men and women regardless of class. It was the task of the priest to instil restraint of sexual passion in the believers. But in the crusade against indecency he should understand

that people are naturally predisposed to act this way as a consequence of their physical development; that the sex drive through its vehement need for satisfaction hinders people in considering the grounds that could keep them from sin, and eliminates the will through the delusion of the greatest satisfaction of the senses.[8]

The idea that abstinence was not conducive to health was contested by the church. In order to give more weight to their arguments churchmen frequently quoted medical doctors who criticized the popular notions on unbridled male sexuality. The women's movement, which took a firm stand against all aspects of the double standard, used these same doctors. This was the only link between the church and the women's movement. Both opposed the scientific legitimation of the double standard, but their proposals for alternative standards were vastly different. The church saw the struggle for women's emancipation as anti-Christian, and the demands of the women's movement as entirely shameless.[9] Christianity had given the woman a calling as mother and wife and only within these functions could she fulfil her earthly duties.[10] Middle-class women were in a position to dedicate their lives entirely to the family, and rebellion against this could in no way be excused.

The women's movement in its turn was not prepared to fight against the double standards in alliance with the church. Rosa Mayreder, a prominent Viennese feminist, wrote in an essay, 'Mutterschaft und doppelte Moral', which appeared in 1905:

> But from the rules of religious morality it would seem that the most fundamental motive is to sanctify the sexual act through sacrament and to justify it by shifting the emphasis to procreation. In modern terms: the rather loose connection between the sex drive and procreation in the human psyche should be tightened under pressure of moral standards, since the sex act itself does not usually evoke images of progeny in the individual consciousness, nor is it usually motivated by it . . ... Religious and bourgeois morality, with their calculated overestimations of virginity, only mean a heteronomous moral law through which an outward order is supposed to be enforced.[11]

Mayreder argued in favour of a change in attitudes: in the modern consciousness sexuality would have to be justified by love. Men should appreciate it when women would, uncalculatingly ('only after we are married'), or without the promise of material gains (presents or money), agree to engage in a sexual relationship out of love. Of course such relationships could be established only after women had gained legal, economic, and social equality.[12] Feminists also refused to believe that it was necessary to sacrifice certain women in order to maintain the achieved level of civilization. Aletta Jacobs had pointed out to her professor that if he saw prostitution as a 'necessary evil' he ought to make his own daughters available as well. The Austrian writer Irma von Troll-Borostyani argued that the only consequence of such arguments would be to introduce a general draft for women into prostitution, analogous to the military draft for men.[13] The argument that abstinence would be detrimental to one's health was scrutinized by, amongst others, Anna Pappritz in her article 'Herrenmoral' (1903):

> While the dangers of abstinence were said to assail *both sexes* they only demanded *satisfaction for men*!! But why should men seek satisfaction in prostitution while there are plenty of unmarried women? some naive provincial might ask who was not trained in logic by the German universities. Well, man does not only

wish to satisfy his legitimate needs, he wishes to be freed from their unpleasant consequences (child, alimony). Thus he created prostitution![14]

She noted sarcastically that the state brothels, governed by educated women – a serious proposal made during the first congress of the German Society Against Venereal Disease held on 9 and 10 March 1903, intended to provide clients with an optimal service without the risk of contamination with sexually transmitted diseases – might lead to a women's state, thus conveniently solving the woman's question since 'all professions from mayor to chimney sweep, would be open to women in Bordelloville'.[15]

No matter how strongly the proponents of the double standard were criticized, the pros and antis agreed that an unbridled expression of sexual needs was socially undesirable. In 1886 Krafft-Ebing demonstrated in his *Psychopathia sexualis* that men were polygamous and women monogamous in nature. His proof was based on the assumption that the world would otherwise have become a brothel and marriage would have been unthinkable.[16] In 1903 the young philosopher Otto Weininger arrived at the opposite conclusion about women. In his thesis *Geschlecht und Character* he 'scientifically proved' the inferiority of women and Jews. To Weininger woman was no mystery. He discovered that she was not only polygamous but also irrational and chaotic. She understood nothing of logic, ethics, and morality and lived only to satisfy her needs. She would have to completely repress her sexuality to become human. Jews were an inferior race because they possessed primarily female characteristics; yes, to the point of being effeminate.

Weininger's book had tremendous impact. It was reprinted many times. The book's reception and the author's success indicate that the ideas about the virtual absence of sexual desire in respectable women had by then lost some of their popularity. Speculation about sexuality now included even women of the higher classes who had thus far been exempted. Now *all* women were controlled, possessed, and determined by their sexuality. Because woman was different, a deviation from the norm – that is, man – she became the subject of research.

Weininger's notion about the nature of women shows a great deal of resemblance to Freud's, despite the reticent attitude of Freud with respect to Weininger. Freud too judged the difference

KARIN J. JUŠEK

of women from men in negative terms, but his theories were more subtle. Weininger's ideas were accepted with far less critical distance in literary circles.

Viennese writers and artists, who could muster only a minimum of interest for the political and social problems of the period, were deeply interested in the 'sexual question'. After 1900 especially, sexuality was a favourite topic of discussion. Through books and plays and their reviews, a polemic about sexual norms was created. Strindberg, 'the representative of poetically worded sex problems',[17] wrote to Weininger with obvious relief: 'Herr Doktor . . . to finally see the woman's question solved comes as a great relief to me, so please accept my admiration and my gratitude!'[18] Also Frank Wedekind, author of the Lulu tragedies, and Karl Kraus, publisher of the magazine Die Fackel, appreciated Weininger. 'An admirer of women enthusiastically underwrites the arguments of your contempt for women,' Kraus wrote to Weininger.[19] This reaction underlines that misogyny and gynolatry are two sides of the same coin, the simple result of absolutizing the model 'woman = sexuality'. Wedekind and Kraus believed in an anarchic primitive force of 'natural sexuality'. They worshipped the prostitute as the one and only real, that is to say sexual, woman. Sexuality to them was not a threat to civilization; on the contrary, culture had had a baneful influence on sexuality from which it should be liberated as quickly as possible. Because women were the epitome of sexuality they fought for the sexual liberation of women. Kraus was furious about the 'Hetzjagd auf das Weib'. Sexual hypocrisy and 'Männermoral' were heavily criticized in his Fackel.[20] Kraus studied vice cases and called the judges and plaintiffs sinners in robes. The newspapers wrote extensively about these court cases as well. The personal data of the accused, names, addresses, testimonies of the witnesses, and gossip from the galleries, everything was published. Kraus accused the legal authorities of openly and systematically humiliating the socially powerless, women in particular. He accused the press of limitless hypocrisy ('Die Presse als Kupplerin') and called the court cases deliberate indecencies that far overshadowed the offences of the accused. And there were many court cases. The authorities had their work cut out for them with all the unwilling subjects who threatened public morals in all possible ways, thereby undermining the roots of civilization as a whole.

130

## 2 GOVERNMENT AND PUBLIC MORALS

The most important governmental instrument for the protection of public morals was the vice squad. Its founder in Austria is thought to have been Ferdinand, who governed the German succession states from 1521 and who succeeded Charles V as the Emperor Ferdinand in 1556. His policy was aimed at the protection of the family and his first step in that direction was to impose stiff fines on all married men caught in brothels (*Frauenhäuser*). In 1542 this was followed by a police decree that made prostitution and procuration criminal offences. Ferdinand also ordered the church to protect morals. The believers should be imbued with the necessity of so doing. His successors, however, paid less attention to public morals until Maria Theresa (1740–80) took up the struggle against indecency again. She went much further than Ferdinand. Her measures in the area of indecency contrast sharply with the enlightened policies that characterize the other domains of her policy. During her reign police attention was directed first and foremost at loose women. They were the ones to be punished now. Her determined struggle against indecency reached its peak with the appointment of a Committee for Public Decency. Large-scale treachery and denunciation were the result. Prostitutes were now even employed as *agents provocateurs* in order to expose indecent citizens and lead them into the arms of the police. Conceivably the committee was abolished during the reign of Joseph II (1780–90), Maria Theresa's son, who had little ambition when it came to upgrading his subjects' morals. When his advisers spoke out in favour of placing the brothels under state control he seems to have said: 'If one wished to implement a brothel system, one would have to bring the entire city under one roof.'[21] Grave concern about public morals does not show up until the second half of the nineteenth century. Children born out of wedlock, a decrease in the number of marriages, and an increase in the number of concubines did cause a certain degree of concern, but the government paid far more attention to the problem of prostitution.

From 1850 on, a number of Viennese medical doctors advocated some kind of legislation with regard to prostitution instead of just prohibiting it, following the example of their colleagues in other countries. 'Polizeiwundarzt' Dr Nusser who raised the matter argued that prostitution was a very old phenomenon that could apparently not be eradicated. This unpleasant fact should therefore be faced and proper measures should be taken. The ban on prostitution should be replaced by legislation and control. The close link between prostitution and syphilis was emphasized. In order to restrict the terrible consequences of prostitution it was deemed necessary to subject prostitutes to regular medical examinations. Dr Nusser stated with remarkable frankness that he was in favour of legislation for two reasons, namely to limit the horrible consequences of contamination with syphilis and also to help doctors get work and appropriate pay.[22] Nusser's proposal divided his colleagues into three groups. One agreed with him, the second found his proposals insufficient and argued in favour of '*Kasernierung*' (the obligatory housing of prostitutes in brothels), and the third, a minority, was opposed to any form of legislation for a variety of reasons. They found that acceptance of prostitution was not in keeping with the dignity of the state and they doubted the effects of legislation in principle. The spokesman for this group, Dr Massari, argued that the problem of venereal diseases and the problem of prostitution should be distinguished. The spread of venereal diseases was caused by loose men and women from all layers of society and legislation that did not address these groups would not, in his opinion, be very effective. He proposed sanitary measures instead, such as the extension of the university clinic, obligatory hospitalization for contaminated people, penalties for men who knowingly spread the diseases (only women could be prosecuted for this), and tighter controls within the army. Massari and his followers did not have a great deal of influence, but they addressed problems that their opponents did not wish to face from the very start of the discussion.

Legislation would take another twenty-three years. It was only because of the expected stream of foreign visitors to the World Exhibition in 1873 that a type of pass law was introduced. The police first opposed any form of legislation. They had their own way of keeping moral law and order, separate from all discussion in medical circles. The female sex, which, in the bigger cities, more or less surrendered to the extra-marital satisfaction of the libido, was seen as the main problem. A very detailed policy statement from the police dating from 1851 states that the following women are a threat to public morals:

1. *the normal prostitutes*, who earn their living from prostitution
2. *the occasional prostitutes*, recruited from the ranks of seamstresses, dressmakers, dancers and other theatre performers and
further from factory girls, servants etc. The occasional prostitutes usually turn into category 1, ordinary prostitutes
3. mistresses
4. concubines[23]

Of interest are the police criteria with respect to the occasional
prostitutes: they are women who were seduced by presents or
invitations to satisfy the sexual needs of men without prospects or
intention of marriage, but they did not associate with just any
man, nor would they necessarily make prostitution their profession. In other words, every woman engaged in an extra-marital
relationship was a whore or in any case an occasional prostitute.
In contrast to all the learned gentlemen who were convinced of the
slight sexual needs of respectable women, the police knew better.
Occasional prostitutes were also those women who agreed to sexual
relationships without accepting presents or money, but merely for
the satisfaction of their immoral instincts. These women could be
found in all layers of society: debauched daughters, unfaithful
wives, and lecherous widows. Some even went so far as to seek out
men and pay them![24] It is clear that the police had an insight
into the hidden lives of the citizens that no other government body
could match, and a know-how encompassing just about everything
humanly possible. It was a good thing that many loose and sinful
daughters, wives, and widows managed to stay out of the hands
of the police, otherwise the enormous apparatus would have been
in need of even further extension.

When medical examinations were finally introduced the government was very careful not to legislate 'the evil practice'. Prostitution was still banned, but a prostitute under medical control was
not punished. Housing prostitutes who practised their profession at
home remained illegal. As a consequence the prostitutes had to
pay exorbitant rents. Also other forms of exploitation and
blackmail were made possible due to contradictions in the law, and
of course the prostitutes were the victims of this.

### The woman-hunt

At the end of the nineteenth century the number of prostitutes in

Vienna was estimated to be between 30,000 and 50,000. Two thousand were – voluntarily or not – placed under medical control. All female prison inmates, including those not involved in any indecency offence, got a pass and were registered as prostitutes. The women who had voluntarily placed themselves under control were so harassed by the police commissioners that they withdrew.[25] There was almost no way back for women who were registered. The police 'guarded' them, which virtually excluded the possibility of another job or of marriage.

The police knew very well that only a small number of prostitutes would be reached in this manner. Therefore they started a witch-hunt for the 'hidden' prostitute. As is clear from the policy statement of the 1850s, all women in extra-marital sexual relationships were considered prostitutes. Since women's appearance does not indicate whether or not they engage in these practices, all women were suspect. The implications of the law were therefore not so much its consequences for prostitution – many prostitutes stayed out of the hands of the police anyway – but rather its consequences for all women. Every woman who aroused suspicion could be arrested and forced to undergo a medical examination.

> Policemen enter the woman's question and fulfil their great cultural mission! They clarify to the Viennese women that every one of them is under the protection of the vice squad.[26]

This was the conclusion of one editor of *Dokumente der Frauen*. The regularity with which the police mistakenly arrested respectable women to have them medically examined caused quite a commotion. Kraus criticized the hypocrisy of this type of indignation in his *Fackel*:

> When the bourgeoisie cries out when the vice squad by mistake brutalizes an 'honourable woman' they merely get a taste of their own legal medicine. One should be outraged by the practice in general, not just by the mistakes, and every 'painful' incident that angers the decent citizen but shows the ordinary beastly treatment of the prostitute, should be welcomed.[27]

Kraus was disgusted by the indignation when an upper-class woman was arrested. He wholeheartedly supported the fact that the bourgeoisie had to swallow a taste of their own medicine, so to speak. But he forgot that the victims of the zealous efforts of the government to raise the moral standards of the citizen were almost exclusively women. It was not the bourgeoisie as a whole that suffered from the vice squad's diligence. Men were never arrested for leading someone on, or for being clients or prostitutes themselves. Men would have trouble with the police only if they tried to defend a woman in their company when she was bothered by the police. If the man in question was a gentleman protecting the woman because she was a member of his family, his servant, or his mistress, then the woman would be relatively fortunate. She was examined in a very humiliating manner, but no further steps would be taken. Far less fortunate were those women who could not count on this type of protection because of their lower-class background or their single status. They were not only arrested but also brought to court. An anonymous accusation would suffice. Here are a couple from many examples:

– a pretty young actress, temporarily out of work, was accused of secret prostitution. The police acted, the actress was taken into custody, all her neighbours were summoned before the court to testify. The caretaker of the house who defended the accused was threatened with arrest by the police commissioner, and the actress was, despite the favourable accounts of all witnesses, sentenced to 48 hours in detention.[28]

– a young girl was reported to the police for leaving her house late in the mornings, wearing striking clothes, and coming home late at night. Her friendly neighbours responsible for doing this to her told the judge that the girl had previously had an older lover. This was immediately taken as an aggravating circumstance. The court case had to be adjourned for the collection of further damaging evidence, because the caretaker maintained that he knew nothing of the late hours of the accused. The prosecutor advised him in a threatening manner to start paying more attention.[29]

The police also used *agents provocateurs* who accosted and invited women on the streets. If a woman responded she was arrested then and there. A week in prison was guaranteed.[30] Because the police suspected vice and hidden prostitution all over, they also made inquiries about men who received women in their homes. A young man complained in the *Fackel* that the police had demanded

information from him. They had received an anonymous tip that
he received lady visitors, which the police informer – undoubtedly
a neighbour – saw as a cause of public nuisance. The police
wanted the name(s) and address(es) of the lady or ladies in order
to investigate whether or not this was a case of hidden prostitution. The young man refused to give this information and was
duly informed that he would be brought to court for this.[31]

A woman who was found in a hotel with someone other than
her husband could, in extreme cases, even be forced to register as
a prostitute, even if she had never accepted money or the man was
her lover.[32]

It is clear that the vice squad was happy to go to any lengths
in order to keep the sexual activities of the citizen under whatever
control they could. The police force itself was, however, frequently
unfaithful to its own high ideals, as was demonstrated in the sensa-
tional court case against Regine Riehl in 1906. The prostitutes
who worked for Madam Riehl under deplorable circumstances had
frequently wanted to file complaints but were always ignored by
the police, who 'could not spend time on futilities like that' or
found their complaints 'childish nonsense'.[33] Before the court
these police officers claimed that it was their duty to protect society
from prostitution and not to protect prostitutes from their madam.
Madam Riehl fully appreciated this approach: her girls were
ordered to be very pleasant towards the officers of the vice squad,
and, needless to say, the gentlemen did not have to pay.[34]

Apart from the diligent government officials social control
played a major role. Secrecy was not the only prerequisite; many
other aspects had to be taken into account as well.

## 3 EROTIC DILEMMAS?

During the course of our conversation the question arose what
a young man ought to do to avoid a conflict with the demands
of morality, society or hygiene. Seduction and divorce being
illegal and dangerous, affairs with 'kokotten' and actresses
dubious and expensive. Then there were the sort of decent girls,
who had left the straight and narrow path, but with whom one
could get stuck, just like with women one seduced. That only
left the 'Dirnen' which, even if one succeeded in protecting one's
health, meant a fairly offensive situation. And I asked my father

for advice in this matter. My father refused to enter into a discussion about this, but with a slight gesture he remarked simply and obscurely: 'One settles these things.'[35]

It is almost impossible to formulate the sexual problems of a young gentleman more clearly than Arthur Schnitzler did in his childhood memories. He mentions the possibilities including the risks. He himself, however, succeeded admirably in finding a solution to the dilemma stated above, without missing out on any one category of women mentioned. Of course many young gentlemen were less successful than the young doctor and poet, but it would seem that the majority of the young men of his class succeeded in solving 'the sexual question' by themselves and to their satisfaction. Naturally there could be no complete sexual freedom for men either, as is shown by the measures against homosexuals. Men of the lower classes were more limited in their options than the gentlemen because the women of higher classes were taboo to them, yet they had many possibilities with women from their own or lower classes.

The greatest risk for men in general – apart from the sexually transmitted diseases, which were a risk to both sexes – was the obligation to pay maintenance for an illegitimate child. In Austria the law had always allowed for paternity orders against the father, but the maintenance payments ordered by the judges were relatively small, certainly in comparison with the burden and costs facing the mother. An illegitimate child did taint the reputation of a man, but far less so than in the case of a woman. Only 'fallen' women could exist. Men, regardless of social class, could never be 'fallen'. Their social position was never dependent on their sexual conduct alone.

For the young woman of the upper classes different rules applied. She was expected to enter marriage, usually with an older man, as a virgin. Her need for love and romance could be expressed after the event, if she had the courage to do so. The bourgeois lady had her romances with young men from her class who were not yet in a position to marry. This was not always free from danger, because if the husband was jealous she risked losing her marriage and social position. It was also a risk to the lover, since he could be challenged to a duel. The biographies of Viennese men of the period indicate that quite a number of women were prepared to take the risk. But undoubtedly there were also women like Stefan Zweig's aunt, who fled back to her parents' house on her wedding night, because her husband, in an apparent state of madness, had made an attempt to undress her.[36] This was the exception rather than the rule, however.

Women from the lower classes had more freedom than the daughters of high birth, but at the same time they were less protected. The rules of the sex game varied according to class. Men from the upper classes could permit themselves far more when dealing with lower-class women than they could with women from their own class. A good example of the problems facing women from the lower middle class is that of Marie Chlum-Glümer. Her father was a government employee in a ministry. After his early demise the family was rather well provided for and his daughters had reasonable prospects. But Marie made mistakes. She let herself be seduced. Because her lover wanted to marry her and rectify *her* indiscretion there was no real problem yet. Then she made an even greater mistake: she fell in love with someone else and broke off the engagement. But now she had fallen into the 'wrong' hands. Her lover told his drinking mates with pride about his little girlfriend and about the fact that he did not risk getting stuck with her since she was, after all, no longer a virgin. His opinion was that 'a decent man only gets involved with girls like that, because he is without obligation'.[37] When he had had enough of her, and because he also wanted to get married, he passed her on to his friend Schnitzler. And once again Marie was unlucky. Schnitzler knew everything about her 'past'. According to official morality she was a fallen woman who could only be passed from hand to hand: '*Freiwild*' at the age of 16. Although Schnitzler loved her inasmuch as he was capable of so doing, he was about the last man on earth who could 'forgive' a woman two previous lovers. He himself had of course had numerous affairs before he met Marie, but he could not get over his 'grief about not being the first' with her. He was a great poet capable of formulating even the most trivial thoughts in elegant words. He presents his emotions after his first night with Marie in a play:

Beträchtlich stört mein junges Liebesglück,
Dass Dich ein anderer hat vor mir besessen,
Ich kann es leider nimmermehr vergessen,

Auf jenem andern glühte dieser Blick.
Und wenn Du Deinen süssen Leib allnächtlich
In wilden Liebesseufzern smiegst an mich,
Denk ich, auch jener hörte Dich wie ich
Und Du begreifst mein Kind, das stört beträchtlich.[38]

But Schnitzler had overestimated Marie's capacities for understanding him. To her it was far from self-evident that her sexual experience excluded the possibility of marriage. So he explained:

Suppose I marry you and introduce you to society . . . where it could certainly happen that in the Salon where I introduce you as my wife, we encounter a man who has held you in his arms, a man who has thrown you on the bed and possessed you while your mother was in the kitchen, a man who, when we leave the Salon, could smirk and think – I have enjoyed that one too, before him – and I was not the first either! . . . I do not know whether you are so blind that you really cannot see the horror of it all, but to believe that one can meet a former lover of one's wife and simply get over that fact, would mean that one is simply out of one's mind.[39]

Marie could be his *Verhältnis*, but never his wife. He could not introduce someone like her to his sister! Now that marriage had become impossible, Marie was forced to seek an occupation. She became an actress. This only complicated her relationship with Schnitzler. When he found out that she had been unfaithful to him (he had had relationships with other women from the start) he called her 'The lowest creature under the sun'.[40] That was the end of their affair.

The daughters of artisans and skilled labourers were very popular as friends of young gentlemen. Thus the girls were free to amuse themselves with the 'fine' young men and later marry someone of their own kind. 'In the city they are loved, in the suburb they are married.'[41] They could be addressed on the streets and be invited. The fine gentlemen brought a bit of glamour into the lives of these women of humble origins. They gave nice presents and had elegant homes in which they could spend quiet and pleasant hours, or they visited a *chambre séparée*, all kinds of things that would normally be outside the young woman's reach. The men appreciated these relationships because they were without problems, did not cause great scenes, did not involve any risks or complications, and could be ended as simply as they had begun. The 'return' of the women to their own kind was not always wholly unproblematic. If a woman managed to marry a man from her own class who would be willing to forget her 'past' she could become a respectable woman. But if no marriage was forthcoming, the *Süsse Mädel* turned into a woman of questionable reputation and started her social downfall. Lower middle-class women were always dependent on others for their material wellbeing: family, lover, or husband. They could not survive on their own income as seamstresses, salesgirls, etc. Women from the proletariat often found lovers in their own class. They were relatively free in sexual matters and starting relationships was not very difficult, given the circumstances of proletarian life. Small, overcrowded houses, bedrooms where strangers sometimes had to share one bed, contacts in the factory, all provided ample opportunity for starting relationships, whether long or short. A child was not so much a scandal, but rather a cause for marriage. Young working girls suffered more sexual abuse than the women from the higher classes. They were entirely at the mercy of the overseers, who determined who would get the nicest and best-paid jobs, not to mention the bosses. Furthermore they were often seen as prostitutes, because women from the lower classes knew no restraint, right?

## CONCLUSIONS

Ideas about sexuality cannot be examined without reference to the social relations between the sexes. In a time where there is 'a women's question' which is the focus of heated debate, there is confusion and disagreement about the place of women in society. The social position of women is directly related to that of men and the relation between the sexes can thus be characterized as 'disturbed'. Strindberg spoke of 'the battle between the sexes'. 'Scientific' excesses such as Weininger's say something about the fierceness and determination of the discussion about sexuality and the relations between men and women. The participants in this discussion are never independent or objective in their investigations, but always parties involved in the fight. Gender determines a human being's background as much as class, race, or religion.

The dominant theories were constructed by men, and the critics – often men as well – emphasized this with remarks like '*Männerstandpunkt*' (male perspective) or '*den Männer-interessen dienend*' (serving the interests of men).

The government's endeavours were to a large extent aimed at controlling sexuality through women. In practice this meant that the sexual behaviour of women should be brought under as much control as possible; by the father, the husband, or, when they were absent or absent-minded, by the police. Vagueness and contradictions in the laws on morals allowed for arbitrary and high-handed police actions, which caused problems for a number of women. Despite this the majority of men and women circumvented formal morals and had more or less secret sexual relationships. The class-specific character of sexual morals meant that greater freedom also implied greater risks for women, as is demonstrated in particular by the weak position of working-class women.

Translation: Women's Translation Collective De Bron, Amsterdam: Rita Gircour

## NOTES

1 Lilian Berna-Simons, *Weibliche Identität und Sexualität. Das Bild der Weiblichkeit im 19. Jahrhundert und in Sigmund Freud*, Frankfurt am Main, 1984, 154.
2 Robert Michels, *Sittlichkeit in Ziffern? Kritik der Moralstatistik*, Munich/Leipzig, 1928, 47.
3 Ibid., 48.
4 *Zur Geschichte einer Petition gegen die Errichtung öffentlicher Häuser in Wien. Protokoll der Frauenversammlung vom 20. Februar 1897 im alten Wiener Rathause*, Vienna, 1897, 25.
5 Ibid., 27.
6 Michael Buchberger (ed.), *Lexikon für Theologie und Kirche*, Freiburg im Breisgau, 1936, 506.
7 *Theologisch-praktische Quartalschrift*, Linz, 1900, 289.
8 Ibid., 295.
9 Augustin Rösler, *Die Frauenfrage vom Standpunkte der Natur, der Geschichte und der Offenbarung*, Vienna, 1893, 6.
10 Ibid.
11 Rosa Mayreder, *Zur Kritik der Weiblichkeit*, reprinted Munich, 1982.
12 Ibid., 48.
13 Sigrid Schmid and Hanna Schnedl, *Totgeschwiegen. Texte zur Situation der Frau von 1880 bis in die Zwischenkriegszeit*, Vienna, 1982.

14 Marielouise Janssen-Jurreit, *Frauen und Sexualmoral*, Frankfurt am Main, 1986, 86.
15 Ibid., 87.
16 Nike Wagner, *Geist und Geschlecht. Karl Kraus und die Erotik der Wiener Moderne*, Frankfurt am Main, 1982, 75.
17 Ibid., 71.
18 Ibid.
19 Ibid., 159.
20 Karl Kraus, *Sittlichkeit und Kriminalität*, reprinted Frankfurt am Main, 1966, 35.
21 H. Montane (Franz Höfberger), *Die Prostitution in Wien. Ihre Geschichte und Entwicklung von den Anfängen bis zur Gegenwart*, Hamburg/Leipzig/Vienna, 1925, 32.
22 J. Schrank, *Die Prostitution in Wien in historischer, administrativer und hygienischer Beziehung*, II, Vienna, 1886, 22.
23 Ibid., 20–1.
24 Ibid., 21.
25 Montane, *Die Prostitution*, 70.
26 Emma Kancler, 'Die österreichische Frauenbewegung und ihre Presse. Von ihren Anfängen bis zum ende des 1. Weltkrieges', Phil. Diss., Vienna, 1947.
27 Kraus, *Sittlichkeit*, 37.
28 Ibid., 35.
29 Ibid., 225–6.
30 Ibid., 337.
31 Ibid., 262.
32 Elga Kern, *Wie sie dazu kamen. Lebensfragmente bordellierter Mädchen*, Munich/Basle, 1928, Darmstadt/Neuweid, 1985; Otto Rühle, *Illustrierte Kultur- und Sittengeschichte des Proletariats*, 2 vols, Giessen, 1977; Otto Henne am Rhyn, *Die Gebrechen und Sünden der Sittenpolizei. Vorzüglich der Gegenwart*, Leipzig, 1893.
33 Kraus, *Sittlichkeit*, 226–50.
34 Ibid.
35 Wagner, *Geist*, 93–4.
36 Stefan Zweig, *Die Welt von Gestern. Erinnerungen eines Europäers*, reprinted Frankfurt am Main, 1979, 66.
37 Renate Wagner, *Frauen um Arthur Schnitzler*, Frankfurt am Main, 1983, 60.
38 Ibid., 63. *Translator's note:* A far less elegantly worded yet no less vulgar rendition of the fragment reads: 'My young love's happiness is quite disturbed / For another possessed you before / Unfortunately I can never forget / That your fiery eyes have rested upon him / And when at night your lovely body touches me / Crying out in the wildest lovers' moans / I think, he too heard you like me / And you understand, my child, that is quite disturbing.'
39 Ibid., 69.
40 Ibid., 76.
41 Ibid., 24.

# 9

# Mannish women of the Balkan mountains:
## Preliminary notes on the 'sworn virgins' in male disguise, with special reference to their sexuality and gender-identity*

*René Grémaux*

One of mankind's most essential distinctions is that between male and female. In spite of this, one occasionally encounters individuals who permanently adopt the dress and behaviour commonly associated with the opposite sex. It may perhaps provoke some astonishment that such an inversion is not restricted to the 'decadence' of urban society but has also existed, and in part still exists today, in more traditional societies. The anthropological information available on the subject is mainly concerned with males who dress and act like females – the Siberian and North American *shamans* and *berdaches* are the outstanding examples; whereas there is a remarkable lack of information about the female-to-male inversion.[1]

It is this latter inversion to which this chapter addresses itself, calling the reader's attention to an interesting custom (oddly rather neglected in international anthropological literature) found among the North Albanians, Montenegrins, and some other ethnic groups in the western Balkans. Unmarried, ideally virginal females who wear male attire, perform men's work, and enjoy, at least to some extent, public recognition as males, have been reported time and time again since the first half of the nineteenth century. Most descriptions of this peculiar practice date back to the turn of our century and concern the area through which the present-day Yugoslav–Albanian frontier runs. Despite considerable linguistic, religious, and other differences, the population of these inhospitable mountains shared until recently a patriarchal warrior-culture and a particular form of tribal organization. Although the numerous tribes have by now lost their autonomy and pacification has gained momentum, local people, especially the old, still cling to a wide variety of archaic values, beliefs, and customs.

In exploring the vast ethnographic literature on this part of South-East Europe (mainly written in Serbo-Croat), I have to date come across more than seventy cases of females who lived their lives, or most of their lives, as males. In my fieldwork in Yugoslavia during the summers of 1985, 1986, and 1987, I had the opportunity to meet personally two of the very few surviving masculine 'sworn virgins' and to gather additional information among people who happened to know them well. For those who are now dead, I have relied on interviews with relatives, friends, and acquaintances.

I begin this chapter with four typical case histories, to some extent based on my own field research, which show the gradual extinction of this phenomenon as a socially recognized institution during the course of the twentieth century. This is followed by a discussion of the sexuality and gender identity of those who belong to this category. Here I focus on two interrelated questions: how do they relate sexually to men and women, and to what extent do they actually identify themselves with the male gender?

## I CASE HISTORIES

### Case One: Mikas

In 1885, the Serbian doctor Jovanovic-Batut reported his strange encounter with Mikas Milicev Karadzic, a 22-year-old soldier in the Montenegrin village of Zabljak. Before examining the assembled soldiers, the doctor was told that Mikas was a 'wonder of the world'. Nevertheless, he was unable to discover anything special about him during the course of a superficial examination in the open air, together with his companions in arms. To his great surprise the doctor was afterwards informed by the commander and the captain that Mikas, whom he considered a 'strong lad', was in fact a girl who had originally been called Milica. Her father, a celebrated hero, had been killed in a battle when she was still very small and she was his only child.

The commander explained as follows:

What could the poor widow do without a male head of the household? In order to console herself she dressed Milica as a man and gave her the new name Mikas. The child got used

144

to it, and later even did not wish it otherwise. With the boys she played, with the boys she tended the sheep, and nobody was allowed to mention that she was not a boy. When her comrades put on a belt with arms, she did not want to remain deprived of them either. Riding on horseback, jumping, shooting a rifle and throwing stones at targets . . . all with them, and all like them as well.

Asked whether the mother and the nearest kin approved of this, the commander answered affirmatively. Their initial expectation that Mikas's tomboy behaviour would end with adulthood was proved false. When she grew up, she did not turn to skirts and distaffs, but continued to work, and to have fun, in the company of males. To the Karadzic clan, however, Mikas was a great embarrassment. The clan advised and reprimanded her, but in vain: 'The more strongly they did so, the more stubborn she became: instead of becoming a real woman she would rather lose her head.'

After listening with disbelief, the doctor sent for Mikas. Behind closed doors and with no one else present, Mikas admitted she was a girl. Her comrades, she said, treated her as their equal, and obtrusive boys had long since stopped being a nuisance to her. Woe betide anyone who dared to mock her! Such a person, she declared convincingly, 'pays with his head'.

Questioned by the doctor about the way she hid her menses (*zenski cvijet*, literally 'women's flower') in the company of men, she denied having them: 'I do not have that. At the age of 13 for some months but afterwards never.' 'Hearing this', the doctor writes, 'was enough for me. I realized that her entire nature had changed.' He added: 'Was this by strong will, or has it come about by force of habit?' Because he thought Mikas to be on the wrong track with much personal trouble ahead, the doctor in a fatherly way admonished her to change her life. But Mikas turned a deaf ear to his words, and expressed her determination to stick to her masculine way of life. Saying farewell to Mikas the doctor cried a little out of sorrow for this 'wretched creature'.[2]

Mikas continued her particular way of life and was observed towards the end of the 1920s by Marijana Gusic, an ethnographer from Croatia. Arriving at Mikas's log cabin, Gusic was given anything but a kind welcome by the aged inhabitant. 'He' refused to receive her and reproached a fellow tribesman: 'Why are you bringing me this stranger-woman?' The ethnographer's husband, however, was not sent away. As a male he was allowed to sit with Mikas in front of the little cabin and to take pictures. Local people still recall Mikas as a person with a great distrust of strangers, who allowed only kinsmen and neighbours to enter her dwelling.

Unable to interview Mikas, Gusic had to rely on information provided by relatives and neighbours. According to them, Milica was 'masculinized out of sorrow', not so much by her young widowed mother, as Jovanovic-Batut's informants claimed, as by her deceased husband's mother. To this I can add that my own informants agreed upon the decisive role played by the grandmother. Gusic also heard that Milica was proclaimed a boy and renamed Mikas (a masculine form of Milica, Milojka, Mika) 'in order to prevent the house, the hearth and the candle from being extinguished'. In this way the girl could act in succession to her famous father.

Probably around 1880, the chieftains of three clans of Jezera (a division of the Drobnjak tribe) put the problem of Mikas to the Orthodox bishop Visarion Ljubisa, when he visited Zabljak. This high traditional authority in both religious and secular matters, according to Gusic, talked with Mikas and instructed that no one should ever insult her in any way. Although the bishop approved of Mikas's masculinity, he still limited her male prerogatives by saying: 'Mikas, never drink brandy, because it might bring shame to you and your house.' Jovanovic-Batut, too, was informed about the bishop's intervention in the Mikas case, at the request of the 'poor' Karadzic clan. Yet according to his information it was ineffective, since Mikas avoided every confrontation with this authority. However, oral tradition today claims that Mikas's special status was sanctioned by the three clans of the Jezera at the intercession of an Orthodox bishop whom she met personally.

In the local vernacular, Gusic goes on to inform us, Mikas was labelled either *ostajnica* ('she who stays', i.e. an unwed female who replaces in her father's house the lacking male heir), or *muskobanja* (manlike woman). Her status required everlasting virginity; violation of this taboo would have called for her death by stoning.

Towards the end of the 1920s, at the time of Gusic's unfortunate visit, Mikas was living alone. In spite of her considerable age she still performed all the hard tasks of a man, such as mowing, hay-stacking, ploughing, and harvesting. She also prepared and cooked her own meals, but refrained from exclusively feminine tasks like handiwork. Female relatives and neighbours performed these tasks for 'him' out of charity, or for a small payment. When Mikas, or 'Mikasu', was addressed by females they used terms such as *djever* (husband's brother), *svekar* (father-in-law), and *kum* (godfather; elderly man). Every November, Mikas celebrated, as a genuine son of her clan, the feast of the Archangel Michael. As master of the house, Mikas received numerous guests, in whose presence 'he' lighted the ceremonial candle and performed other ritual acts which were normally strictly reserved for males. By visiting and congratulating Mikas on this occasion the community paid tribute to 'him' as the descendant of the late Milic Karadzic. In official documents she was registered under the male name Mikas Milicev Karadzic, which enabled her, for instance, to vote in parliamentary elections at a time when female suffrage was non-existent.

In the late 1920s Mikas was living in reduced circumstances, owing to several successive dry, infertile years. Three cows and some land was all that was left of her initially much bigger patrimony. I was told that Mikas in her younger years owned a good deal of fertile land and a flock of fifty sheep of the best quality. Cattle-breeding and cattle-trading occupied her so much that she was forced to lease out her arable land for sharecropping. Gusic describes the aged Mikas as an unhappy, mentally deranged person with clearly visible misogynous and misanthropic traits. In the opinion of the ethnographer, the enforced celibacy and male role were to blame for this. The high status Mikas enjoyed in the local community was too small a compensation for her 'unnatural' way of life.[3]

When I visited Jezera, I learned that several old people still have a vivid memory of Mikas, who died more than half a century ago. All my informants stressed Mikas's striking masculinity in spirit, appearance, and behaviour, as well as her fierce insistence on being treated and respected as a genuine male, which seems to have been her main task in life. Though they doubted Mikas's claim of not having monthly periods, women – including the one who washed her during her final illness – had noticed extremely ill-developed breasts, a condition caused, they said, by tying them up.

Mikas is said to have always used the male gender when talking about herself,[4] and her general way of speaking and her voice must also have been quite manlike. Talking about Mikas, my informants alternately used 'he' and 'she', as was also observed by Gusic when Mikas was still alive. In her presence, however, nobody would have had the insolence to call her a woman, though everyone in Jezera knew that she was a female by nature. Feelings of reverence, but also of fear, prevented them from doing so. Mikas's utmost sensitivity to even the slightest defilement of her much cherished manliness was well known, and her resoluteness to avenge such an indecency, too. Being called by female names like Milica or Mika outraged her very much, and induced her to throw stones at the evil-doer or to punch the top of his head with her *cibuk* (a long Turkish pipe). One expression in particular would stir her fury beyond all limits: 'Mika-puklaca', which related her female name to an obscene word for female genitals. Such an insult would cause her to draw her pistol and fire without compassion. It was above all young people, fond of teasing, who nicknamed her 'Mika-puklaca', but they had to reckon with her bullets if it reached her ears. Meanwhile 'puklaca' has become obsolete in Jezera, but the combination 'Mika-puklaca' is still a winged word among youngsters nowadays, even among those who have never heard the story of Mika-Mikas.

Mikas used her masculinity in a far from opportunistic way, as is shown by the following tragi-comic event which occurred in 1916 when the tiny kingdom of Montenegro was occupied by the Austrian army. Mikas happened to be among the numerous soldiers who fell into the hands of the enemy. With resignation she awaited deportation with the other prisoners-of-war to Austria, but this was prevented by the intervention of Vasilije Pipovic, her first neighbour, who was fully aware that she would never disclose her femininity in order to be released. He applied to the *Wachtmeister* on duty and informed him about Mikas's true sex, upon which she was promptly released. According to one version of this story the Austrian refused to believe that Mikas was a woman until she was forced to show what her clothes hid.

Females used to kiss Mikas's hand submissively, as they were expected to do whenever they met a venerable elderly male. Friends presented her with coffee and tobacco, since she was a great 'coffee-lover' and 'tobacco-lover'. Like a male, she used to smoke the *cibuk* and to drink coffee without sugar. Her favourite pastime was to sit in one of the Zabljak inns. Though she was referred to as a *pasalija*, i.e. someone who enjoys life like the men in the company of a Turkish pasha, she is said to have spent her lifetime without any sexual intercourse – she did not want anything to do with males. In her younger days, it is said, a reckless youth made an attempt to assault Mikas indecently when she was asleep, upon which she immediately reacted by drawing her inseparable pistol. With women too – whom she overtly treated with contempt – she did not have intimate relations, though she was not totally indifferent to their beauty. She is said to have expressed in the company of men her eagerness for touching females in a lascivious way. She once, so a woman told me, grasped with passion the legs of a girl sitting next to her and paid the girl compliments on her charm. According to this informant, Mikas was physically attracted to females, but had never been able to have a woman like ordinary males. 'Poor Mikas!' she concluded. Referring to her youth the aged Mikas once sighed, 'When we were boys', the local shoemaker told me cheerfully.

In June 1933, the sick and weakened Mikas was carried on the back of an ox from her home to the house of Muso (Milutin) Baranin, to spend her last days in the care of Jelena Simicevic, Muso's young bride. As Mikas's father's sister's grandson, Muso was the heir presumptive. I was told by the widowed Jelena that she used to call Mikas *svekar* (father-in-law) or *strika* (from *stric*, meaning father's brother, elderly man), and that she herself was called *snaha* (daughter-in-law, sister-in-law) by 'him'. Feeling her end drawing near, Mikas called Jelena, whom she seemed to have loved in spite of her general attitude towards females, and said in a deep, dark, masculine voice, '*Snaha*, please do not disgrace me!' for she was deadly afraid of being buried in female dress. Mikas gave her money and sent her to the tailor in Zabljak to buy a proper outfit for the last journey. Jelena did what she was asked and bought her a new costume consisting of white socks, woollen trousers, a vest, and a cap. When Mikas passed away in the autumn of 1934 she was actually dressed in this manly costume, and, with the approval of the Orthodox priest, Bogdan Cerovic, buried like a man in the Zabljak churchyard.

## Case Two: Tonë

On 17 June 1971 the cemetery of Tuzi, close to the Albanian border in Montenegro, was the scene of the funeral of Tonë Bikaj, a *virgjinéshë* (sworn virgin) wearing male dress, born exactly seventy years previously. Fifteen years later I paid a visit to the village where she had spent the last decades of her life with Gjelosh, a brother much younger than she. On that occasion, Gjelosh proudly told me the fascinating story of Tonë's life.[5]

Tonë was born in the predominantly Catholic Kelmënd tribe of the highlands of adjacent North Albania. She was the first child of Tom Lule Bikaj and his wife Katarinë. Her parents' wedding had been delayed by twelve years, since Bikaj was arrested for taking part in the armed struggle against Turkish rule in Albania. The death sentence originally passed on him was commuted to long-term penal servitude in faraway Anatolia.

Tonë's birth was followed by the birth of two sons and two daughters. However, both sons – the pride and joy of every patriarchal family – succumbed at an early age to the much-feared endemic malaria. Left without brothers, Tonë decided at about the age of 9 years to become the son and brother her parents and sisters needed so much. She promised never to marry and exchanged her girl's clothes for a boy's. Instead of the female tasks she used to perform at her mother's side, she started to help her father with male tasks. This radical change, however, was not completed by the adoption of a masculine name.[6]

The decision to behave like a boy pleased her parents very much. When he visited peasants in the neighbourhood, the father proudly introduced his 'new son' to them. Like all the other sons in these unsafe mountains, Tonë received weapons from her father's hands when she reached the age of 15. A happy event occurred in the Bikaj family when Tonë was 20 years of age: the 49-year-old mother gave birth to a son, who was given the name Gjelosh. For little Gjelosh, Tonë performed the role of the older brother who would look after him and protect him in times of trouble – all the more necessary because of the advancing age of the parents. As the years passed, Tonë succeeded in changing her voice, her way of speaking, her posture and manners to such a degree that it was hard to distinguish her from a male. Her tribe recognized and honoured her as a man. When her sisters reached the nubile age, they were handed over to their grooms by Tonë, who acted in this respect just like an older brother.

The attitude Tonë displayed at the end of the Second World War, when the communist victory was on its way in Albania, may serve as a proof of her fighting spirit. Together with her brother, she joined the nationalist guerrilla movement in her native area. Tonë, who was in command of an all-male resistance fighters' unit, was forced to surrender after a three-month struggle, and so was her brother. In the mean time their mother, who had actively supported the resistance by providing food, was shot by a people's commissar for refusing to co-operate in persuading the guerrillas to agree to a cease-fire.

Tonë's surrender was followed by an imprisonment which lasted more than a year. During this confinement, she was deeply upset at being treated as a woman and being separated from her comrades. When finally in 1951 Gjelosh was released, both he and Tonë – their father had died immediately after the war – ventured to cross the Albanian border illegally. This hazardous enterprise turned out well, and both arrived on Yugoslav territory safe and sound. Completely destitute, they settled among the Grudë, a Catholic Albanian tribe in Montenegro close to the Albanian border. In this new environment they founded a communal household headed by Tonë. In her quality of *zot shtëpie* (master of the house) she received guests and participated in traditional all-male gatherings. At her brother's wedding in 1953 she acted as *vëllam*, i.e. the male (commonly the groom's father, uncle, or brother) who goes for the bride and leads her to the groom. Tonë continued to live with Gjelosh and his wife, and the couple's children used to call Tonë respectfully *babá* (father). The acceptance of Tonë as a male within the family seems to have been so complete that some members, at least, were ignorant of her female sex. 'It was only after his death that I realized Uncle Tonë had in fact been a woman,' a young man of about 25 years old told me.

Gjelosh's earnings as a carpenter in nearby Titograd allowed them to buy some land and build a house. Tonë mainly stayed in the village during the years that her brother commuted. Outdoors she performed exclusively tasks which were in accordance with her male status, like the heavy and prestigious mowing and hay-stacking. Indoors she occupied herself with cooking and the preparation of meals, but not with womanly handicraft. Initially the house and land were registered in the name of Tonë, but by the late 1950s this was changed in favour of her brother Gjelosh. Her retreat from the position of master of the house, however, was just a formality: in real terms nothing changed. Tonë remained in charge of the house and continued to take part in gatherings of the male heads of households. Her brother, who had gradually become a successful farmer and all-round craftsman, always escorted Tonë to these meetings with pride.

Among the Albanians living on the Montenegrin side of the border Tonë gained a considerable popularity as a singer and musician, and many people I met remember her as such. Like a genuine male she used to sing 'mountaineer songs', holding one hand behind the ear, and she performed other traditional songs accompanying herself on the *lahutë* or *gusle*, a bow-and-string instrument. One of them sang the praises of a beauty from her native soil beyond the frontier. In addition to this, she was known to be a good player of the *fyell*, an end-blown flute. Singing and making music for an audience including males, activities which were traditionally considered improper for females, used to be a kind of speciality of many an Albanian sworn virgin.[7]

Unlike her experience with Mikas, Gusic was given a warm welcome by Tonë when she visited her in 1960. In her opinion Tonë was a pleasant and satisfied person, who was thoroughly enjoying the high esteem allotted to her both by the family and by the wider community. Gusic found no trace of the psychological mutilation which she discerned in Mikas.[8]

Tonë's death in 1971 was preceded by three years of serious illness, during which people often paid her visits. Among those who stood at her bedside were several Franciscan nuns, with whom she felt a strong bond both as a pious Catholic and as a virgin. In accordance with her will she was buried in the antiquated male costume she used to wear on special occasions. At the funeral a photograph taken some years before, of Tonë wearing that costume, figured on top of the coffin (Plate 15). At the cemetery some men, relatives and friends of the deceased, wanted to start the *vajtim*, a traditional impromptu lamentation or funeral oration in verse, but were kept from performing it. The custom of the local Grudë tribe allegedly did not allow a female to be publicly lamented by males. Gjelosh still feels sorry that in this way Tonë was deprived of the last honours of a man, to which she was entitled according to the customs of the native Kelmënd tribe.

### Case Three: Stana

In a small mountain village of central Montenegro lives Stana Cerovic, who dresses and behaves like a man. Although everyone there knows that she is not a male, she counts as a distinguished *domacin*, 'master of the house'. After having heard that Stana, who is now about 50 years of age, appreciated well-intended interest in her special position, of which she is proud, I visited her house in 1986 and again in 1987. On both occasions I was kindly received by Stana's eldest sister Borka, while Stana herself was away with the cattle in the summer pastures. The first time, I could not go out into the vast highland pastures to look for Stana, neither having the time nor being prepared; the second time, I had to refrain from going to see her out of respect since she had recently lost her most beloved sister, Vukosava. They are pictured together in Plate 16.

Stana is, so I was informed by Borka in 1986, the youngest of the five children – all female – of Milivoj Cerovic and his spouse. Two of them married, and the others – Borka, Vukosava, and Stana – stayed unwed and continued to live together in the parental home after the death of their father (1953) and their mother (1958).

As is usual in this region, during the cold season the family occupies a house made of stone in a village in the valley where the arable and meadow land is situated; during the warm season they live in a log cabin in the upland pastures. In the past, when Borka was still a good walker, each of the three unwed sisters used to live in these pastures, where Borka and Vukosava occupied themselves with female tasks such as dairy production and raking, while Stana performed male tasks like mowing, hay-stacking, and the protection of their cattle. In recent years, Stana and Vukosava always worked as brother and sister in the summer pastures, but now a sudden death has deprived Stana of her dedicated companion Vukosava, her dear 'Koka' (hypocoristic of *kokos*, 'hen').

Stana's house is a heroic one. Her father was the grandson of a well-known captain in the Montenegrin army, and a close relative of the legendary Novica Cerovic, famous throughout the Orthodox South Slav lands for his share in the killing of the detested Turkish lord Smail-aga Cengic in 1840. Her father Milivoj was overtaken by disaster when, after the death of Milos, Borka's twin brother who died at the age of 2 months, no more sons were born to him. Without a male child, Milivoj's house, for all its glorious history, would suffer a humiliating decline. To avert still more daughters being born, the fifth was called Stana, a name signifying something like 'Stay!' or 'Stop!' But in spite of all their hopes, no son was born to prevent the extinction of the house, and Stana remained the lastborn. For the purpose of delaying the inevitable fate by one generation the young Stana was encouraged by the parents to adopt the male role. Her father, whose Benjamin she was, used to call her coaxingly 'My son!', and at the age of 5 she was already smoking the left-overs of his tobacco. Borka watched with sorrow as Stana, twelve years younger than she, gradually came to resemble boys in dress and behaviour. 'I considered it unnatural,' Borka confided to me, 'and I have told my parents this time and again, but on every occasion I was given to understand: Let Stana dress and behave as she pleases.' Once it became fully clear that Stana would never marry, nor retreat from her male way of life, Borka and Vukosava decided not to leave their sister alone at home, and thus they stayed single too.[9]

Stana's formal education consisted of eight years attending primary school in the nearby village, where she excelled in mathematics and ball games, as well as in boyish pranks. The grown-up Stana is praised by her eldest sister for her keen mind, diligence, and strength, but she is also characterized as being 'furious'. When it comes to alcohol, Stana holds her own and is even capable of drinking male comrades under the table. Even though she has never adopted a male name herself, she is sometimes called in joke 'Stancane', a peculiar masculine adaptation of Stana.

As a real son of the Montenegrin highlands Stana displays a passion for hunting and shooting. She usually joins the men in the wolf-hunt, though she has no hunting licence. She has been trying for years to obtain one, citing the menace which the increasing number of wolves constitutes to the livestock. As soon as a shooting-club was founded in a neighbouring village, Stana applied for membership, but her request was turned down. Stana is nevertheless an excellent marksman, as she showed at a tournament organized about nine years ago by the club; seeing all the male competitors missing the mark, she abandoned the passive role of spectator and grabbed a rifle, saying that she would give it a try. Much to the dishonour of the competitors Stana's first shot hit the mark.

Towards the end of 1985 the journalist Petar Milatovic managed to interview Stana. From this interview, in which Stana consistently used the male gender while talking about herself, I would like to quote some revealing statements. 'When I grew up I told my father that I would be his son. I took an oath never to marry or to abandon his house as long as I live.' And she added as if she was looking for approval: 'Do I really have to let it happen that after him there won't be anyone in this house to light the fire!' Pointing at a sewing-machine, the reporter provocatively questioned Stana if she was perhaps the one in the house who used it. Indignantly she replied: 'No, really, and it doesn't suit me either . . . I am the master of the house! . . . That is for these two sisters, they potter around it . . .. And they do the milking, of course . . .. That's not for a man. I plough, mow, gather wood.' And, in the context of the rejected request for membership of the shooting-club, 'Most of all I detest being a female . . . nature is mistaken.' She clearly expressed misogyny and denounced women for their chatter and preoccupation with clothing. Instead of 'wasting' her time in female company she preferred to go 'with the men, to have a conversation, to play cards'. When the interview was over, the reporter was informed by an insider about Stana's frequent attendance at the dances in the local cultural centre, where she associates and drinks with the men. On one such occasion she is reported to have said, chuckling, to her companions: 'Oh, if I could somehow drive that daughter of Milovan into a corner . . .. Come across her in seclusion.'[10]

### Case Four: Durgjan

In a Yugoslavian town in the vicinity of the Albanian border resides Durgjan Ibi Gllavolla, a teacher of Albanian extraction, working in a local primary school. In August 1985, at the recommendation of the headmaster, I made my way to a tea room – an outstanding example of a men's space – where Durgjan kills time. When I arrived there, she appeared to be elsewhere, but she showed up as soon as she was informed that a stranger was looking for her. At first glance, it was not quite easy to discern a

155

female in Durgjan, wearing grey trousers and a white shirt, and with a short hair-style. The person's voice, bearing, and movements further strengthened the masculine image. This impression changed when I perceived the curve of the chest and the expression of the eyes. The sole unusual features about Durgjan were big reddish birthmarks on the face and neck.

Kind but decisive, she said hallo to me, and after a short while proposed we leave the tea-room to do the talking at her uncle's house in the same street. This we did and in the lengthy conversation that ensued she responded in a friendly but quite pompous way to my questions. Answering in fluent Serbo-Croat she consistently made use of the female gender while talking about herself.

She demonstrated herself to be fully aware of the fact that she constitutes by apparel, behaviour, profession, and way of thinking a rare exception among the local female population, in particular among her Muslim Albanian contemporaries. This exceptional position, as she clearly stated, does not displease her; it fills her with a certain pride.

The story of Durgjan's life commences in 1937, when she was born in the same town where she now lives, the last child of poor and simple parents. Prior to Durgjan's birth, her father Ibush (Ibi) and her mother Lutvijë had been mercilessly ravaged by child mortality resulting from diseases and malnutrition. Out of nine children they had buried eight, including all their four dear sons. To prevent the newborn child from facing the same fate, the desperate parents turned to a wise Muslim priest for advice. He recommended calling the child Durgjan, a Turco-Arabic name with the magical meaning 'Stay, my soul!' On his advice the parents also searched trees for a stone that happened to be in such an unlikely place. In the end their efforts were rewarded. According to the priest's instructions the precious object was put in the child's bath and afterwards safely stored in a high place in the room, where it remained for some decades until the old house was deserted. 'That no evil falls upon the child': so the explanation of the magic ran. Describing her parents' 'superstition' in this matter, Durgjan smiled scornfully.

Her father, it is claimed by usually reliable sources, secretly declared the small Durgjan *virgjinéhë* or *tybeli*, i.e. sworn virgin, so that she could be his fictitious son.[11] Yet another authority relates this case to a folk-belief according to which infants could be prevented from dying by dressing them up as members of the opposite sex.[12] To me Durgjan vehemently denied becoming a sworn virgin at the instigation of her father during infancy. Claiming to be averse to everything that smells of tradition, Durgjan does not consider herself to be a sworn virgin, and utterly dislikes being compared to those virgins of the 'backward' countryside. 'Not incited by my parents' wish but because I wanted it that way, I started to dress and behave like a boy. As far as I remember I have always felt myself more like a male than a female.' On the subject of her parents Durgjan added this: 'At my birth it was of secondary importance to them whether I was a boy or a girl; the only thing that really did matter was saving my life.' This insistence on her own responsibility, I presume, originates in the need to clear her parents from the charge of having pursued an 'unnatural' procedure, which is nowadays increasingly vilified as a manifestation of sheer traditionalism. Durgjan considered it even necessary to take the entire Albanian population, which is in general heavily stigmatized for its alleged backwardness, under her wing by stating: 'I can't imagine that our parents could have done such a thing to their children.' By claiming all responsibility herself, Durgjan emphasizes moreover her manliness, since according to the standards of our time more honour is derived from a self-chosen than from a superimposed 'deviant' way of life.

In her youth she was taken by many people to be a boy, and since she did not mind it at all she tried not to spoil their illusions. She used to join the boys in their horseplay, and attended school with them when it was still unusual for Albanian Muslim girls to follow formal education. At the teacher training college, where she was enrolled after the technical school that she originally attended was transferred to a distant city, a certain event occurred which still fills her with malicious pleasure. 'As there are no girls in our class,' the teacher said when he wanted to treat a subject he considered to be unfit for female ears. To his great surprise he was told by one of the pupils that Durgjan was not a boy but a girl. 'Oh, how stupid I have been. Am I supposed to be a teacher?' While uttering these words the teacher is reported to have beaten his head.

In the early 1950s the young Durgjan was appointed to a teaching post in a village close to her native town. Originally she was registered as a schoolmaster. As I was assured by the primary school inspector of those days, Mr Mehdi Bardhi, Durgjan was appointed as a male teacher, even though it was known to him, as well as to others, that she was in fact female. They let her pass as a male, assuming she had good reasons to do so. I do not know exactly when Durgjan was officially turned from a schoolmaster into a schoolmistress, but by 1957 she was already designated as a female teacher at a village school.[13] In 1966 Durgjan was working as a schoolmistress in her native town, as was observed by Mirko Barjaktarovic.[14] Notwithstanding her downright masculine behaviour and appearance, he writes, she used to talk about herself as a female. Twenty years later I saw her name on the list of teachers written in its feminine form, Durgjane. In the teachers' room my attention was drawn to a framed colour photograph of the assembled staff, females as well as males. Wearing a two-piece man's suit Durgjan's figure looms large in the foreground surrounded by her junior female colleagues in dresses and with long hair.

Durgjan likes to show off as a sports enthusiast. In her youth she played football with the boys; later she settled down to handball. She played in a ladies' handball team, which was almost invincible during the years 1957–8. Her personal fame spread throughout the country and she was given the opportunity to join the team of the capital, Belgrade. Since she did not want to leave her family she had to reject this attractive offer. Looking back now, Durgjan regrets not having utilized her talents as a trainer.

As I have stated already, Durgjan claims to be the sole person responsible for her way of life. Above all she is protective about her mother, who died in 1979 and whose ring she wears as a loving souvenir: 'Though she didn't know how to read or write she certainly was not a conservative person. After my father's death in 1950 she tried together with my father's brother to prevail on me to behave and dress as a woman. Both of them preferred me to marry.' As Durgjan confided to me, she had by then already grown too much attached to her masculine way of behaviour to be able to comply with their wishes. Neither could she give up her manliness – which she seems to consider her second nature – when males courted her. When Barjaktarovic asked the 28-year-old Durgjan why she didn't adopt female attire and get married, she responded in a resigned way that such a thing would be 'very difficult' to do at that time. Her one and only sister had just passed away and Durgjan had decided to raise the deceased's children 'like her own', yet 'differently' from the way she herself had been raised.

Today Durgjan is living alone in an apartment, but still spends a lot of time with her foster children, who respect her and call her *tèto* (aunt) Dan. She is fond of doing the housework and boasts of her cleanliness. According to her the only thing good about marriage is having children. Though she would like to have a child she never would have sacrificed her independence to a male for this reason only. The traditional submissive role of married women is abhorrent to Durgjan. Fortunately her job enables her to be in close contact with children. 'Year after year', she conceitedly informed me, 'my class receives many more applications than there are places.'

Durgjan's favourite way of passing time is a good, serious conversation with males, in the course of which alcohol is not despised. She heartily dislikes stupidity and garrulousness in women, and even more when they are found in men. Durgjan is a popular customer of the tea-room where I met her. In this all-male meeting-place she is respected and treated as an equal, so the manager and some of his habitués told me.

Durgjan likes to advertise herself as a worldly-wise person who is free from the blinkers and prejudices of tradition. Unlike most women of her generation and ethnic background who never look beyond the horizon of their native area, Durgjan is much travelled. In her small car she has made trips to metropolises like Istanbul and Paris, where 'curiosity' drove her to visit gay bars and the like. Without expressing her sexual preference or tendencies clearly, Durgjan declared herself disappointed by what she observed in those establishments.

At least some of her fellow townsmen appear to consider her hermaphroditic, i.e. combining physical characteristics of both sexes. A middle-aged Serbian lady who was convinced of this herself, however, frankly admitted she was completely ignorant of Durgjan's antecedents. Durgjan's 'unnatural' appearance evokes so much aversion in this informant that she cannot even stand facing her while shopping or walking in the street. This avoidance seems not to be restricted to the informant. To me Durgjan repeatedly and emphatically declared she had a perfectly normal female physique. The obvious psychological predilection for masculinity and the alleged biological femaleness seem to have found a livable balance in her personality. Anyway she let me know: 'I'm really satisfied with my life.'

## II

All four persons described in the previous section have in their youth 'crossed over' to the male gender on the initiative of, or at least by the consent of, their (grand-)parents in order to substitute for a male heir. A structural precondition of this 'gender-crossing' was the extremely high appreciation of males and masculinity in the culture under study. The house – a unit combining social, economic, moral, and cultic functions – was doomed to disappear in the absence of a male heir. The extinction of a house, symbolized by the quenching of fire, caused profound distress to its members, and was much feared by them. The revenge of the ancestral spirits for the termination of their worship was viewed with fear and trembling. In everyday life, parents who failed to produce a son suffered a loss of status, or downright ostracism.

In the traditional context these masculinized individuals were in principle bound to perpetual virginity, normally by oath. This is the reason why they are often referred to in the vernacular as 'sworn virgins'. Virginity was conceived of by the patriarchal culture to be synonymous with 'masculine' virtues like purity and strength. The intact, impermeable body symbolized the moral integrity of the person in question as well as of the group whose member it was.[15] Moreover, virginity performed an important practical function: it prevented these non-nubile females from bringing forth children who would be *a priori* considered 'bastards' and have no legitimate place within the system of patrilineages. According to the indigenous cosmology children spring from the 'blood' of the father; whereas the mother's part in procreation is confined to that of incubating; 'The woman is a sack for carrying,' as a costumier of tribal North Albania perceptively stated.[16]

Much uncertainty and dissension exists concerning the meaning of 'virginity' as applied to the person in question. Did they always have to refrain from sexual contacts with males, or did they rather enjoy some kind of freedom in the realm of (hetero-)sexuality?[17] Or, using a distinction common in classical antiquity, should such a person be labelled *virgo intacta* or simply *virgo*, the latter term denoting 'unattached, unwed female'?[18] The case histories known to me all seem to point in the direction of complete heterosexual abstinence; yet some general statements on those who became sworn virgins in order to escape an arranged marriage – a type of sworn virginity almost exclusively found among North-Albanians – indicate the opposite in relation to their itinerant life-style. Statements of this kind date back to the turn of the century. Spiridion Gopcevic (*nom de plume* of Leo Brenner) informs us about the girls in the Catholic tribes of Mirditë who moved over to the male gender: 'On his travels this new man only has to take care not to become pregnant, for that would cause his death.'[19] And concerning the wandering sworn virgins of the tribes of Malësi an all but chaste behaviour is mentioned by Karl Steinmetz.[20] However, with regard to these statements made by foreigners the question arises whether they are based on actual evidence or just on impressions.[21] It is possible after all that the foreigners were deluded by the 'non-virginlike' audacious manners in male company. Rude language was not seldom heard from the mouths of sworn virgins, especially in public drinking-places, and sometimes they even engaged in public flirtations with males.[22]

Sworn virgins among Catholic Albanian tribes are reported not to have taken the oath of chastity. According to Ernesto Cozzi, an Italian missionary working in Malësi, only the (very few) nuns of this area were really bound to perpetual chastity.[23] And his contemporary, the Czech traveller Viktor Dvorsky, noted that at Zatrijebac on the Montenegrin side of the border, 'a "virgin" promises only not to enter matrimony, but does not promise to remain a chaste maiden'.[24] In any case, the alleged heterosexual liberty of these 'virgins', assuming normal fertility and lack of prophylactics, must have been severely restricted by the danger of pregnancy. Capital punishment (by stoning in Montenegro and by burning alive in North Albania) was prescribed by customary law for pregnant nubile girls and sworn virgins. My material, however, does not include a single enactment of this draconian punishment on the latter.[25]

Pelja Osman mentions an alternative procedure allegedly pursued by Albanians at the Montenegrin border: 'Should a *tombelija* [sworn virgin] accidently become pregnant (which is a very rare event) then she has to denounce that man [the father]

and marry him. If he disagrees a blood feud arises between the
lineage of the *tombelija* and the lineage of that man.' The need to
avenge a sworn virgin's honour could cause a bloodbath: 'In
1894', Pelja Osman continues, 'Boca Preljina became pregnant,
and because of her 72 men were killed.'[26] Though we remain
ignorant of Boca's own destiny, her case perfectly shows how risky
it could be for males to have illicit relations with sworn virgins.

Of the very few persons I know of, who, after having lived for
considerable time as sworn virgins in male disguise, returned to
the female gender and married, one case in particular appeals to
the imagination. This is a case clearly reflecting the waning
influence of tradition on the individual's life.

The person concerned was born in 1926 in Nisor, a village near
Suva Reka in Kosovo, the fourth daughter of a simple Muslim
Albanian peasant family called Ejupi. Since the parents lacked a
son, they decided to let the new-born girl pass off as a boy and
to conceal the true sex from the outside world. The father forbade
the girl to be called by her original female name Fatime and gave
her the male name Fetah. Widowed at an early age, the mother
was charged with the difficult task of guiding Fetah undetected
through the first stages of life. Proceeding cunningly she managed
to by-pass the *synét* (circumcision) of her 'son' and postponed the
search for a future bride indefinitely. To have a son was of great
importance since a childless widow or a widow with only daughters
by custom had no right to occupy her deceased husband's homestead; she had to return to the house of her birth or was married
off once again.

Perhaps the mother's success would have continued had Fetah
not been recruited in 1944 by the conquering Yugoslav partisans.
Only after she had been two years in the army did a medical
check-up expose her as a female, upon which she was promptly
discharged from military service. Returning to her native village
she kept on dressing and behaving as a man. She was appointed
a member of the revolutionary community council, in which
capacity she participated actively in the struggle for equal rights
for Muslim women. Seclusion and veiling were the main targets
for Fetah's partisan enthusiasm.

In the following years the local community grew more and more
aware of the fact that Fetah was a female. The final unmasking
occurred in 1951 when, much to the discontent of the mother,

Fetah married Asllan Asllani whose wife she still is. Her husband once declared that he had to 'seize' the resisting Fetah, who was at that time still wearing male clothing, in order to make her his bride. At marriage, her female name Fatime was reinstated and the tight manly trousers exchanged for wide harem trousers. It was far from easy to get used to the role of housewife. In retrospect, Fatime claims to be content with having become a woman. Recently she declared to a journalist: 'I'm happy with my son and two daughters.' To conclude this story a moving detail ought to be mentioned: the mother never resigned herself to the loss of her only 'son' and died without granting Fatime forgiveness.[27]

## III

Having considered relations with males, we must turn our eyes to relations with females. Belonging primarily to the man's world the transvestite sworn virgins often took part in the open disdain of the second sex. In the matter of misogyny they sometimes rivalled true males, as Gusic's experience with Mikas shows (pp. 145–6, above). In the early years of our century, Edith Durham went through a similar example of overacting by an Albanian virgin in male dress she happened to meet among the Hot, a tribe of Malësi. 'She treated me with the contempt she appeared to think all petticoats deserved – and turned her back on me', writes Durham, annoyed.[28] As a matter of fact, this independent, unmarried English lady, who had moreover a short hair-style, was during her extensive travels through the 'wild' tribes of Highland Albania more or less considered a sworn virgin by male natives, and hence treated respectfully.[29]

Sexual tendencies towards females seem to be present in the cases of Mikas (p. 149, above) and Stana (p. 155, above), albeit in a rather restrained and repressed way. Of liaisons with females, however, I found no trace whatsoever. Yet cohabitation of masculine sworn virgins with female partners is not completely unknown. I know of three such couples; for two of which a sexual relationship is actually indicated. At least two out of these three couples were bound by 'blood–sisterhood', a kind of ritual or spiritual kinship which, however, does not usually include living together.[30] According to Tatomir Vukanovic, sworn virgins were

163

in some places quite ill-reputed for 'certain abnormal sexual relations' with their blood-sisters.[31]

The first couple belonged to the Kuci, a mixed Montenegrin-Albanian tribe, and consisted of the Orthodox Montenegrin Djurdja Popovic and her *posestrima* (blood-sister) and fellow *tombelija* (sworn virgin) Curë Prenk Rexhinaj, a Catholic Albanian. Stevan Ducic, a fellow tribesman and contemporary has depicted this 'interesting pair of blood-sisters' briefly in a book probably written about 1910. Coming from the neighbouring village of Koce and bringing along the paternal inheritance, Curë settled down fifteen years earlier in the house of Djurdja's father, the former captain of Medun. They formed a joint household and lived together 'in the greatest harmony'. 'Only very seldom are they apart; they are always working together', Ducic wrote.[32] His words leave us guessing at the nature of this relationship, and no other known source provides information about it.

In 1939 Barjaktarovic met Djurdja, but does not report anything about this relationship. He just informs his readers about Djurdja, who was at that time residing in Tuzi. Betrothed at the age of 18, Djurdja started preparing the wedding gifts. She noticed that her mother, whose third child and eldest daughter she was, watched her doing the needlework for the presents with sadness. 'Mother, it looks as if you're not glad that I'm getting married.' On this question from Djurdja the mother replied affirmatively by saying: 'Because if you get married I'll be left alone, but if you stay with me, I'll have a son.' On hearing those words Djurdja threw down her embroidery. She came to the decision to stay in her parental house, and changed her appearance by cutting off her hair, taking a shepherd's crook, and putting on a black cap and a coat; however, she kept the skirt. From then on she devoted herself to tending cattle. She started to smoke and mixed increasingly with males. Barjaktarovic goes on to tell that Djurdja lost her father shortly after her decision not to marry her fiancé; her mother, however, lived until 1937. As long as the mother was alive, Djurdja's means of subsistence were satisfactory due to the father's pension, but afterwards she became poor.[33]

The second couple consisted of Shefkije Rexhepi Cur and her companion Rukë, who both belonged to the Magjyp (sedentary Muslim Gypsy) community of Djakovica, a small town in Metohija near the Albanian border. Vukanovic knocked in 1958 at the door of the manly dressed Shefkije who was at that time about 47 years old. Her earnings as a singer and player of the *dájre* (tambourine) were insufficient to support her and accordingly she had to rely on social assistance. After having become a sworn virgin at the age of 15 she first continued to live with her brother, but about 1938 left him in order to found a joint household with her friend Rukë, with whom she concluded the solemn bonds of blood-sisterhood.[34] From neighbours in the Gypsy quarter Vukanovic understood that this relationship also had a sexual component.[35] When I made enquiries in 1985 I found out that Shefkije and Rukë had died several years previously. Some local informants had a vivid memory of the small Shefkije with her man's clothes and cap and the feminine-looking Rukë, famous for their performances at wedding-parties: this eccentric couple had left an indelible memory.

The third couple is a contemporary one among the Orthodox population of northern Montenegro. Curious about the vicissitudes of N. N., who was recognized in 1955 during a medical screening of the population, I paid a visit to her native village in 1986. According to Gusic, whose husband took part in the screening, the person concerned was born in 1941 to a poor peasant family, and at the age of 10 declared *ostajnica* (p. 46, above) out of nine daughters by the widowed mother. Ever since, she wore boy's clothes, except for special occasions such as the medical check-up where she arrived dressed as a girl.[36] Villagers told me that this person, who is still dressed as a man, is nowadays living and working in a town. She is said to live together with a 'beautiful' and 'feminine' friend of good family. They are inseparable and cause quite a stir. In the modern usage they are referred to as *lesbeke* (lesbians).

In discussing this kind of relationship it is hard to disregard a tradition from Bosnia-Herzegovina published towards the end of the last century by Ivan (Johann) Zovko. Among the heroines (Amazons) reviewed by this author are a kind called *muskobaraca's*, according to him meaning approximately 'mannish women' (German: *Mannweiher*). In translation the German text offers the following description of these women (italics added):[37]

They fight like males and are crazy about doing everything in the way males do. Unfortunately our Lord has created them as women! They dress themselves like males, talk like males; in brief, do everything like males. *Several* muskobaraca's *are even claimed to have fallen in love with other girls and married them*, but are said to have treated them roughly, as if God hadn't created them for that purpose. They hate every woman's adornment as the devil hates the baptized soul.

The original Serbo-Croat text, however, indicates that these marriages were brought about by deception;[38] the brides were apparently under the illusion that the grooms were of the male sex. Marital deceit of this type is occasionally reported in early modern western Europe,[39] but as far as the Balkans are concerned it is very hard to find actual proof of its occurrence. I only know of one single instance, badly documented at that. Immediately after the Second World War two Bosnians got married, but later their marriage was annulled because the bride had found out that she was married to a female. This case, which is mentioned by Vukanovic in passing, is all the more mysterious since both partners were subsequently hospitalized for months in Belgrade for an unspecified disease.[40]

It is not inconceivable that in the earlier history of the Balkans females could be classified as men, to the extent of acting as husbands without let or hindrance. In fact an institutionalized 'woman-marriage' is known from some parts of the non-western world, most notably from Africa, where it is predominantly found in patrilineal and patrilocal tribes. There the custom enables, for instance, rich widows without heirs to obtain a wife. By paying the customary bride-price the female husband is the father (*pater*) to the children, who result from a liaison with some male (*genitor*). Alternative strategies to provide heirs are also to be found in tribal Africa, such as the 'ghost marriage', in which a girl is married to a deceased male, and the 'marriage with the house' in which a girl is not given in marriage but remains in the paternal home; in both cases sexual encounters with males are to secure offspring.[41]

In view of the eye-catching similarities regarding classificatory fictions in service of a strict observance of the principles of patrilineality and patrilocality, one would expect to find in the tribal part of the Balkans ingenious emergency measures like the ones mentioned above. On the basis of the logic intrinsic to this particular Balkan culture it appears rather unsatisfactory to induce females to embrace the male gender-role when the male line is threatened with extinction, if they are not also granted the right to ensure progeny themselves.[42] Viewed from this perspective, the Balkan institution of sworn virgins who administer the parental homestead until death, upon which it is transferred to kinsmen seems to be merely rudimentary. Much research into the historical development of this institution will be needed to test this conjecture.

## IV

The difficult question now arises of how far the masculine behavioural pattern, manifest in so many sworn virgins, is actually supported by identification with manliness in the minds of these persons. When trying to deal with this topic, one should be fully aware of the limitations imposed by the character of the available data. To determine the individual gender-identity one should actually have at one's disposal data gathered by the method of depth psychology, and revealing ego documents such as diaries and autobiographies. Instead of this I have to rely upon verbal and non-verbal behaviour observed by myself and others in sworn virgins, behaviour which is most probably biased by their obedience to rules of conduct and by their 'impression management' (Erving Goffman).

The four persons described in the first section differ to a considerable extent in claiming masculinity. Mikas, whose intense claim is perhaps connected with a hormonal disorder, constitutes one pole, and Durgjan, who seems to have totally abandoned this claim, the other. Some, such as Stana and Durgjan, are not secretive about their female physique, though they respond to it in different ways: to Stana it seems to be a matter of regret and to Durgjan of indifference. Others renounce their femaleness completely and are hypersensitive about allusions to it, as the case of Mikas shows. It stands to reason that the latter are almost inaccessible for research, since they consider every kind of special attention paid to them a manifestation of doubt concerning their cherished masculinity.

In such a case the researcher might try a white lie, as I have done in 1985 when visiting a Muslim village in the Sandzak, the area around the city of Novi Pazar in south-western Serbia. In

order to meet the retired local photographer, so far unapproach-
able to other researchers, I pretended to be interested in old
photographs of local buildings, costumes, and the like. In this way
I managed to get introduced and admitted by 'him'. Referring to
information provided by a relative of the person concerned, the
Serbian legal-ethnologist Ljiljana Gavrilovic states that she had
been raised as a man since infancy, because the well-to-do parents
were without a son. Later a son was born, but this happy event
did not change the status of the appointed son. Only the oldest
and closest relatives seem to know that the person was born as a
girl, but they try to hush it up as much as they can.[43] During
the hours I spent at 'his' place I noticed that the members of the
household, as well as the visitors on occasion of the *kurban-bajram*
(a Muslim festival), all respected the person as a man. 'Uncle' and
'brother' were the words used by relatives in referring to the
person in 'his' absence. I had to take care not to reveal my
foreknowledge by slips of the tongue which would have offended
the person's masculine status. In the domestic circle and in the
village I found no trace of scepticism regarding the person's male
sex, but aged males from surrounding villages told me they had
once heard the person being referred to as *hadum* (eunuch) and as
'*ni zensko ni musko*' (neither female nor male).

Apart from those socialized as males since infancy, persons who
were brought up as girls sometimes also laid claim to masculine
prerogatives, as is shown by the following two examples. A case
probably dating from the mid-nineteenth century is mentioned by
Dervis Korkut. In Gora near the river Lasva in Bosnia lived a
'very pretty' Muslim girl of aristocratic family, about whom we
are informed:[44]

> when her lover died, she put on a man's suit and started to live
> entirely like a man, she rode horseback, smoked, carried arms,
> and even went to girls 'under the window' and knew the art of
> *asikovati* [courting by means of reciting poems]. She adopted a
> male name and allowed nobody to mention her girl's name, nor
> to make an allusion to her sex in general.

The next case, reported by Vukanovic, originates from the turn of
the century and concerns not a girl but a widow. Badë, a Muslim
Albanian from the village of Spiljanije by the river Ibar, had
become a sworn virgin after her husband died. Being armed,

dressed up accordingly, and with the typical pony-tail on top of her smooth-shaven head she must have had a quite manly appearance. Once a man 'mocked' her for being a female, and for this reason she thought it necessary to avenge her masculine honour by killing him. For this crime the Turkish authorities of the day sentenced her to several years of hard labour, after which she returned to the house of her deceased husband to continue her life as a sworn virgin.[45]

Taking into account the limitations mentioned at the beginning of this section, I would like to conclude this chapter by stating that the considerable differences in the extent to which the masculine gender *seems* to be internalized by the transvestite sworn virgins can be in my opinion attributed to combinations of the following groups of variables: (1) starting age, duration, and consistency of the socializing process; (2) function and esteem within family and local community; and, last but not least, (3) personal predisposition, fitness, and preference.

## NOTES

*I wish to thank Dr Ken Dowden for his comments on the English of the first draft of this chapter.

1 See on the male-to-female inversion, e.g.: G. Bleibtreu Ehrenberg, *Der Weibmann. Kultische Geschlechtswechsel im Schamanismus: Eine Studie zur Transvestition und Transsexualität bei Naturvölkern*, Frankfurt am Main, 1984. One of the rare articles devoted to the opposite inversion is E. Blackwood, 'Sexuality and gender in certain native American tribes: The case of the cross-gender females', *Signs*, 1984, 10: 27–42.

2 M. Jovanovic-Batut, 'Cudna prilika (S moga puta po Crnoj Gori)', *Branik*, 1885, 12/24, XII. Instead of Mikas this source mentions the (more usual) male name Miras, which must be either a misunderstanding or a printer's error, since Gusic (see note 3) as well as my informants all agree on the name Mikas.

3 M. Gusic (-Heneberg), 'Etnografski prikaz Pive i Drobnjake', *Narodna starina*, Zagreb, 1930, 9: 191–205, 198; M. Gusic, 'Ostajnica-tombelija-virdzin kao drustvena pojava', *Treci kongres folklorista Jugoslavije*, Cetlnje, 1958 (55–64), 57–8; M. Gusic, 'Pravni polozaj ostajnice-virdjinese u stocarskom drustvu regije Dinarida', in *Odbrede pozitivnog zakonodavstva i obicajnog prava o sezonskim kretanjima stocara u jugoistocnoj Evropi kroz vekove* (Zbornik radova), Belgrade, 1976, (269–95): 180.

4 In Serbo-Croat the past participle displays gender clearly.

5 Compare P. Milatovic, 'Tobelija: Obicaj koji prkosi prirodi', *Politikin zabavnik*, Belgrade, 29.XI.1985, 14–15. I thank Father Gjergj Marstijepaj, OFM, of Tuzi for providing me with information on Tonë from the death register.

6 Tonë (definite form: Tona) is the female derivation of Ton (definite form: Toni).

7 K. Steinmetz, *Ein Vorstosz in die nordalbanischen Alpen*, Vienna/Leipzig, 1905, 50–2; D. Antonijevic, 'Die Frau als Träger epischen Tradition bei einigen Balkanvölkern', *Balcanica*, Belgrade, 1970, 1 (217–38): 221, 225; T. Djordjevic, *Nas narodni zivot*, Belgrade, 1984, II, 277.

8 Gusic, 'Pravni polozaj', 272–3.

9 The son of Borka's married sister confided to me that the Cerovic family has about twenty female members who have stayed single because partners from equal or higher ranking families were unavailable.

10 Milatovic, 'Tobelija', 14–15.

11 M. Barjaktarovic, 'Problem tobelija (virdzina) na Balkanskom poluostrvu', *Glasnik etnografskog muzeja*, Belgrade, 1966, 29: (273–86), 276–7; V. Begolli, *Pozita e gruas në Kosovë me nje vështrim të posaçem në të drejtën zakonore*, Pristina, 1984, 40.

12 T. Vukanovic, 'Virdzine', *Glasnik muzeja Kosova i Metohije*, Pristina, 1961, 6: (79–120) 92. Compare T. Djordjevic, *Nas narodni zivot*, Belgrade, 1923, 62.

13 Vukanovic, 'Virdzine', 92.

14 Barjaktarovic, 'Problem', 276–7.

15 A similar interpretation of virginity was originally put forward in the thought-provoking articles of Kirsten Hastrup: 'The sexual boundary – purity: heterosexuality and virginity', *Journal of the Anthropological Society of Oxford*, 1974, 5: 137–47; Kirsten Hastrup, 'The semantics of biology: virginity', in S. Ardener (ed.), *Defining Females: The Nature of Women in Society*, London, 1978, 49–65.

16 Sh. K. Gjeçov, *Kanuni i Lekë Dukagjinit*, Shkodër, 1933, 19, art. 29.

17 In Serbian ethnography there has been a controversy on this issue between M. Filipovic and M. Barjaktarovic in which the first claimed sexual freedom and the latter sexual continence: M. Filipovic, 'M. Barjaktarovic – Prilog proucavanju tobelija (zavjetovanih devojaka)', *Glasnik etnografskog instituta Srpske Akademije*, Belgrade, 1952, 1: 614–17; M. Barjaktarovic, 'Odgovor D-ru Milenku Filipovicu', *Glasnik etnografskog instituta Srpske Akademije*, Belgrade, 1953–4, 2/3: 979–82.

18 See, e.g., G. Rattray Taylor, *Sex in History*, New York, 1954, 215.

19 Spiridion Gopcevic, *Oberalbanien und seine Liga. Ethnographisch-politisch-historisch*, Leipzig, 1881, 460; Spiridion Gopcevic, *Das Fürstentum Albanien*, Berlin, 1914, 109–10.

20 Steinmetz, *Ein Vorstosz*, 50.

21 Carlton Coon met during his stay in tribal North Albania in the late 1920s a womanly dressed sworn virgin who 'spent the night' with one of his horse-drivers; cf. C. Coon, *The Mountains of Giants. A Racial and*

*Cultural Study of the North Albanian Mountain Ghegs*, Cambridge, Mass., 1950, 25.

22 M.E. Durham, *High Albania*, London, 1909, 80; T. Djordjevic, *Nas narodni zivot*, Belgrade, 1984, I, 134; M. Filipovic, 'Has pod Pastrikom', *Djela*, Sarajevo, 1958, 2: (1–130) 59; D. Korkut, 'T. Djordjevic, Nas narodni zivot VI, Beograd 1932', *Zapisi*, Cetinje, September 1932, (169–173) 172.

23 E. Cozzi, 'La donna albanese con speciale riguardo al diritto consuetudinario delle Montagne di Scutari', *Anthropos*, 1912, (309–35, 617–26) 321.

24 V. Dvorsky, *Cernohorskoturecke hranice od usti Bojany k Tare*, Prague, 1909, 130.

25 See also Coon, *Mountains*, 25.

26 Pelja Osman, 'Tombelije', *Gajret. Kalendar za godinu 1940/1358–1359 po hidzri*, Sarajevo, 1939,(166–9), 167. This slaughter is perhaps the same one as mentioned by M. Wesnitsch, 'Die Blutrache bei den Südslaven', *Zeitschrift für vergleichende Rechtswissenschaft*, 1889, 8 (443–70), 470.

27 V. Milosavleviq, 'Virgjineshat (tybelijet) – Fli të votrës familjare', *Rilindja*, Pristina, 16.X.1958, 12; Vukanovic, 'Virdzine', 92; Barjaktarovic, 'Problem', 274–6; R. Reshitaj, 'Fshehtësia e gjatë njëzet vjet', *Rilindja* 11.XI. – 22.XI.1978 (serial). Rexhai Surroi's novel *Besniku* (first edition Pristina, 1959) is based on this case.

28 Durham, *High Albania*, 80. Fortunately Durham also had less negative experiences with 'Albanian virgins', as she preferred to call them. See, e.g., ibid, 101–2.

29 M. E. Durham, 'High Albania and its customs in 1908', *Journal of the Royal Anthropological Institute of Great Britain and Ireland*, 1910, 40: (453–73) 460–1.

30 The institution of blood-sisterhood (Serbian: *posestrimstvo*; Albanian: *motëri*) is the counterpart of blood brotherhood (Serbian: *pobratimstvo*; Albanian: *vëllami*). For both forms of ritual kinship see, e.g., F. S Krauss, *Sitte und Brauch der Südslaven*, Vienna, 1885, 619–43; S. Ciszewski, *Künstliche Verwandtschaft bei den Südslaven*, Diss. Leipzig, 1897.

31 Vukanovic, 'Virdzine', 111. In some parts of Montenegro blood-sisterhood was 'very rare', and the few who concluded this bond made a secret of it 'so that they could not be blamed for it'; A. Jovicevic, 'Svagdasnji obicaji-Rijecka Nahija u Crnoj Gori', *Zbornik za narodni zivot i obicaja Juznih Slovena*, Zagreb, 1906, 11, 1 (52–79) 65, to whom we owe this information, explains it by reference to the minor social function and importance of blood-sisterhood as compared to blood-brotherhood. In my opinion the alleged objectionable sexual practices between blood-sisters need to be included in the explanation. See also: E. E. Evans-Pritchard, 'Sexual inversion among the Azande', *American Anthropologist*, 1970, 72 (1428–34) 1432.

32 S. Ducic, *Zivot i obicaji plemena Kuca*, Belgrade, 1931, 235–6.

33 M. Barjaktarovic, 'Prilog proucavanju tobelija (zavjetovanih

devojaka)', *Zbornik filozofskog fakulteta*, Belgrade, 1948, 1 (343–53): 346.

34 Vukanovic, 'Virdzine', 97–8; T. Vukanovic, 'The position of women among gypsies in the Kosovo-Metohija region', *Journal of the Gypsy Lore Society*, 1961, 40, 3/4 (81–100): 92; T. Vukanovic, *Romi (Cigani) u Jugoslaviji*, Vranje, 1983, 152. My informants called Shefkije's partner Rukë (Ruka) and not 'Madzupka', the name mentioned by Vukanovic.

35 Vukanovic, personal communication.

36 Gusic, 'Ostajnica', 57, 64; Gusic, 'Pravni polozaj', 274–5.

37 Johann Zovko, 'Ursprungsgeschichten und andere Volksmeinungen', *Wissenschaftliche Mittheilungen aus Bosnien und der Hercegovina*, Sarajevo/Vienna, 1893, 1 (426–44): 444.

38 Ivan Zovko, 'Junakinje', *Glasnik zemaljkog muzeja u Bosni i Hercegovina*, Sarajevo/Vienna, 1892, 6, 1: (269–70) 270.

39 See, e.g., W. Tegg, *The Knot Tied: Marriage Ceremonies of All Nations*, London, 1877, 250–1; R. Dekker and L. van de Pol, *The Tradition of Female Transvestism in Early Modern Europe*, London, 1989.

40 Vukanovic, 'Virdzine', 81, 96; Vukanovic, personal communication.

41 See, e.g., E. Tietmeyer, *Frauen heiraten Frauen: Studien zur Gynaegamie in Afrika*, Hohenschäftlarn, 1985.

42 Compare I. Whitaker, '"A sack for carrying things": the traditional role of women in northern Albanian society', *Anthropological Quarterly*, 1981, 54: (146–56) 151. Several classificatory fictions in an African society are dealt with in F. Klausberger, 'Die Hochzeit des toten Jünglings: Rechtsfiktionen im Dienst der Fortpflanzung (Boma-Murle)', *Anthropos*, 1986, 81: 65–74.

43 Lj. Gavrilovic, 'Tobelije: Zavet kao osnov sticanje prava i poslovne sposobnosti', *Glasnik etnografskog muzeja*, Belgrade, 1983, 47: (67–80) 78–9; Lj. Gavrilovic, personal communication; see also Vukanovic, 'Virdzine', 92.

44 D. Korkut, 'T. Djordjevic', 172.

45 Vukanovic 'Virdzine', 89. For Albanian widows from Kosovo who adopted male clothing and assumed the position of master of the house, see S. Tomic, 'Jedan pogled na pogrebne narodne obicaje', *Brastvo*, Belgrade, 1939, XXX, 50 (91–102): 101.

## NOTE ON SPELLING

The diacritical signs on Serbo-Croat consonants have been omitted. Albanian nouns are as much as possible given in their indefinite form. For geographical terms the Serbo-Croat spelling is used for the territory of the Yugoslav state (with the exception of Belgrade instead of Beograd), and the Albanian for the Albanian state. Personal names are spelled according to the language actually spoken by the people concerned.

# 10

## A history of sexology:
### social and historical aspects of sexuality

*Gert Hekma*

Nowadays we speak without hesitation about sexuality, homosexuality, heterosexuality, as if the meaning of the word 'sexuality' were totally clear. This is certainly not the case. In the nineteenth century, when the concept of sexuality was being introduced, a Dutch dictionary gave 'sexuality' quite another definition than the one we are used to: 'sex system' (with sex in the meaning of biological gender), according to Linnaeus, and derived from the Latin *sexus*. It is likely that biology, especially the theory of evolution that attributes an essential role to propagation, led to the entanglement of gender and sexuality which still prevails today.

In recent years, historians have debated at length the social construction of homosexuality by physicians in the nineteenth century. Inspired by Foucault, Weeks in particular has focused on this 'making of the modern homosexual'.[1] Such medical attention had far-reaching consequences for the 'perverts' and the 'perversions', since turn-of-the-century doctors changed what had once been considered lust beyond and after the saturation of normal desires into a psychopathological constitution. According to them, sexual aberrations were not learned, but biologically determined. Once the good doctors had discovered the perversions and sexual psychopathology, they became interested in 'normal' sexuality as well and founded the discipline of sexology. Since these developments have not been analysed very often, I shall concentrate in this final chapter on the emergence of 'Sexualwissenschaft' or sexology, and its crucial role in the modernization of sexuality.[2]

## PRELUDE

Several modern historians have discerned a sexual revolution halfway through the eighteenth century.[3] They may not agree about the character of the change, but consensus does exist that something happened to Western sexualities. Prior to this, all sexual acts that either occurred outside of marriage or did not intend procreation had been considered sinful and criminal. *'Philosophes'* of the Enlightenment, such as Montesquieu and Voltaire, started opposing the stringent practices which resulted from this moral-theological outlook. They defended lust within marriage, regardless of procreative intent, and, moreover, did not condemn libertine pleasures. The materialist Lamettrie, especially, defended a philosophy of hedonism in eating, drinking, and loving. But two forms of sexuality were still abhorred: masturbation and Socratic love (as Voltaire put it; nowadays we would speak of homo-sexuality). However, these expressions of lust were not to be criminalized, but rather prevented.[4]

Masturbation aroused a particularly enormous panic.[5] It was the enlightened physician Tissot who attracted world-wide attention with his *De l'onanisme* (1760). His treatise was chiefly important for two reasons. First, in the Age of Reason the child was imagined to embody a natural innocence which only a bad education could spoil. Onanism was an unmistakable indicator of poor upbringing and thus the struggle against self-abuse provided the basis for a new and enlightened pedagogy. Because any mistake in the child's rearing could induce masturbation – wrong food, wrong sleeping and clothing habits, wrong upbringing, wrong life-styles – the educator had to pay attention to every facet of the child's life. Secondly, Tissot also detected a connection between sexuality and insanity: masturbation led to all kinds of diseases of wasting, including shrinkage of the spinal cord and the brain. Non-acceptable sexual behaviour caused insanity, whereas masturbation itself was generated by social and cultural factors: misguided education, overheated fantasy. After the French Revolution, Pinel reorganized psychiatry thoroughly, and Tissot's schemata were adopted in psychiatric models of explanation. A new generation of psychiatrists considered insanity the outcome of 'excesses of sex and alcohol' (*in venere et baccho*). Only at the end of the nineteenth century was a more precise connection set forth: the fourth stage of syphilis appeared to be identical with 'dementia paralytica', a deadly brain disease. But we need not take these 'explanations' of eighteenth- and nineteenth-century psychiatrists too seriously. Negative social, geographical, climatological, cultural, and hereditary circumstances could all lead to insanity. In the mid-nineteenth century, the theory of degeneration was such a comprehensive system that almost anything could be imagined as a cause or consequence of insanity.[6]

With Tissot's focus on masturbation and the corresponding reorientation in psychiatry, a new interest in 'sexual aberrations' was awakened, but it was often merely anecdotal. In his book with the promising title *La médecine des passions* (1844), Descuret devoted more attention to suicide than to love. Among the 'beastly' passions he included drunkenness, gluttony, rage, anger, laziness, and libertinism, while the 'social' passions were love, pride, ambition, envy, greed, gambling, suicide, duelling, and nostalgia. Finally, he considered the 'intellectual' passions, the manias for study, order, music, and collecting, and also artistic, religious, and political fanaticism. Descuret's medicine of passions is a fascinating museum of curiosities which enjoyed a certain success (and numerous reprints), although thanks more to his marvellous stories than any theoretical or therapeutic insight. Let me recapitulate one example of his 'passion of love'. An 18-year-old Spanish girl, Maria de los Dolores, lived with her father, a shepherd. Their life together went well until Maria fell in love with Juan. This love was reciprocal but Maria's father forbade the alliance. The enamoured's supplications were to no avail against the father's stubbornness. The proud Juan decided not to pursue an impossible love-affair, and Maria had to stay with her father. Once, when her father roasted a piece of meat, Maria flared up and acted out her bitter thoughts; she grabbed a knife, stabbed her father to death, and cut his heart out of his body. She roasted the heart and devoured it 'while she uttered terrible cries . . . "See, he took my Juan from me, I killed him; he broke my heart, see here his!"' The metaphor of the heart cost the father his life, and Maria 'of the Sorrows' was locked up in a madhouse in Saragossa.[7]

Apart from the realms of masturbation and psychiatry, enlightened philosophy had a third consequence for sexual life. Sodomy, defined as anal penetration or any sexual act that did not intend procreation, was until the eighteenth century a sin for which the death penalty could be imposed. The '*philosophes*' of the

GERT HEKMA

Enlightenment criticized the severe penalties for sodomy, and indeed this 'infamous crime' disappeared from many lawbooks after the criminal code reform in France: France itself in 1791, the Netherlands in 1811, Bavaria in 1813. Wherever sodomy remained a crime, forensic medicine continued to discuss evidence of it, especially involving the penetrated partner's anus. Since the founding of forensic medicine at the beginning of the seventeenth century, most handbooks had given attention to sodomy or 'unnatural vices'. However, they discussed only the consequences of a given act, not the causes of sodomy or the character of sodomites.[8]

## BACKGROUND OF SEXOLOGY

This changed after 1800, when sodomy was decriminalized and the articles on it in handbooks of forensic medicine became outdated. In 1843, three French doctors no longer examined the anus of a pederast's victim, but instead studied the mental state of the pederast himself.[9] One year later, Kaan wrote his dissertation *Psychopathia sexualis*, a work whose content was typical for his transitional period but bearing a title that would later become proverbial through the famous handbook of Krafft-Ebing. Kaan's theoretical basis was Tissot's theory of masturbation, but he discussed other sexual perversions as well. According to Kaan, onanism was the result of excessive fantasizing and led in turn to all other perversions. His formula was that self-abuse was the *pars pro toto* of all debauchery. He mentioned all the vices that were known to forensic medicine: pederasty; tribadism (from the Greek *tribein*, 'rubbing'; here he does not mean only a lesbian act but also a certain form of male homosexuality); bestiality; violation of corpses and statues. Onanism and ultimately all perversions must, according to Kaan, lead to insanity.[10]

Michéa's article 'Des déviations maladives de l'appétit vénérien' (1849), though a relatively obscure publication, represented a breakthrough in theorizing about sexuality. For him, the perversions were not acts caused by an excessive fantasy; they were not socio-psychological, but rather physiological phenomena. Perverted behaviour implied a changed biological functioning. Michéa reversed the relationship between sexual behaviour and nervous damage. The brain was not damaged by sexual acts; instead, sexual aberrations were produced by neurological or other

176

physiological changes. Michéa once again reiterated the classical classification of vices, but he stressed *philopédie* – his neologism for pederasty – notwithstanding that the starting-point for his article was a case of corpse violation. Michéa stated that the *philopédes* were feminine and explained their femininity by the existence of a female organ in their bodies, responding to the then recent discovery of a rudimentary uterus in some males. His theory was thus biological and deterministic, and he realized so himself, for he cited the eighteenth-century materialist Lamettrie with approval.[11]

Michéa's discovery of the *philopédie* came about in a turbulent period, immediately after the revolution of 1848, when Haussmann started to reconstruct Paris and men of science began to replace a biblical history of mankind with a natural history of the human race, primarily with theories of evolution and degeneration: Darwin, Morel, Gobineau, Marx.[12] The reorganization of social and urban life, especially the growth of the police force, caused the number of apprehended sex-delinquents to rise steadily. The life stories of many of them were reported as medical cases in Casper's and Tardieu's handbooks of forensic medicine. Their works occupy a special position in the flow of such handbooks, since they treated sodomy not just as an abstract issue, but provided authentic case studies of 'wrong lovers'.[13]

Following Michéa, the Berlin professor of forensic medicine Casper stressed the feminine qualities of pederasts, calling them 'hermaphrodites of the mind'. Why did these doctors stress the feminine character of wrong lovers? On the one hand, they were simply reporting their own observations. For 150 years, a subculture of sodomites had existed in which forms of transvestism played a significant part.[14] But, more importantly, men of science were starting to discover the deviant personality behind different kinds of 'abnormal' behaviour (insanity, crime, perversion), and it was principally physicians who connected deviant behaviour with the physiological and psychological development of individuals. At the same time, Lombroso was developing a new science of criminology, the study of the 'born criminal' and the 'criminal constitution'. Behind crime, the criminal now became visible.[15] Thus doctors saw in homosexuals a new race, a third sex between men and women. They conceived of sexuality as an attraction between opposite poles (man and woman), and consequently, if a man felt attracted to a man, he must according to them be a woman.

The homosexual lawyer and classicist Ulrichs developed this notion into an elaborate theoretical construct and authorized twelve treatises about it (1864–70 and 1880).[16] He had a fine and oft-cited formula for 'uranism', his neologism for what in 1869 became known as homosexuality: *anima muliebris in corpore virili inclusa*, or 'a woman's soul enclosed in a male body'. Basing his theory on what was known about hermaphroditism, he suggested that uranism came about as a psychic hermaphroditism in the first thirteen weeks of embryonic life. Uranism was thus an inborn capacity which had its place in the body: in his first booklets, he located it in the brain; later, in the testicles.

It is remarkable that it was a classicist who was the first to break with the traditional apology of male love that had heretofore been based on Socratic philosophy and Plato's *Symposium*. But this classicist, Ulrichs, had a clear message for his times. In the 1860s, Bismarck was forging the unification of Germany, and divergent criminal codes had to be integrated. Whereas Bavaria had no criminal law concerning homosexual acts, 'unnatural fornication' was the object of severe penalties in Prussia. Precisely this illiberal law was to become the national German standard. Ulrichs's treatises were directed against the criminalization of homosexual acts and, in the heyday of European liberalism, his message got a rather friendly reception. A blue-ribbon medical commission, which included the leading German physiologist Virchow, prepared for the Prussian minister of law a report on the dangers posed by unnatural vice and concluded that such acts, both sodomy and mutual masturbation, were not injurious unless practised to excess.[17] Despite this report, the German penal code got its infamous Paragraph 175 criminalizing unnatural fornication. According to Ulrichs it was the pressure of Christian groups that led to this atavistic situation, one which persisted well into the twentieth century. Nevertheless, Ulrichs's apology in biological terms had more chance of succeeding than a cultural-historical approach now that materialism and positivism were on the rise.[18]

Ulrichs's lonely struggle for uranian emancipation was destined to fail, and he fled to Italy. But his biologistic theory had an enormous, if unintended success. The leading Berlin psychiatrists endorsed his theory while giving it another direction. They considered uranism, which Westphal christened 'sexual inversion', a psychopathological condition that should be an object of psychiatric study.[19] Especially thanks to Krafft-Ebing, who likewise was inspired by Ulrichs, the psychiatric doctrine of homosexuality became known world-wide as the keystone of his sexual psychopathology.[20] Psychiatrists gave increasing attention to homosexuality, which was now regarded as the precise reversal (sexual inversion) of heterosexuality, in turn deemed the 'normal' form of sexuality. Up to 1880, it was mostly Germans who discussed the new invention, but after 1880 a lively interest in homosexuality emerged throughout the western world, especially in France. Most prominent French psychiatrists published on sexual aberrations in the 1880s.[21]

The introduction of sexual psychopathology was a scientific revolution in Kuhn's sense.[22] Several decisive points in the breakthrough can be delineated. First of all, the proper focus of the new subject was a matter of debate. Was the central theme sexual behaviour or sexual identity? In forensic medicine, attention was always devoted to the physical consequences of sexual practices. After 1880, the interest centred on the personality of individuals who had other than 'normal' sexual desires. A second point was the continuing uncertainty about sexual vocabulary. Each author invented new terms for sexual aberrations such as exhibitionism, fetishism, sadism, and masochism. Other psychiatrists coined terms which are now quite obscure: 'mixoscopism' (voyeurism), 'copromania' (sexual desire for excrement), 'pagism' (the sexual subjugation of a male to a beautiful girl), 'picacism' (non-coital heterosexuality).[23]

A third element of this scientific revolution was the classification of perversions. The old system of forensic medicine sank into oblivion. Moreau (1880) divided the perversions into 'abnormal intelligences', nymphomania and satyriasis (heightened sexual lust in the female and male), erotomania and absolute sexual perversion: bestiality and the violation of corpses and of women. Homosexuality belonged to the abnormal intelligences.[24] A Russian psychiatrist divided the 'diseased phenomena of the sexual sense' (1885) into hereditary, learned, and compound forms of pederasty.[25] The classification proposed by Lacassagne and Krafft-Ebing became the most successful. They distinguished quantitative (large, limited, or lacking sexual desire) and qualitative forms, such as pederasty, tribadism (female homosexuality), necrophilia, bestiality, and the 'nihilistes de la chair', who were shortly afterwards dubbed 'fetishists'.[26]

A fourth element of the scientific revolution in sexual thinking was the confusion concerning explanations. Binet proposed to explain all perversions through 'association of ideas' in youth. He meant that the linkage of sexual lust with a specific object gave the perversion its particular form; therefore he spoke of 'fetishism in love'. The case of the sleeping-cap became famous: a girl had a strong sexual obsession for white sleeping-caps since she once slept with her grandmother who wore one. According to Binet, such perversions could develop only on a degenerate base; his psychological explanation implied a physical pathology.[27] This theory was the most important new explanation of the stormy 1880s. Most physicians still distinguished between biologically based 'perversions' and 'perversities' resulting from sexual exhaustion. Whereas earlier authors held that perversity was more widespread than perversion, Krafft-Ebing stated in 1901 that homosexuality was always a perversion and never a perversity. Thus the balance had shifted dramatically.

In the 1880s, two theories survived: first the biological, according to which all sexual perversions were inborn forms of degeneration, and secondly the psychological, which stressed the importance of upbringing. The biological theory predominated and slowly replaced older notions of exhaustion, lust, and excessive fantasy. Whereas most physicians considered homosexuality a degeneration, homosexuals such as Ulrichs used the biological model to stress that uranism was a normal, non-pathological variation of the sexual drive. From 1896 on, Hirschfeld emerged as the foremost proponent of this view and in 1901 he succeeded in bringing Krafft-Ebing over to his side.[28] Binet was the first to propose a psychological explanation, and others soon followed his lead. A therapy for homosexuality was developed, bringing an end to the phase of 'therapeutic nihilism' which had prevailed up till then. Whereas other psychiatrists paid no attention to prevention or cure, 'suggestion therapy' yielded good results according to the doctor who developed it.[29] Another doctor explained perversion by pointing to the existence of a period of sexual non-differentiation in which not only the perversions, but also heterosexuality developed. For Dessoir, procreation and the sexuality directed towards it were no longer self-evident and natural facts.[30] Discussion of sexual psychopathology ended up problematizing heterosexuality itself. Thus, and also because of state policies concerning population growth, the need for good sexual politics was slowly becoming evident.

The emergence of sexual psychopathology signalled a paradigmatic shift. Forensic medicine with its classification of vices was abandoned, to be supplanted by a psychiatry of perversions. In the period 1880–95, sexual psychopathology was a developing science; classification, terminology, and the precise nature of its object were hotly debated. A shift away from sexual practices to the psychology of perversion was the general trend, and the focus of attention was changed: previously, the bodily consequences of certain acts had been the primary consideration; now the question was how acts were caused by physiological and psychological determinants. Krafft-Ebing's *Psychopathia sexualis* (1886) was the standard work of the new field and appeared nearly every year in a revised and enlarged edition, each time incorporating new ideas and new terms.[31] It marked the first shift in a paradigmatic change of which the second shift would be the creation of '*Sexualwissenschaft*' or sexology.

## FROM ABNORMAL TO NORMAL SEXUALITY: THE RISE OF SEXOLOGY

Interest in sexuality in general originated after 1890. In the 'purity crusade' which sprang up at the end of the nineteenth century all over the western world, social interest in the various forms of sexual life developed quickly.[32] Especially because of the debate on prostitution, sexuality became a major topic among many social groups.[33] Condoms became available to a large segment of the population. Due to new printing techniques, pornography could be sold on an unprecedented scale. Sexuality became a social question for which liberals had no good answer because of their reluctance to interfere in private life. In the last quarter of the nineteenth century, such groups as fundamentalist Christians, socialists, and feminists rejected liberal sexual politics, which for them led to satanic vices, capitalist degeneracy, or male contempt of women. In a remarkable coalition, they managed in many countries to bring about an end to medical control of prostitution and the enactment

181

of stricter criminal laws concerning sexuality. Within sexual psychopathology interest shifted, due to social pressure as well as the discipline's inner logic, from perversions to 'normal' forms of sexuality, which some experts now regarded not as self-evident, but as tenuous results of human development.

A major development towards a general theory of sexuality, towards a sexology in the modern sense, was the appearance of Moll's *Untersuchungen über die Libido sexualis* (1897), the first standard work in sexology. Moll unlinked sexuality and procreation, challenging the notion of a 'procreative drive'; procreation, he suggested, was the coincidental result of certain sexual acts.[34] In addition, he argued that attitudes towards perversion should be liberalized radically, for he was a strict Darwinist and believed that the human race could survive only through bitter struggle. He regarded heterosexual marital life as the social precondition for biological propagation. He distinguished two drives: first, '*Detumeszenz*' (discharge), as the narrow definition of the sexual drive, and secondly, '*Kontrektation*' (relationship drive, we would say now), as the social side of the sex drive. As a Darwinist, Moll stressed the importance of stimulating the heterosexual relationship drive in order to guarantee human survival. This was a time when western European population growth was levelling off while the western nations were seeking a rapid expansion into their colonial territories. He acknowledged the existence of biologically determined variations of the relationship drive, especially homosexuality, but because of his Darwinist outlook he simultaneously stressed the importance of preventing learned homosexuality. Through the centrality of Moll's relationship drive within sexology, the modern stalemate-dichotomy of homo- and heterosexuality came into being. Sexologists increasingly came to interpret non-homosexual perversions as specific forms of hetero- or homosexual relationship drive. By so strongly interpreting sexuality as a relationship, sexologists were turning homosexuality into the sole systematic aberration of the man-wife pattern and locating it in the centre of the domain of sexual perversions. Homosexuality now became the most important qualitative variation of the sex drive, and numerous books were published on the subject with such subtitles as 'with special attention to sexual inversion'.

Following Moll, sexology developed quickly, especially in the

German-speaking countries. He wrote *Das Sexualleben des Kindes* ('The sexual life of the child') (1909) and edited the *Handbuch der Sexualwissenschaft* ('Handbook of sexology') (1908), to which Freud also contributed, and a journal was published using the same term. From the turn of the century onward sexology prospered, particularly in Germany, and this era came to an end only when Hitler took power – and then not because the National Socialists opposed sexology *per se*, but because so many sexologists were Jewish.[35]

It would be incorrect to regard Freud as a thinker who was radical because he was the first to dare to discuss sexuality, especially that of children. Most French and German psychiatrists before Freud had paid attention to sexual life, and to their astonishment they had to acknowledge how early the sexual drive manifested itself. The most important contribution of psychoanalysis was incorporating the shocking revelations of sexual psychopathology into the Oedipal system and thus rendering them harmless. Freud subsumed the sexual perversions under 'normal' sexual development and suggested therapeutic cures for them. Psychoanalysis was a method of social adaptation, not a radical social theory. Therefore, it could succeed even more quickly than sexology.[36]

From its beginnings, sexology was an applied science. While basic research was being conducted elsewhere in medicine and biology, sexologists appropriated analytical devices developed elsewhere and applied them to sexology. Research on hermaphroditism led to theories of homosexuality; the discovery of hormones and chromosomes made explanations of sexual differences possible. Thus sexology functioned from its beginnings as a social science with the pretension of being a natural science, a status to which it could aspire only through analogic thinking. Sexologists had the same problems as psychoanalysts. As social scientists they wanted to be natural scientists, but with their ambiguous strategy they were only occasionally successful in achieving respectability. The significance of the confessions of psychiatric patients remained contested, especially by medical positivists.

A clear example of the ambiguities of the work of sexologists was given by the Eulenburg affair. At the end of the nineteenth century, forward-looking scientists in Germany had started to campaign against the criminalization of unnatural fornication (anal and intercrural homosexual intercourse as well as bestiality). Because they considered homosexuality a natural variation of the sexual drive, they regarded the criminalization of homosexual acts entered into freely by adult men as a remnant of medieval superstition in an otherwise enlightened age. All the leading sexologists, from Krafft-Ebing to Freud, signed a petition to the German parliament or made statements to this gist. Hirschfeld took the initiative in this campaign. He was a leading sexologist, the founder of the world's first homosexual rights organization, the WHK (Wissenschaftlich-humanitäres Komitee, or Scientific-Humanitarian Committee), and editor of the *Jahrbuch für sexuelle Zwischenstufen* ('Annual for sexual intermediates', 1899–1923).

The scientific and political activities of sexologists furthered the general awareness of homosexuality but also provoked a backlash effect, evident, for example, in the spectacular homosexual scandals of the turn of the century: Oscar Wilde in 1895, Alfred Krupp in 1902. In 1907, the final and biggest scandal of all broke out when the journalist Maximilian Harden began to attack the 'Camarilla of Liebenberg'. He was referring to Prince Philipp zu Eulenburg, a close friend and adviser to Emperor Wilhelm II and at the same time an acquaintance of the secretary of the French embassy. Harden intended to expose the covert influence of this circle on German politics and its direct link with France. In order to achieve this goal more quickly, he hinted broadly at the existence of homosexual relations between the key figures of the circle, Eulenburg and Count Kuno von Moltke, the military commandant of Berlin. The latter brought a libel suit against Harden. The first trial he lost, amongst other reasons because Hirschfeld testified as an expert witness that Moltke was indeed a homosexual. His testimony was based in part on Moltke's physical attributes, but even more on the declarations of his former wife, who revealed to the court her sexless marital life with the count. In a second trial, it was successfully argued that her testimony was both hysterical and libellous. Hirschfeld was forced to reverse his opinion: Moltke was no homosexual. His psychological assessment had been based on vicious backbiting and his biology on extravagant conclusions derived from the human form. Hirschfeld's reputation suffered in two ways: he had to repudiate in public one of his 'expert' pronouncements, and homosexuals, observing that his theories could have negative consequences for themselves, abandoned the WHK in droves.[37]

The German social democracy was especially interested in sexology; furthermore, it was the only political group that championed more liberal sexual policies and was able to implement them. The liberals did not want to do so because of their dislike of political engineering in the private sphere, while Christians as well as conservatives were staunch supporters of marriage and opposed any sex reform. In the turbulent years after the First World War socialists and sexologists worked together closely, and in the revolutionary era of 1918–19, Hirschfeld succeeded with socialist help in founding his 'Institute for Sexology'. Its scientific pretensions notwithstanding, it became an institution which specialized primarily in social and therapeutic help in sexual matters.[38]

Aided by other pioneers in sexology, Hirschfeld convened in 1921 the first world congress on sexology in Berlin. At the second congress in Copenhagen, 1928, he founded the World League for Sexual Reform. This group organized three more conferences: in London in 1929, Vienna in 1930, and Brno in 1932. The goals of the league comprised themes still current today, such as equality of women and men, freedom to marry and divorce, access to birth control, a rational attitude towards homosexuals, systematic sex education, as well as some aims which would be out of place in a contemporary, progressive organization: racial betterment through eugenics, prevention of venereal diseases and prostitution, and treatment for disturbances of the sex drive instead of regarding them as vices or crimes while it remains unclear what these disturbances might be.[39] Not only in its goals, but also in its publications, the league linked up with the international, leftist movement; its proceedings were even partially published in Esperanto. The Soviet Union was held up as a prime example of an enlightened state with advanced sexual politics, despite the chilly '*raison d'état*' of the Russian sexologists' contributions to the conferences.[40] According to them, such sexual practices as bestiality and prostitution were no longer dealt with as crimes in their country, but instead were handled by medical therapy and social help. Thus, 'labor-prophylaxis' was required of prostitutes who were to learn how to carry out real work.[41]

Notwithstanding its social character, sexology was primarily founded on biology. Sexologists believed in the rational transmission of biological 'facts' within social reality and stressed the necessity of sex education based on these biological facts or, as they put it using a terrible term, 'reproductive biology education'.[42] Sexology wanted to be biological, rational, and social – Hirschfeld's motto was *'per scientiam ad justitiam'* – as well as relation-oriented: thus the dichotomization of homo- and heterosexuality gained strength. Interest in masturbation was limited, in transvestism and pornography even more so, while fetishism and sadomasochism did not seem to be fit subjects for sexology at all. In Kaan's *Psychopathia sexualis* (1844), onanism had been the *'pars pro toto'* for all sexual aberrations, whereas after 1900 it became at most of marginal interest for sexology. Masturbation was no longer regarded as pathological because it led to physical exhaustion, but rather because it implied the absence of a social relationship. Before 1800, sodomy had been far worse a sin than self-abuse; after 1900, homosexuality could be regarded as better sex than masturbation, because it at least was social whereas onanism was asocial.

After the Second World War, the United States became the centre of sexology, and with the research of the biologist Kinsey it acquired a sociological character. But Kinsey's books were still based on biological premises, especially the notion of the sexual outlet presupposing a sexual drive. His starting point was not the social construction of sexualities, but statistics on the innumerable orgasms in white, puritan America. His classification scheme was based on social relations: heterosexual relations before, inside, and outside marriage, or with prostitutes, homosexuality, bestiality, and masturbation as relationless sex. Pornography, transvestism, sadomasochism, and fetishism were rarely touched upon.[43] In sexual terminology and classification, Kinsey did not go beyond Moll's dichotomy of 1897: Kinsey's 'sexual outlet' is a semantic equivalent of discharge, and his statistics are based on relations or, as Moll would have said, on contraction. The new feature in Kinsey's work is his statistical scale of findings on sexual outlets and pairings. The subsequent study carried out by the Kinsey Institute in the 1970s marks a further retreat into biology. In *Sexual Preference* (1981) the authors test all socio-psychological theories concerning homosexuality, arrive at the conclusion that none is reliable, and aver that homosexuality is probably biologically determined![44]

# A HISTORY OF SEXUALITY?

The nineteenth century witnessed a paradigmatic revolution in the scientific approach to sexuality. The term itself was introduced and denoted new meanings. Moll's splitting of sexuality into discharge and relationship drive became the foundation of modern sexology. The idea of a drive to sexual discharge made sexology first of all a biological science, and secondly the idea of sexual relations and sexual object choice made sexology a science of intimate relations. Emphasis was placed first on biology and medicine, and only later on psychology. Sexuality was regarded as a universal category, not as a product of social and historical developments. Certain forms of sexual behaviour received considerable attention, especially hetero- and homosexuality, whereas interest in other forms, such as sodomy and masturbation, dissipated. With his statistics on sexual outlets, Kinsey extended sexology into the realm of sociology. Because of the stress on biological foundations and psychological forms, certain erotic preferences received scant attention in sexology: fetishisms of body parts or clothes, the everyday forms of sadomasochism, sexual fantasy. Because sexuality has been interpreted as a private matter, social and historical forms have remained insufficiently analysed. Its biological premisses have gone unquestioned, which has been detrimental to the quality of sexology.

Sociological and historical investigations of sexuality have been impeded by the biological and psychological foundations of sexology. Another problem has been the flight from empirical behaviour into theoretical speculation. Embarrassment about sexual acts continues to make it difficult to study such social facts. Moreover, many researchers quickly pass over actual sexual phenomena in order to discuss them in light of other social facts; for example, homosexuality in terms of the relation with the parents, prostitution in terms of poverty and social class, transvestism in terms of gender, sadism in terms of power relations, or sexual rituals in terms of symbolic systems. Such analyses are legitimate, but they often hinder deeper insights into the sexual phenomena themselves. Also, the reverse is hardly ever done: analysing family life, politics, or the economy in terms of sexuality. Psychoanalysis alone did so by systematically reducing psychic mechanisms to sexual phases, but it aimed at the therapeutic goal of preventing neuroses and sexual aberrations.

Social prejudices as well as biological, psychological, and theoretical premises continue to impede the development of sociological and historical research on sexuality – all the more so since all the approaches interpret sexuality itself as a natural phenomenon that is constant over time and place. Despite a well-developed scientific debate on culture and nature, and despite the importance researchers from the humanities and social sciences attribute to the cultural construction of social relations, analyses of sexual behaviour are still determined by theories of biological drive and psychological development. Thus cultural-historical studies on sexuality have rarely been undertaken, while in sociology collating statistics on sexual outlets has proved to be the limit of what seems possible.

Historians and sexologists need to devote more attention to the social formation of sexual mores, to their choreography and architecture, to representations and preliminaria of sexual acts. There is no sociology or history of sexual fashions, and no research has been conducted on the relationship between sexual fantasies and sexual modes of behaviour, or on the connection between social circumstances and sexual practices.

Sexuality is a constantly changing phenomenon; it is one manifestation of the culture of the body. Since Kinsey, sociologists have regarded sexual outlets as a biological phenomenon, as a natural preserve in a social environment, and thus they have not felt called upon to analyse the social nature of this act. Moreover, they have relegated sexuality as an intimate affair to psychology, ignoring the historical, social, and political implications of sexual mores. Many questions remain which never have been analysed historically and sociologically. Why did the bordellos with their 'madams' disappear? Why did leather replace fur as a sexual fetish in sado-masochism? Why did the 'normal' boy or young man as a sexual object disappear from the homosexual imagination, whereas he was such a familiar figure at the turn of the century in novels by Forster, Ackerley, and Proust, and how should this be related to the homogenization and integration of homosexuality in modern society?

Sexuality is a plastic social and historical phenomenon, not a clinical or natural entity as even sociological and historical researchers have claimed.[45] Not only do views on sexuality change, but

188

also sexuality and sexual behaviour themselves change in an even more radical way than many sociologists and historians suppose. Why should we be surprised that biologists have such a central place in sexology and concern themselves with the social formation of sexuality when sociologists and historians refuse to research sexual mores, relegating sexuality as an analytical topic to biology? In light of the clinical speculations in which biologists rejoice and to which sociologists and historians submit, research on the social formation of sexualities cries out for more thorough and systematic pursuit.

## NOTES

I want to thank James D. Steakley and Mattias Duyves for their help with this chapter.

1 Foucault 1976; Weeks 1981. See also Bray 1982, Van der Meer 1984, and the articles by Boon, Chauncey, and Hekma in Duyves 1984.
2 Hekma 1987. See for a history of psychopathia sexualis Wettley 1959; Lanteri-Laura 1979 and Sulloway 1979, ch. 8.
3 Shorter 1975; Trumbach 1985.
4 See Hekma 1987, ch. 1, and Stockinger 1979.
5 An article of mine on the presentation of self-abuse as the functional groundwork for an enlightened pedagogy was published in G. Hekma and H. Roodenburg (eds), *Soete minne en helsche boosheit. Geschiedenis van seksuele voorstellingen in Nederland*, Nijmegen, 1988, 232–54.
6 See previous note, and Stengers and Van Neck 1984.
7 Descuret 1844, 315.
8 See Hekma 1987, chs 1 and 2.
9 Ferrus 1843.
10 Kaan 1844, 47–8, 43–5, and 64–7.
11 Michéa 1849, 338–9.
12 Darwin 1859; Morel 1857; and Gobineau 1853–5; also the Marxist theory. See for degeneration theory Chamberlain 1985.
13 Casper 1852 and 1858; Tardieu 1857.
14 See Van der Meer 1984, *passim*; Trumbach 1977; Bray 1982, ch. 4.
15 Lombroso 1876. The degeneration theory of Morel (n. 12) was the basis as well for Lombroso's criminal anthropology and for Krafft-Ebing's psychopathia sexualis.
16 Ulrichs's brochures were reprinted in Leipzig, 1898, and New York, 1975, as *Forschungen über das Rätsel der mannmännlichen Liebe*. Therein: *Vindex* (1864), *Inclusa* (1864), *Vindicta* (1865), *Formatrix* (1865), *Ara spei* (1865), *Gladius furens* (1868) *Memnon* (1868), *Incubus* (1869), *Argonauticus* (1869), *Prometheus* (1870), *Araxes* (1870), and *Kritische Pfeile* (1880).

17  Reprinted in: *Jahrbuch für sexuelle Zwischenstufen*, Berlin, 1905, 7: 5–8.
18  For law reform, see Ulrichs (1975, *Kritische Pfeile*), 106–7.
19  Griesinger 1868–9 and Westphal 1869.
20  Krafft-Ebing 1877 and 1886.
21  See Courouve 1978; Binet 1888.
22  Kuhn 1962.
23  Lasègue 1877; sadism and masochism in Krafft-Ebing 1886, 1891[6]; pagism and mixoscopism in Gallus 1905, 74 and 298; copromania and picacism in Eulenburg 1895, 103 and 98.
24  Moreau 1880.
25  Tarnowsky 1886.
26  Lacassagne, as cited in the dissertation of his student J. Chevalier 1885, 10–11; Krafft-Ebing 1877.
27  Binet 1888.
28  Hirschfeld 1896; Krafft-Ebing 1901, who stated that he considered homosexuality a normal variant of the sexual drive.
29  Schrenck-Notzing 1892.
30  Dessoir 1894.
31  From 1886 to 1894, an enlarged and improved version of the book appeared each year. It grew from 110 to 414 pages. The 17th edition, by A. Moll, was 838 pages. Translations in Italian, Russian, English, French, and Dutch appeared in 1886, 1887, 1892, 1895, and 1896.
32  Ussel 1968 and Pivar 1973.
33  See Walkowitz 1980; Corbin 1978; for the Netherlands, Hekma 1984.
34  Moll 1897, 4.
35  See for persons, books, and journals of this first period of German sexology Haeberle 1983.
36  Freud 1915 and Sulloway 1979.
37  See for the Eulenburg scandal Hirschfeld 1908; Friedländer 1909, ch. 9; Young 1959; Hull 1982; Steakley 1983.
38  See for Hirschfeld Seidel 1969; Steakley 1975, ch. 3; Steakley 1985 and *Magnus Hirschfeld* 1985.
39  See for the conferences Haeberle 1983. For the goals *Sexualnot und Sexualreform. Verhandlungen der Weltliga für Sexualreform. IV. Kongress (1930)*, ed. H. Steiner, Vienna, 1931, xix.
40  The Russian law reform was valued positively by Hirschfeld, In *Sexualnot*, 383–4; there also the contribution of the Russian G. Batkis, 338–45; see also *Sexual Reform Congress, Copenhagen . . . 1928 . . . Proceedings of the second congress*, ed. H. Riese and J. H. Leunbach, Copenhagen/Leipzig, 1929; Russian contributions, 37–63 and 228–39.
41  Ibid., 230–2 (N. Pasche-Oserski: 'Sexualstrafrecht in der Sowjet-Union').
42  'Resolution: Sexualpädagogik', in ibid., 148.
43  Kinsey 1948.
44  Bell 1981, ch. 19.
45  See Tielman 1982, *passim*, especially 295; and Kooy 1976, especially 64, where even a hierarchy of sexual behaviour is given, from petting to coitus. Other sexual acts are termed preliminaria. For an example

of a historian with the same natural attitude to sexuality, see Gay
1983.

# BIBLIOGRAPHY

Bell, A. P., M. S. Weinberg, and S. K. Hammersmith, *Sexual preference:
its development in men and women*, Bloomington, Ind., 1981.
Binet, A., *Du fétichisme dans l'amour*, Paris, 1888.
Boon, L. J., 'Dien godlosen hoop van menschen', in Duyves 1984,
57–66.
Bray, A., *Homosexuality in Renaissance England*, London, 1982.
Casper, J. L., 'Ueber Nothzucht und Päderastie', *Vierteljahrschrift für
gerichtliche und öffentliche Medicin*, I, Berlin, 1852, 21–78.
Casper, J. L., *Handbuch der gerichtlichen Medizin*, Vol. 2, Berlin, 1858.
Chamberlain, J. E., and S. L. Gilman (eds), *Degeneration: the dark side of
progress*, New York, 1985.
Chauncey, G., 'Mietjes, buikschuivers en christenbroeders', in Duyves
1984, 92–103.
Chevalier, J., *De l'inversion de l'instinct sexuel au point de vue médico-légale*,
Lyon, 1885.
Corbin, A., *Les filles de noce*, Paris, 1978.
Courouve, C., *Bibliographie des homosexualités*, new edn, Paris, 1978.
Darwin, C., *The Origin of Species* . . ., London, 1859.
Descuret, J. B. F., *La médicine des passions*, 3rd edn, Liège, 1844.
Dessoir, M., 'Psychologie der Vita sexualis', *Allgemeine Zeitschrift für
Psychiatrie und psychisch-gerichtliche Medicin*, 1894, vol. 50, 941–75.
Duyves, M., G. Hekma, and P. Koelemij (eds), *Onder mannen, onder
vrouwen*, Amsterdam, 1984.
Eulenburg, A., *Sexuale Neuropathie*, Berlin, 1895.
Ferrus, Foville and Brierre de Boismont, 'Attentat aux moers', *Annales
médico-psychologiques*, 1843, I, 289–99.
Foucault, M., *Histoire de la sexualité, Vol. 1, La volonté de savoir*, Paris,
1976.
Freud, S., *Drei Abhandlungen zur Sexualtheorie*, Vienna/Leipzig (1905) 1915[3].
Friedländer, B., *Die Liebe Platons im Lichte der modernen Biologie*, Berlin,
1909.
Gallus, *L'amour chez les dégénérés*, Paris, 1905.
Gay, P., *The Enlightenment: an interpretation, Vol. 2, The science of freedom*,
New York, 1969.
Gay, P., *The Bourgeois Experience, Vol. 1, Education of the senses*, New York,
1983.
Gobineau, J. A. de, *Essay sur l'inégalité des races humaines*, 4 vols, Paris,
1853–5.
Griesinger, M., 'Vortrag zur Eröffnung der psychiatrischen Klinik zu
Berlin', *Archiv für Psychiatrie und Nervenkrankheiten*, 1, Berlin, 1868–9.
Haeberle, E. J., *The Birth of Sexology: a brief history in documents*, n.p.,
1983.

Hekma, G., 'Getemde ontucht', *Verzorging*, Amsterdam, 1984, I, 3: 19-38.
Hekma, G., 'Sociale filosofie, sociale praktijk', in Duyves 1984, 67-78.
Hekma, G., *Homoseksualiteit, een medische reputatie. De uitdoktering van de homoseksueel in negentiende-eeuws Nederland*, Diss., Amsterdam, 1987.
Hirschfeld, M. (under the pseudonym Ramien), *Sappho und Socrates*, Leipzig, 1896.
Hirschfeld, M., 'Jahresbericht 1906/8', *Jahrbuch für sexuelle Zwischenstufen*, 1908, 9: 621-3.
Hirschfeld, M., *Die Homosexualität des Mannes und des Weibes*, Berlin, 1914.
*Magnus Hirschfeld, Leben und Werk, Eine Ausstellung . . .*, Berlin, 1985.
Hull, I. V., 'Kaiser Wilhelm and the "Liebenberg Circle"', in J. C. G. Rohl and N. Sombart (eds) *Kaiser Wilhelm II: New Interpretations*, Cambridge, 1982, 193-220.
Kaan, H., *Psychopathia sexualis*, Diss., Leipzig, 1844.
Kinsey, A. C., *et al.*, *Sexual Behaviour in the Human Male*, Philadelphia/London, 1948.
Kooy, G. A., *Jongeren en seksualiteit*, Deventer, 1976.
Krafft-Ebing, R. von, 'Über gewisse Anomalien des Geschlechtstriebes/ . . .', *Archiv für Psychiatrie und Nervenkrankheiten*, 1877, 7: 291-312.
Krafft-Ebing, R. von, *Psychopathia sexualis, mit besonderer Berücksichtigung der konträren Sexualempfindung*, Stuttgart, 1886.
Krafft-Ebing, R. von, 'Neue Studien auf dem Gebiete der Homosexualität', in *Jahrbuch für sexuelle Zwischenstufen*, 1901, 3: 1-36.
Kuhn, T.S., *The Structure of Scientific Revolutions*, Chicago, 1962.
Lanteri-Laura, G., *La lecture des perversions. Histoire de leur appropriation médicale*, Paris, 1979.
Lasègue, C., 'Les exhibitionistes', *Union médicale*, 1 May 1877.
Lombroso, C., *L'uomo delinquente*, Rome, 1876.
Meer, T. van der, *De wesentlyke sonde van sodomie en andere vuyligheden. Sodomieten vervolgingen in Amsterdam 1730-1811*, Amsterdam, 1984.
Michéa, C. F., 'Des déviations maladives de l'appétit vénérien', *Union médicale*, 17 July 1849.
Moll, A., *Untersuchungen über die Libido sexualis*, Berlin, 1897.
Moreau, P., *Des aberrations du sens génésique*, Paris, 1880.
Morel, B. A., *Traité des dégénérescences physiques, intellectuelles et morales de l'espèce humaine . . .*, Paris, 1857.
Pivar, D. J., *Purity Crusade: sexual morality and social control, 1868-1900*, Westport, Conn., 1973.
Schrenck-Notzing, A. von, *Die Suggestionstherapie bei krankhaften Erscheinungen des Geschlechtssinnes . . .*, Stuttgart, 1892.
Seidel, R., *Sexologie als positive Wissenschaft und sozialen Anspruch. Zur sexualmorphologie des Geschlechtssinnes . . .*, Stuttgart, 1969.
Shorter, E., *The Making of the Modern Family*, New York, 1975.
Steakley, J. D., *The Homosexual Emancipation Movement in Germany*, New York, 1975.
Steakley, J. D., 'Iconography of a scandal . . .', *Studies in Visual Communication*, 1983, IX, 2: 20-51.

Steakley, J. D., *The Writings of Dr Magnus Hirschfeld: a bibliography*, Toronto, 1985.

Stengers, J. and A. Van Neck, *Histoire d'une grande peur: la masturbation*, Brussels, 1984.

Stockinger, J., 'Homosexuality and the French Enlightenment', in G. Stambolian and E. Marks (eds), *Homosexualities and French Literature*, Ithaca, NY, 1979, 161–85.

Sulloway, F. J., *Freud as a Biologist of the Mind*, New York, 1979.

Tarczylo, T., *Sexe et liberté au siècle des Lumières*, Paris, 1983.

Tardieu, A., *Étude médico-légale sur les attentats aux moeurs*, Paris, 1857.

Tarnowsky, B., *Die krankhaften Erscheinungen des Geschlechtssinnes*, Berlin, 1886.

Tielman, R. A. P., *Homoseksualiteit in Nederland*, Meppel, 1982.

Trumbach, R., 'London's sodomites: homosexual behaviour and Western culture', *Journal of Social History*, 1977, 11: 1–33.

Trumbach, R., 'Sodomitical subcultures, sodomitical roles, and the gender revolution', *Eighteenth-Century Life*, 1985, 9: 109–21.

Ulrichs, K. H., *Forschungen über das Rätsel der mannmännlichen Liebe*, Leipzig, 1898, reprinted New York, 1975.

Ussel, J. M. W. van, *Geschiedenis van het seksuele probleem*, Meppel, 1968.

Walkowitz, J. K., *Prostitution and Victorian Society: women, class and the state*, Cambridge, 1980.

Weeks, J., *Sex, Politics and Society: the regulation of sexuality since 1800*, London, 1981.

Westphal, K. F. O., 'Die conträre Sexualempfindung', *Archiv für Psychiatrie und Nervenkrankheiten*, 1869, 2: 73–108.

Wettley, A., *Von der 'Psychopathia sexualis' zur Sexualwissenschaft*, Stuttgart, 1959.

Young, H. F., *Maximilian Harden, Censor Germaniae*, The Hague, 1959.

# Notes on contributors

**Jan Baptist Bedaux** b. 1947, is Associate Professor in Art History at the Free University, Amsterdam. He is the author of *The Reality of Symbols. Studies in the Iconology of Netherlandish Art 1400–1800* (1990), co-author and editor of *Tot Lering en Vermaak* (1976), and editor of *Annus qaudriga mundi. Opstellen over middeleeuwse kunst* (1989).

**Jan Bremmer** b. 1944, is Professor of History of Religion at the University of Groningen. In addition to many articles on social and religious aspects of ancient Greece, he is author of *The Early Greek Concept of the Soul* (1983, paperback edition 1987), co-author (with Nicholas Horsfall) of *Roman Myth and Mythography* (1987) and (with Jan den Boeft) of *Martelaren van de Oude Kerk* (1987), editor of *Interpretations of Greek Mythology* (1987) and co-editor (with Herman Roodenburg) of *A Cultural History of Gestures* (1991).

**René Grémaux** b. 1952, studied social anthropology at the University of Nimwegen and is currently preparing an anthropological thesis on mannish women of the Balkan mountains. He also published 'Politics in 19th-century Montenegro', *Current Anthropology*, 25 (1984); 'Males in Female Robes, Females in Trousers. On the Involvement of Franciscan Friars with the Sworn Virgins of North Albanian Tribes', *Focaal Tijdschrift voor antropologie* (Nijmegen), 1990, no. 13: 85–111.

**Gert Hekma** b. 1951, is Lecturer in Gay Studies at the University of Amsterdam. He is the author of *De uitdoktering van de homoseksueel in negentiende-eeuws Nederland* (1987), and co-editor (with M. Duyves and P. Koelemij) of *Onder mannen, onder vrouwen* (1984), (with Kent Gerard) of *The Pursuit of Sodomy – Male Homosexuality from the Renaissance throughout the Enlightenment* (1989), and (with Herman

194

Roodenburg) of *Soete Minne en Helsche Boosheit. Seksuele voorstellingen in Nederland, 1300–1850* (1988).

**Arnold Heumakers** b. 1950, works as literary critic for the Dutch national newspaper *De Volkskrant*. Amongst his publications on de Sade, Stendhal, and Céline are 'Elites, gelijkheid en anarchie: een verkenning van Sade's politiek', *Bzzlletin*, 83 (1981) and 'Céline en Drumont', *Maatstaf*, 34 (1986).

**Mayke de Jong** b. 1950, is Professor of Medieval History at the University of Utrecht. She is the author of *In Samuel's Image: Child Oblation in the Early Middle Ages* (forthcoming, 1991). Amongst her other publications are 'De boetedoening van Iso's ouders', in *Ad Fontes. Feestbundel C. van der Kieft* (1984) and ' "Volk" en geloof in vroegmiddeleeuwse teksten', in G. Rooijakkers and Th. van der Zee (eds), *Religieuze volkscultuur. De spanning tussen de voorgeschreven orde en de geleefde praktijk* (1986).

**Karin Jušek** b. 1953, studied history at the University of Groningen and is currently preparing a thesis on sexual morality and prostitution in Vienna around 1900.

**André Lardinois** b. 1961, studied classics at the Free University, Amsterdam, and the University of Utrecht and is now following the Princeton Classics Graduate Program. He is the co-author (with Th. C. W. Oudemans) of *Tragic Ambiguity. Anthropology, Philosophy and Sophocles' Antigone* (1987).

**Herman Roodenburg** b. 1951, is Fellow in Cultural History at the P. J. Meertens-Instituut, Department of Folklore, of the Koninklijke Nederlandse Akademie van Wetenschappen at Amsterdam. He is the author of *Onder censuur: de kerkelijke tucht in de gereformeerde gemeente van Amsterdam, 1578–1700* (1990), and co-editor (with Gert Hekma) of *Soete Minne en Helsche Boosheit: Seksuele voorstellingen in Nederland, 1300–1850* (1988), (with Rudolf Dekker) of Aernout van Overbeke's *Anecdota sive historiae jocosae* (1991), and (with Jan Bremmer) of *A Cultural History of Gestures* (1991).

**Mirjam Westen** b. 1956, art historian, is Assistant Professor of Art and Management at the University of Utrecht. She is the author of *Pearl Perlmuter. Beeldhouwster* (1988). Amongst her publications is 'Over het naakt in de Noordnederlandse kunst in de periode 1770–1830', *De negentiende eeuw*, 4 (1986).

# Select bibliography
*Gert Hekma and Herman Roodenburg*

What follows is a personal sampling of the vast literature on the history of sexuality. The subject is of course endless and we have therefore concentrated, although not exclusively, on those areas in which the most innovative modern studies have appeared: England, France, Holland, and the United States. Popular accounts or 'coffee-table' histories of sexuality have been omitted, even though these publications are often valuable for their rich illustrations.

The first part of the bibliography (A) contains the general studies of heterosexuality and homosexuality; studies of the family which are relevant to the subject have also been included. The second part (B) lists studies of individual aspects of sexuality.

We would like to thank Jan Bremmer, Florence Koorn, and Lotte van de Pol for their suggestions and Alexandra van Hensbergen for technical assistance.

## A GENERAL STUDIES OF HETEROSEXUALITY AND HOMOSEXUALITY

### A.0 Historiography and methodology

Davidson, A. I., 'Sex and the Emergence of Sexuality', *Critical Inquiry*, 1987, 14: 16–48.
*Journal of the History of Sexuality*, 1990.
Padgug, R. A., 'Sexual Matters: on Conceptualising Sexuality in History', *Radical History Review*, 1979, 20: 3–23.
Ross, E., and Rapp, R., 'Sex and Society: a Research Note from Social History and Anthropology', *Comparative Studies in Society and History*, 1981, 23: 51–72.
Stone, L. *The Past and the Present Revisited*, London, 1987, 344–82, 434–8 ('Sexuality').

Vicinus, M., 'Sexuality and Power: a Review of Current Work in the History of Sexuality', *Feminist Studies*, 1982, 8: 133–56.


## A.1 Through the ages

Ariès, P., and Bejin, A. (eds), *Western Sexuality*, Oxford, 1985.
Bloch, I., *Das Geschlechtsleben in England*, 3 vols, Berlin, 1901–3.
Bottomley, F., *Attitudes to the Body in Western Christendom*, London, 1980.
Bullough, V. L., *Sexual Variance in Society and History*, New York, 1976.
────── and Bullough, B., *Sin, Sickness and Sanity: a History of Sexual Attitudes*, New York, 1977.
D'Emilio, J., and Freedman, E.B., *Intimate Matters. A History of Sexuality in America*, New York, 1988.
Deschner, K., *Das Kreuz mit der Kirche. Eine Sexualgeschichte des Christentums*, Munich, 1974.
Flandrin, J.-L., *Le sexe et l'occident. Evolution des attitudes et des comportements*, Paris, 1981.
Foucault, M., *The History of Sexuality*, Vol. 1: *An Introduction*, New York, 1978; Vol 2: *The Use of Pleasure*, New York, 1985; Vol. 3: *The Care of the Self*, New York, 1987.
Fuchs, E., *Le désir et la tendresse. Sources et histoire d'une éthique chrétienne de la sexualité et du mariage*, Geneva, 1979.
Goody, J., *The Development of the Family and Marriage in Europe*, Cambridge, 1983.
Hekma, G., and Roodenburg, H. W. (eds), *Soete Minne en helsche boosheit. Seksuele voorstellingen in Nederland 1300–1850*, Nijmegen, 1988.
*Histoire et sexualités = Annales ESC*, 1974, 29: 973–1057.
Levin, E., *Sex and Society in the World of the Orthodox Slavs, 900–1700*, Ithaca, 1989.
Murstein, B. I., *Love, Sex and Marriage through the Ages*, New York, 1974.
Rath-Vegh, I., *Die Geschichte der Liebe*, Leipzig/Weimar, 1982.
*Sexuality in History = Journal of Contemporary History* 1982, 17: no. 2.
Tannahill, R., *Sex in History*, New York, 1979.
Taylor, G. R., *Sex in History: Society's Changing Attitudes to Sex throughout the Ages*, London, 1953.
Ussel, J. W. M. van, *Geschiedenis van het seksuele probleem*, Meppel, 1968.
Vandenbroecke, C., *Vrijen en trouwen van de Middeleeuwen tot heden*, Brussels, 1986.
Wheaton, R., and Hareven, T. K. (eds), *Family and Sexuality in French History*, Philadelphia, Pa., 1980.


## A.2 Antiquity

Blok, J., and Mason, P. (eds), *Sexual Asymmetry*, Amsterdam, 1987.
Brown, P., *The Body and Society: Men, Women and Sexual Renunciation in Early Christianity*, New York, 1988.
Halperin, D. M., Winkler, J. J., and Zeitlin, F. I. (eds), *Before Sexuality.*

*The construction of erotic experience in the ancient world*, Princeton, 1990.

Keuls, E., *The Reign of the Phallus*, New York, 1985.

Parker, R., *Miasma*, Oxford, 1983, 74–103 ('The Works of Aphrodite').

Rousselle, A., *Porneia: On Desire and the Body in Antiquity*, Oxford, 1988.

Sissa, G., *Le corps virginal*, Paris, 1987.

Veyne, P., 'La Famille et l'amour sous le Haut-Empire Romain', *Annales ESC*, 1978, 33: 35–63.


## A.3 Middle-Ages

Browe, P., *Beiträge zur Sexualität des Mittelalters*, Breslau, 1932.

Brundage, J. A., 'Carnal Delight: Canonistic Theories of Sexuality', in *Proceedings of the VIth International Congress of Medieval Canon Law*, Vatican City, 1980, 361–85.

———— Law, Sex and Christian Society in Medieval Europe, Chicago, 1987.

Bullough, V.L., and Brundage, J. (eds), *Sexual Practices and the Medieval Church*, Buffalo, N.Y., 1982.

Demyttenaere, B., 'Vrouw en seksualiteit. Een aantal kerkideologische standpunten in de vroege middleleeuwen', *Tijdschrift voor Geschiedenis*, 1973, 86: 236–61.

Derouet-Besson, M.-C., '"Inter duos scopulos". Hypothèses sur la place de la sexualité dans les modèles de la représentation du monde au XIe siècle', *Annales ESC*, 1981, 36: 922–45.

Dinzelbacher, P., 'Ueber die Entdeckung der Liebe im Hochmittelalter', *Saeculum*, 1981, 32: 185–208.

Dufresne, J.-L., 'Les comportements amoureux d'après le registre de l'officialité de Cerisy', *Bulletin philologique et historique (jusqu'à 1610) de Comité des travaux historiques et scientifiques*, 1973, 131–56.

Flandrin, J.-L., *Un temps pour embrasser. Aux origines de la morale sexuelle occidentale (VIe–XIe siècles)*, Paris, 1983.

Jeay, M., 'Sexuality and Family in 15th Century France: Are Literary Sources a Mask or a Mirror?', *Journal of Family History*, 1979, 4: 328–45.

Lemay, H., 'The Stars and Human Sexuality: Some Medieval Scientific Views', *Isis*, 1980, 71: 127–37.

Manselli, R., 'Vie familiale et éthique sexuelle dans l'Occident médiéval, Rome, 1977, 363–82.

Pavan, E., 'Police des moeurs, société et politique à Venise à la fin du Moyen Age'. *Revue Historique*, 1980, 104: 241–88.

Payer, P.J., *Sex and the Penitentials: the Development of a Sexual Code*, 550–1150, Toronto, 1984.

Ruggiero, G., 'Sexual Criminality in the Early Renaissance: Venice 1338–1358', *Journal of Social History*, 1974–5, 8: 18–37.

———— Boundaries of Eros: Sex Crime and Sexuality in Renaissance Venice, New York/Oxford, 1985.

Schroeter, M., 'Staatsbildung und Triebkontrolle. Zur gesellschaftlichen

Regulierung des Sexualverhaltens vom 13. bis 16. Jahrhundert',
*Amsterdams Sociologisch Tijdschrift*, 1981, 8: 48–89.
———— *'Wo zwei zusammenkommen in rechter Ehe'. Sozio- und psychogenetische
Studien über Eheschliessungsvorgänge vom 12. bis 15. Jahrhundert*, Frankfurt
am Main, 1985.
Weir, A., and Jerman, J., *Images of Lust: Sexual Carvings on Medieval
Churches*, London, 1986.


## A.4 The Early Modern Period

Bieler, A., *L'homme et la femme dans la morale calviniste. La doctrine reformée
sur l'amour, le mariage, le célibat, le divorce, l'adultère et la prostitution,
considérée dans son cadre historique*, Geneva, 1963.
Boucé, P. G. (ed.), *Sexuality in Eighteenth-Century Britain*, Totowa, N.J.,
1982.
Dulong, C., *L'amour au XVIIe siècle*, Paris, 1969.
Flandrin, J.-L., *Les amours paysannes. Amour et sexualité dans les campagnes de
l'ancienne France, XVIe–XIXe siècle*, Paris, 1975.
———— *Families in Former Times*, Cambridge, 1979.
Hagstrum, J.-H., *Sex and Sensibility: Ideal and Erotic Love from Milton to
Mozart*, Chicago, 1980.
Haks, D., *Huwelijk en gezin in Holland in de 17e en 18e eeuw. Processtukken en
moralisten over aspecten van het laat 17e-en 18e-eeuwse gezinsleven*, Assen, 1982.
Hunt, D., *Parents and Children in History: the Psychology of Family Life in
Early Modern France*, New York, 1970.
Leites, E., 'The Duty to Desire: Love, Friendship, and Sexuality in
Some Puritan Theories of Marriage', *Journal of Social History*, 1982, 15:
383–408.
———— *The Puritan Conscience and Modern Sexuality*, New Haven/London,
1986.
Maccubin, R.P. (ed.), *Unauthorized Sexual Behavior during the Enlightenment
= Eighteenth Century Life*, 1985, 9: no. 3.
Morgan, E.S., 'The Puritans and Sex', *New England Quarterly*, 1942, 15:
591–607.
Neret, J. A., *Documents pour une histoire de l'éducation sexuelle en France du
seizième siècle à nos jours*, Paris, 1957.
Quaife, G. R., *Wanton Wenches and Wayward Wives*, London, 1979.
*Représentations de la vie sexuelle = Dix-huitième siècle. Revue annuelle*, 1980, 12.
Rowse, A. L., *Simon Forman: Sex and Society in Shakespeare's Age*, London,
1971.
Sharpe, J. A., *Defamation and Sexual Slander in Early Modern England: the
Church Courts at York*, 1900.
Shorter, E., *The Making of the Modern Family*, New York, 1975.
Solé, J., *L'amour en Occident à l'époque moderne*, Paris, 1976.
Steinberg, L., *The Sexuality of Christ in Renaissance Art and in Modern
Oblivion*, New York, 1983.
Stone, L., *The Family, Sex and Marriage in England, 1500–1800*, London,

1977.
Storme, H., 'Het 18de-eeuwse katholiek discours over huwelijk en seksualiteit in de Mechelse kerkprovincie', *Documentatieblad Werkgroep Achttiende Eeuw*, 1985, 17: 29–50.
Vandenbroeke, C., 'Seksualiteit en huwelijksbeleving in Vlaanderen'. *Spiegel Historiael*, 1979, 14: 425–33.
Wagner, P. *Eros Revived: Erotica of the Enlightenment in England and America*, London, 1988.


## A.5 The Nineteenth Century

Barker-Benfield, G. J., *The Horrors of the Half-Known Life: Male Attitudes towards Women and Sexuality in Nineteenth Century America*, New York, 1976.
———— 'The Spermatic Economy', *Feminist Studies*, 1972, 1: 45–74.
Boyd, K. M., *Scottish Church Attitudes to Sex, 1850–1914*, Edinburgh, 1980.
Branca, P., *Silent Sisterhood: Middle Class Women in the Victorian Home*, London, 1975.
Callagher, C., and Laqueur, Th. (eds), *Sexuality and the Social Body in the Nineteenth Century* = *Representations*, 1986, 14.
Cominos, P. T., 'Late Victorian Sexual Respectability and the Social System', *International Review of Social History*, 1963, 8: 18–48.
Copley, A., *Sexual Moralities in France, 1780–1980*, London, 1989.
Degler, C.N., 'What Ought to Be and What Was: Women's Sexuality in the Nineteenth Century', *American Historical Review*, 1974, 79: 1468–90.
———— *At Odds: Women and the Family in America from the Revolution to the Present*, New York, 1980.
*Dénatalité: l'antériorité française, 1800–1914* = *Communications*, 1986, 44.
Gathorne-Hardy, J., *Love, Sex, Marriage and Divorce*, London, 1981.
Gay, P., *The Bourgeois Experience: Victoria to Freud*, Vol. 1: *Education of the Senses*, New York/Oxford, 1984: Vol. 2: *The Tender Passion*, New York/Oxford, 1986.
Harrison, F., *The Dark Angel: Aspects of Victorian Sexuality*, London, 1977.
Kern, L. J., *An Ordered Love: Sexual Roles and Sexuality in Victorian Utopias: the Shakers, the Mormons, and the Oneida Community*, Chapel Hill, 1981.
Marcus, S., *The Other Victorians: a Study of Sexuality and Pornography in Mid-Nineteenth Century England*, London, 1966.
Pearsall, R., *The Worm in the Bud: the World of Victorian Sexuality*, New York, 1969.
———— *Public Purity, Private Shame: Victorian Sexual Hypocrisy Exposed*, New York, 1976.
Phayer, J. M., *Sexual Liberation and Religion in Nineteenth Century Europe*, London, 1977.
Shorter, E., '"La vie intime": Beiträge zu einer Geschichte am Beispiel des kulturellen Wandels in den bayrischen Unterschichten im 19. Jahrhundert', in P. C. Ludz (ed.), *Soziologie und Sozialgeschichte*, Opladen, 1972, 530–49.
Smith, F. B., 'Sexuality in Britain, 1800–1900: Some Suggested

Revisions', in M. Vicinus (ed.), *A Widening Sphere: Changing Roles of Victorian Women*, Bloomington/London, 1977, 182–98.

Smith-Rosenberg, C., *Disorderly Conduct: Visions of Gender in Victorian America*, New York, 1985.

Smout, T. C., 'Aspects of Sexual Behaviour in Nineteenth Century Scotland', in A. A. Maclaren (ed.), *Social Class in Scotland: Past and Present*, Edinburgh, 1976.

Trudgill, E., *Madonnas and Magdalens: the Origins and Development of Victorian Sexual Attitudes*, London, 1976.

Weeks, J., *Sex, Politics and Society: the Regulation of Sexuality since 1800*, London, 1981.

# B SPECIAL THEMES

## B.I CONTRACEPTION AND ILLEGITIMACY

### B.I.1 Through the Ages

Berguès, H., *La prévention des naissances dans la famille, ses origines dans les temps modernes*, Paris, 1960.

Flandrin, J.-L., *L'Eglise et le contrôle des naissances*, Paris, 1970.

Himes, N. E., *Medical History of Contraception*, New York, 1970.

Laslett, P., *The World We Have Lost*, London, 1965.

———— *Family Life and Illicit Love in Earlier Generations: Essays in Historical Sociology*, Cambridge, 1977.

———— (ed.), *Bastardy and Its Comparative History: Studies in the History of Illegitimacy and Marital Nonconformism in Britain, France, Germany, Sweden, North America and Japan*, London, 1980.

Noonan, J. R., J. T., *Contraception: A History of Its Treatment by the Catholic Theologians and Canonists*, Cambridge, Mass., 1965.

Walle, E. van de, and Walle, F. van de, 'Allaitement, stérilité et contraception: les opinions jusqu'au XIXe siècle', *Population*, 1972, 27: 685–701.

### B.I.2 Antiquity

Hopkins, K., 'Contraception in the Roman Empire', *Comparative Studies in Society and History*, 1965, 8: 124–51.

Krenkel, W. A., 'Familienplanung und Familienpolitik in die Antike', *Wurzburger Jahrbücher für die Altertumswissenschaft*, 1978, 4· 197–203,

### B.I.3 Middle-Ages

Biller, P. A., 'Birth Control in the Medieval West', *Past and Present*, 1982, 94: 3–26.

## B.I.4 The Early Modern Period

Chamoux, A., and Dauphin, R., 'La contraception avant la révolution française. L'exemple de Châtillon-sur-Seine', *Annales ESC*, 1969, 24: 662–84.

Depauw, J., 'Amour illégitime et société à Nantes au XVIIIe siècle', *Annales ESC*, 1972, 27: 1155–82.

Dupaquier, J., and Lachiver, M., 'Les débuts de la contraception en France ou les deux malthusianismes', *Annales ESC*, 1969, 24: 1391–1406, [cf. the discussion in *Annales ESC*, 1981, 36: 473–95].

Fairchilds, C., 'Female Sexual Attitudes and the Rise of Illegitimacy: a Case Study', *Journal of Interdisciplinary History*, 1977–8, 8: 627–67.

Gyssels, M. C., 'Het voorechtelijk seksueel gedrag in Vlaanderen', *Tijdschrift voor Sociale Geschiedenis*, 1984, 10: 71–104.

Knodel, J., and van de Walle, E., 'Lessons from the Past: Policy Implications of Historical Fertility Studies', *Population and Development Review*, 1979, 5: 1–20.

Lachiver, M., 'Fécondité légitime et contraception dans la région parisienne', in *Hommage à Marcel Reinhard: sur la population française au XVIIIe et XIXe siècles*, Paris, 1978, 383–402.

Lebrun, F., 'Démographie et mentalités: le mouvement de conception sous l'Ancien Régime', *Annales de Démographie Historique*, 1974, 45–50.

Lottin, A., 'Naissances illégitimes et filles-mères à Lille au XVIIIe siècle', *Revue d'Histoire Moderne et Contemporaine*, 1970, 17: 278–322.

Maclaren, A., 'Some Secular Attitudes towards Sexual Behaviour in France, 1760–1860', *French Historical Studies*, 1973–4, 8: 604–25.

Ranum, O., and Ranum, P. (eds), *Popular Attitudes toward Birth Control in Pre-Industrial France and England*, New York, 1972.

Schnucker, R. V., 'Elizabethan Birth Control and Puritan Attitudes', *Journal of Interdisciplinary History*, 1974–5, 5: 655–67.

Vandenbroeke, C., 'Het seksueel gedrag van de jongeren in Vlaanderen sinds de late 16de eeuw', *Bijdragen tot de Geschiedenis*, 1979, 62: 193–230.

Wrigley, E. A., 'Family Limitation in Pre-Industrial England', *Economic History Review*, 1966, 19: 82–109.

## B.I.5 The Nineteenth Century

Banks, J. A., *Prosperity and Parenthood. A Study of Family Planning Among the Victorian Middle Classes*, London, 1954.

——— *Victorian Values: Secularism and the Size of Families*, London/Boston, 1981.

——— and Banks, O., *Feminism and Family Planning*, Liverpool, 1964.

Langer, W. L., 'Origins of the Birth Control Movement in England in the Early Nineteenth Century', *Journal of Interdisciplinary History*, 1975, 5: 669–86.

Ledbetter, R., *A History of the Malthusian League, 1877–1927*, Columbus, Oh., 1976.

Maclaren, A., *Birth Control in Nineteenth-Century England*, London, 1978.
Matras, J., 'Social Strategies of Family Formation: Data for British Female Cohorts Born 1831–1906', *Population Studies*, 1965/6, 19: 167–82.
Scott Smith, D., 'Family Limitation, Sexual Control, and Domestic Feminism in Victorian America', *Feminist Studies*, 1972, 1: nos 3 and 4.
Stengers, J., 'Les pratiques anticonceptionnelles dans le mariage au XIXe et XXe siècles', *Revue Belge de Philologie et d'Histoire*, 1971, 49: 403–81, 1119–74.

## B.II HOMOSEXUALITY

### B.II.0 Bibliographies

Bullough, V.L., *et al.*, *An Annotated Bibliography of Homosexuality*, New York, 1976.
Courouve, C., *Bibliographie des homosexualités*, Paris, 1978[2].
Dall'Orto, G., *Leggere Omosessuale. Bibliografia*, Turin, 1984.
Dynes, W., 'A Bibliography of Bibliographies of Homosexuality', *The Cabirion and Gay Books Bulletin*, 1984, 10: 16–22.
—— *Homosexuality: a Research Guide*, New York, 1987.
Herzer, M., *Bibliographie zur Homosexualität. Verzeichnis des deutschsprachigen nichtbelletristischen Schrifttums zur weiblichen und männlichen Homosexualität aus den Jahren 1466 bis 1975*, Berlin, 1982.
Weinberg, M. S., and Bell, A. P., *Homosexuality: An Annotated Bibliography*, New York, 1972.

### B.II.1 Through the Ages

*Among Men, Among Women: Sociological and Historical Recognition of Homosocial Arrangements*, Amsterdam, 1983.
Bailey, D. S., *Homosexuality and the Western Christian Tradition*, Hamden, Conn., 1975[2].
Bleibtreu-Ehrenberg, G., *Tabu Homosexualität. Geschichte eines Vorurteils*, Frankfurt am Main, 1978.
Bonnet, M. J., *Un choix sans équivoque*, Paris, 1985.
Bullough, V. L., *Homosexuality, a History: from Ancient Greece to Gay Liberation*, New York, 1979.
Courouve, C., *Vocabulaire de l'homosexualité*, Paris, 1985.
Crompton, L., 'Gay Genocide from Leviticus to Hitler', in L. Crew (ed.), *The Gay Academic*, Palm Springs, Ca., 1978.
Dynes, W. (ed.), *Encyclopedia of Homosexuality*, New York, 1900.
Duberman, M., Chauncey, G., and Vicinus, M., *Hidden from History, Reclaiming the Gay and Lesbian Past*, New York, 1989.
Gollner, G., *Homosexualität. Ideologiekritik und Entmythologisierung einer Gesetzgebung*, Berlin, 1974.

Greenberg, D. F., *The Construction of Homosexuality*, Chicago, 1989.
Hirschfeld, M., *Die Homosexualität des Mannes und des Weibes*, Berlin, 1914.
Hyde, H. M., *The Love That Dare Not Speak Its Name*, New York, 1970.
Hohmann, J. S. (ed.), *Der unterdrückte Sexus. Historische Texte und Kommentare zur Homosexualität*, Lollar, 1977.
Katz, J. N. (ed.), *Gay American History*, New York, 1976.
Licata, S. J., and Petersen, R. P. (eds), *Historical Perspectives on Homosexuality*, New York, 1981 = *Journal of Homosexuality*, 1980/1, 6: nos 1 and 2.
Plummer, K. (ed.), *The Making of the Modern Homosexual*, London, 1981.
Rowse, A. L., *Homosexuals in History: a Study of Ambivalence in Society, Literature, and the Arts*, New York, 1977.
Sedgwick, E.K., *Between Men: English Literature and Male Homosocial Desire*, New York, 1985.

## B.II.2 Antiquity

Bremmer, J., this volume, ch. 1.
Dover, K. J., *Greek Homosexuality*, Oxford, 1978.
Lardinois, A., this volume, ch. 2.

## B.II.3 Middle-Ages

Boswell, J., *Christianity, Social Tolerance and Homosexuality: Gay People in Western Europe from the beginning of the Christian Era to the Fourteenth Century*, Chicago/London, 1980.
Goodich, M., *The Unmentionable Vice: Homosexuality in the Later Medieval Period*, Santa Barbara, 1979.
Kuster, H. J., *Over homoseksualiteit in middeleeuws West-Europa*, Diss. Utrecht, 1977.
Relinquet, P., *Le moyen âge: Gilles de Rais, maréchal, monstre et martyr*, Paris, 1982.

## B.II.4 The Early Modern Period

Bray, A., *Homosexuality in Renaissance England*, London, 1982.
Brown, J. C., *Immodest Acts. The Life of a Lesbian Nun in Renaissance Italy*, Oxford, 1986.
Burg, B. R., *Sodomy and the Perception of Evil: English Sea Rovers in the Seventeenth-Century Caribbean*, New York/London, 1983.
Coward, D. A., 'Attitudes to Homosexuality in Eighteenth Century France', *Journal of European Studies*, 1980, 10: 231–55.
Faderman, L., *Surpassing the Love of Men: Romantic Friendship and Love between Women from the Renaissance to the Present*, London, 1981.
Gerard, K., and Hekma, G. (eds), *The Pursuit of Sodomy: Male Homosexuality in Renaissance and Enlightenment Europe*, New York, 1989 =

*Journal of Homosexuality*, 1988, 15: nos 1/2.
Gilbert, A. N., 'The Africaine Court-Martial: A Study of Buggery and the Royal Navy', *Journal of Homosexuality*, 1974, 1:111–22.
Hentze, H., *Sexualität in der Pädagogik des späten 18. Jahrhunderts*, Frankfurt am Main, 1979.
Hernandez, L., *Les procès de sodomie aux XVIe, XVIIe et XVIIIe siècles*, Paris, 1920.
Huussen, Jr., A. H., 'Sodomy in the Dutch Republic during the Eighteenth Century', *Eighteenth Century Life*, 1985, 9: no. 3, 169–78.
Lever, M., *Les bûchers de Sodome*, Paris, 1985.
Meer, Th. van der, *De wesentlijke sonde van sodomie en andere vuyligheeden. Sodomietenvervolgingen in Amsterdam, 1730–1811*, Amsterdam, 1984.
Rey, M., 'Police et sodomie à Paris au 18ième siècle: du péché au désordre', *Revue d'histoire moderne et contemporaine*, 1982, 113–24.
Ruig, R. de, *In de schaduw van de Grand Seigneur*, Utrecht, 1984.
Saslow, J. M., *Ganymede in the Renaissance: Homosexuality in Art and Society*, New Haven/London, 1986.
Stockinger, J., 'Homosexuality and the French Enlightenment', *Homosexuality and French Literature: Cultural Contexts/Critical Texts*, Ithaca/London, 1979, 161–85.
Trumbach, R., 'London's Sodomites: Homosexual Behaviour and Western Culture', *Journal of Social History*, 1977, 11: 1–33.

## B.II.5 Nineteenth Century

Aron, J.-P., and Kempf, R., *Le pénis et la démoralisation de l'Occident*, Paris, 1978.
Crompton, L., *Byron and Greek Love: Homophobia in 19th-century England*, Berkeley, Los Angeles/London, 1985.
Hahn, P., *Nos ancêstres les pervers. La vie des homosexuels sous le Second Empire*, Paris, 1979.
Hekma, G., *Homoseksualiteit, een medische reputatie. De uitdoktering van de homoseksueel in negentiende-eeuws Nederland*, Diss. Amsterdam, 1987.
Hocquenghem, G., *Race d'Ep. Un siècle d'images de l'homosexualité*, Paris, 1979.
Hyde, H. M., *The Strange Death of Lord Castlereagh*, London, 1959.
Jenkyns, R., *The Victorians and Ancient Greece*, Oxford, 1980.
Mayer, H., *Aussenseiter*, Frankfurt am Main, 1975.
Moers, E., *The Dandy: Brummell to Beerbohm*, London, 1960.
Mosse, G. L., *Nationalism and Sexuality: Respectability and Abnormal Sexuality in Modern Europe*, New York, 1985.
Reade, B. (ed.), *Sexual Heretics: Male Homosexuality in English Literature from 1850 to 1900*, London, 1970.
Steakley, J. D. (ed.), *The Homosexual Emancipation Movement in Germany*, New York, 1975.
Weeks, J., *Coming Out: Homosexual Politics in Britain, from the Nineteenth Century to the Present*, London, 1977.

# B.III PROSTITUTION

## B.III.0 Bibliography

Bullough, V. L. and Deacon, M. (eds), *A Bibliography of Prostitution*, New York, 1977.

## B.III.1 Through the Ages

Bloch, I., *Die Prostitution*, 2 vols, Berlin 1912/25.
Bullough, V. L., *The History of Prostitution*, New Hyde Park, N.Y., 1964.
Chauvin, C., *Les chrétiens et la prostitution*, Paris, 1983.
Evans, H., *Harlots, Whores and Hookers: a History of Prostitution*, New York, 1979.
Henriques, F., *Prostitution in Europe and the New World*, London, 1963.
Vandenbroeke, C., 'De prijs van betaalde liefde', *Spiegel Historiael*, 1983, 18: 90–4.

## B.III.2 Antiquity

Herter, H., 'Die Soziologie der antiken Prostitution im Lichte des heidnischen und christlichen Schrifttums', *Jahrbuch für Antike und Christentum*, 1960, 3: 70–111.

## B.III.3 Middle-Ages

Larivaille, P., *La vie quotidienne des courtisans en Italie au temps de la Renaissance. Rome et Venise, XVe et XVIe siècles*, Paris, 1975.
Otis, L.L., *Prostitution in Medieval Society: the History of an Urban Institution in Languedoc*, Chicago/London, 1985.
Rossiaud, J., 'Prostitution, jeunesse et société dans les villes du Sud-Est au XVe siècle, *Annales ESC*, 1976, 31: 289–325.
Trexler, R.C., 'La prostitution florentine au XVe siècle: patronages et clientèles', *Annales ESC*, 1981, 36: 983–1015.

## B.III.4 The Early Modern Period

Benabou, E.-M., *La prostitution et la police des moeurs au dix-huitième siècle*, Paris, 1987.
Perry, M. E., '"Lost Women" in Early Modern Seville: The Politics of Prostitution', *Feminist Studies*, 1978, 4: 195–214.
Davis, N. Z., 'Scandale à l'Hotel-Dieu de Lyon (1537–1543)', in *La France d'Ancien Régime. Etudes réunies en l'honneur de Pierre Goubert*, Toulouse, 1984, 175–87.

SELECT BIBLIOGRAPHY

### B.III.5 Nineteenth Century

Corbin, A., *Les Filles de noce. Misère sexuelle et prostitution (19e et 20e siècles)*, Paris, 1979.

Evans, R. J., 'Prostitution, State and Society in Imperial Germany', *Past and Present*, 1976, 70: 106–29.

Finnegan, F., *Poverty and Prostitution: a Study of Victorian Prostitutes in York*, London/New York, 1979.

Kaplan, M., 'Prostitution, Morality Crusades and Feminism: German Jewish Feminists and the Campaign against White Slavery', *Women's Studies International Forum*, 1982, 5: 619–27.

McHugh, P., *Prostitution and Victorian Social Reform*, London, 1980.

Riegel, R. E., 'Changing American Attitudes towards Prostitution (1800--1920)', *Journal of the History of Ideas*, 1968, 29: 437–52.

Sigsworth, E. M., and Wyke, T. J., 'A Study of Victorian Prostitution and Venereal Disease', in M. Vicinus (ed.), *Suffer and Be Still. Women in the Victorian Age*, Bloomington/London, 1972, 77–99.

Trudgill, E., 'Prostitution and Pater Familias', in H. J. Dyos and M. Wolff (eds), *The Victorian City*, London, 1973.

Walkowitz, J. R., and Walkowitz, D. J., *Prostitution and Victorian Society: Women, Class, and the State*, New York, 1980.

## B.IV GYNAECOLOGY

### B.IV.1 Through the Ages

Fischer-Homberger, E., *Krankheit Frau und andere Arbeiten zur medizingeschichte der Frau*, Berne, 1979.

Knibiehler, Y., and Fouquet, C., *La femme et les médecins. Analyse historique*, Paris, 1983.

Shuttle, P., and Redgrove, P., *The Wise Wound*, London, 1978.

### B.IV.2 Antiquity

Lefkowitz, M., *Heroines and Hysterics*, London, 1982.

Rousselle, A., 'Observation féminine et idéologie masculine: le corps de la femme d'après les médecins grecs', *Annales ESC*, 1980, 35: 1089–115.

### B.IV.3 Middle-Ages

Delva, A., *Vrouwengeneeskunde in Vlaanderen tijdens de late middeleeuwen*, Leiden, 1983.

Diepgen, P., *Frau und Frauenheilkunde in der Kultur des Mittelalters*, Stuttgart, 1963.

Jacquart, D., and Thomasset, C., *Sexualité et savoir médicale au moyen âge*, Paris, 1985.

Wood, Ch. Th., 'The Doctor's Dilemma: Sin, Salvation, and the Menstrual Cycle in Medieval Thought', *Speculum*, 1981, 56: 710–27.


*B.IV.4 The Early Modern Period*

Beall, O. T., '"Aristotle's Masterpiece" in America: a Landmark in the Folklore of Medicine', *The William and Mary Quarterly*, 1963, 20: 207–22.
Crawford, P., 'Attitudes to Menstruation in Seventeenth-Century England', *Past and Present*, 1981, 91: 47–73.
Darmon, P., *Le mythe de la procréation à l'âge baroque*, Paris, 1977.
——— *Le tribunal de l'impuissance. Virilité et défaillances conjugales dans l'Ancienne France*, Paris, 1979.
Donegan, J. B., *Women and Men Midwives: Medicine, Morality, and Misogyny in Early America*, Westport, Conn., 1978.
Donnison, J., *Midwives and Medical Men: a History of Inter-Professional Rivalries and Women's Rights*, London, 1977.
Eccles, A., *Obstetrics and Gynaecology in Tudor and Stuart England*, Kent, Oh., 1982.
Ehrenreich, B., and English, D., *Witches, Midwives, and Nurses: a History of Women Healers*, Old Westbury, N.Y., 1973.
Fox, C. E., *Pregnancy, Childbirth and Early Infancy in Anglo-American Culture, 1675–1830*, Philadelphia, 1966.
Gélis, J., 'Sages-femmes et accoucheurs. L'obstétrique populaire au XVIIe et XVIIIe siècles', *Annales ESC*, 1977, 32: 927–57.
——— *L'arbre et le fruit. La naissance dans l'occident moderne, XVIe–XIXe siècle*, Paris, 1984.
———, Laget, M., and Morel, M.-F., *Entrer dans la vie. Naissances et enfances dans la France traditionelle*, Paris, 1978.
Laget, M., 'La naissance aux siècles classiques. Pratiques des accouchements et attitudes collectives en France aux XVIIe et XVIIIe siècles, *Annales ESC*, 1977, 32: 958–92.
——— *Naissances. L'accouchement avant l'âge de la clinique*, Paris, 1982.
MacLaren, A., *Reproductive Rituals: the Perception of Fertility in England from the Sixteenth to the Nineteenth Century*, London/New York, 1984.
Porter, R., 'Spreading Carnal Knowledge or Selling Dirt Cheap? Nicolas Venette's *Tableau de l'Amour Conjugal* in Eighteenth Century England', *Journal of European Studies*, 1984, 14: 233–55.
Roger, J., *Les sciences de la vie dans la pensée française du XVIIIe siècle*, Paris, 1971.
Shorter, E., *A History of Women's Bodies*, New York, 1982.


*B.IV.5 Nineteenth Century*

Blackman, J., 'Popular Theories of Generation: The Evolution of "Aristotle's Works", the Study of an Anachronism' in J. Woodward and D. Richards (eds), *Health Care and Popular Medicine in Nineteenth-Century England*, London, 1977, 56–88.

Douglas Wood, A., ' "The Fashionable Diseases": Women's Complaints and their Treatment in 19th Century America', *Journal of Interdisciplinary History*, 1973, 4: 25–52.

Haller, J. S., and Haller, R. M., *The Physician and Sexuality in Victorian America*, London, 1974.

Knibiehler, Y., 'Les médecins et la "nature féminine" au temps du Code Civil', *Annales ESC*, 1981, 31: 824–45.

Shorter, E., 'L'âge des premières règles en France, 1750–1950', *Annales ESC*, 1981, 36: 495–511.

Smith-Rosenberg, C., and Rosenberg, C. E., 'The Female Animal: Medical and Biological Views of Women and Her Role in 19th Century America', *Journal of American History*, 1973, 60: 332–56.

Showalter, E., and Showalter, E., 'Victorian Women and Menstruation', *Victorian Studies*, 1970–1, 14: 83–9.

# B.V. OTHER THEMES

## B.V.0 Bibliographies

Langer, W. L., 'Infanticide: a Historical Survey', *History of Childhood Quarterly*, 1973, 1: 353–65.

Loth, D., *The Erotic in Literature: a Historical Survey of Pornography*, London, 1961.

Pisanus Fraxi (= H. S. Aschbee), *Index Librorum Prohibitorum*, London, 1877; repr. 1960.

———— *Centuria Librorum Absconditorum*, London, 1879; repr. 1960.

———— *Catena Librorum Tacendorum*, London, 1885; repr. 1960.

## B.V.1 Through the Ages

Bäumler, E., *Amors vergifteter Pfeil*, Hamburg, 1976.

Kearney, P., *A History of Erotic Literature*, London, 1982.

Legman, G., *The Horn Book*, New York, 1964.

Nater, J. P., *Kwik, pokhout en arseen*, The Hague, 1975.

Quetel, C., *Le mal de Naples. Histoire de la syphilis*, Paris, 1987.

*Sexuality and Madness* = *Social Research*, 1986, 53: 211–385.

Stengers, J., and Neck, A. van, *Histoire d'un grand peur. La masturbation*, Brussels, 1984.

## B.V.2 Antiquity

Nardo, E., *Procurato aborto nel mondo greco romano*, Milan, 1971.

Oldenziel, R., 'The Historiography of Infanticide in Antiquity', in

J. Blok and P. Mason (eds), *Sexual Asymmetry*, Amsterdam, 1987, 87–107.

## B. V. 3 Middle-Ages

Brissard, Y.-B., 'L'Infanticide à la fin du Moyen Age. Ses motivations psychologiques et sa répression', *Revue Historique du Droit Français et Etranger*, 1972, 50: 229–56.

Coleman, E. R., 'L'Infanticide dans le haut Moyen Age', *Annales ESC*, 1974, 29: 315–35.

Helmholz, R. H., 'Infanticide in the Province of Canterbury during the Fifteenth Century', *History of Childhood Quarterly*, 1974/5, 2: 379–90.

Kellum, B. A., 'Infanticide in England in the Later Middle-Ages', *History of Childhood Quarterly*, 1973/4, 1: 367–88.

Trexler, R. C., 'Infanticide in Florence: New Sources and First Results', *History of Childhood Quarterly*, 1973/4, 1: 98–116.

## B. V. 4 The Early Modern Period

Dekker, R. M., and Roodenburg, H. W., 'Humor in de zeventiende eeuw. Opvoeding, huwelijk en seksualiteit in de moppen van Aernout van Overbeke', *Tijdschrift voor Sociale Geschiedenis*, 1984, 35: 243–66.

Dekker, R. M., and Pol, L. C. van de, *The Tradition of Female Transvestism in Early Modern Europe*, London, 1989.

Foxon, D., *Libertine Literature in England, 1660–1743*, New York, 1965.

Hoffer, P. C., and Hull, N. E. H., *Murdering Mothers: Infanticide in England and New England, 1558–1803*, New York, 1981.

Jongh, E. de, 'Erotica in vogelperspectief. De dubbelzinnigheid van een reeks 17de-eeuwse genrevoorstellingen', *Simiolus*, 1968/9, 1:22–72.

Malcolmson, R. W., 'Infanticide in the eighteenth century', in J. S. Cockburn (ed.), *Crime in England*, London, 1977, 187–209, 336–9.

Roodenburg, H. W., 'The Autobiography of Isabella de Moerloose: Sex, Childrearing and Popular Belief in Seventeenth Century Holland', *Journal of Social History*, 1985; 18: 517–40.

Tarczylo, Th., *Sexe et liberté au siècle des Lumières*, Paris, 1983.

Thalhofer, F. X. *Die sexuelle Pädagogik bei den Philantropen*, Kempten/Munich, 1907.

Thompson, R., *Unfit for Modest Ears: a Study of Pornography, Obscene and Bawdy Works Written or Published in England in the Second Half of the Seventeenth Century*, London, 1979.

Ussel, J. M. W. van, *Sociogenese en evolutie van het probleem der sexuele propedeuse tussen de 16e en 18e eeuw, vooral in Frankrijk en Duitsland. Bijdrage tot de studie van de burgerlijke sexuele moraal*, Amsterdam, 1967.

Vandermeersch, P., 'Simon-André Tissot (1728–1797) en de strijd tegen het onanisme: mythe of realiteit?', *Documentatieblad Werkgroep Achttiende Eeuw*, 1985, 17: 173–94.

Wächtershäuser, W., *Das Verbrechen des Kindermordes im Zeitalter der Aufklärung. Eine Rechtsgeschichtliche Untersuchung der dogmatischen, prozessualen und rechtssoziologischen Aspekte*, Berlin, 1973.
Wrighton, K., 'Infanticide in earlier seventeenth-century England', *Local Population Studies*, 1975, 15: 10–22.


B.V.5 Nineteenth Century

Brandt, A. M., *No Magic Bullet: a Social History of Venereal Disease in the United States since 1880*, New York/Oxford, 1985.
Dekker, R. M., 'De fatale voet in de literatuur van de negentiende eeuw', *De Gids*, 1980, 143: 420–8.
Gibson, I., *The English Vice: Beating, Sex, and Shame in Victorian England and after*, London, 1978.
Lanteri-Laura, G., *Lecture des perversions: histoire de leur appropriation médicale*, Paris, 1979.
Lasowski, P. W., *Syphilis. Essai sur la littérature française du XIXe siècle*, Paris, 1982.
Wawerzonnek, M., *Implizite Sexualpädagogik in der Sexualwissenschaft, 1886 bis 1933*, Cologne, 1984.
Westen, M., 'Over het naakt in de Noordnederlandse kunst in de periode 1770–1830', *De negentiende Eeuw*, 1986, 10: 209–31.
Wettley, A., *Von der 'Psychopathia sexualis' zur Sexualwissenschaft*, Stuttgart, 1959.

# Index